MW01131116

Bringing the Prophets to Life

Bringing
the Prophets
to Life

A Timely Look
at a Timeless Story

Neil N. Winkler

gefen
publishing house בית הוצאה לאור
JERUSALEM ◆ NEW YORK   Est. 1981

Cover Design: Stephanie & Ruti Design
Typesetting: Gittel Kaplan

ISBN: 978-965-229-478-4

1 3 5 7 9 8 6 4 2

Gefen Publishing House Ltd.
6 Hatzvi Street
Jerusalem 94386, Israel
972-2-538-0247
orders@gefenpublishing.com

Gefen Books
11 Edison Place
Springfield, NJ 07081, USA
1-800-477-5257
orders@gefenpublishing.com

www.gefenpublishing.com

Printed in Israel

Send for our free catalogue

DEDICATIONS

YOUNG ISRAEL OF FORT LEE

Alex and Marina Balanevsky

Ulo and Ethel Barad
In Memory of Gedalia and Cilla Barad

Rabbi Shaya and Nechi Kilimnick

Jack and Sally Wimmer
**In Honor of Our Children, Grandchildren and
Great-Grandchildren**

Dr. David and Shaindy Zigelman
**In Honor of Our Beloved Parents
Rabbi Abraham and Beatrice Zigelman
Who taught us to appreciate the beauty and
importance of *Sefarim*.
In Memory of Our Beloved Parents
Mr. Herbert and Frieda Hauser
Who taught us, guided us and inspired us בדרך התורה**

Jack and Miriam Zwas
In Memory of Our Sons Mark and Jeffrey

SEPHARDIC CONGREGATION OF FORT LEE

Joseph and Lydia Abergel

NIERENBERG FAMILY

Mrs. Laura Nierenberg

In Memory of My Beloved Husband
A Caring Father, Loving Grandfather
And Doting Great-Grandfather
Dr. Harold Nierenberg
And in Honor of My Wonderful Children
Grandchildren and Great-Grandchildren

ROSENBLUM FAMILY
In Memory of our Beloved Parents, Grandparents and Great-Grandparents Who Brought Torah to Life For Us All

In Memory of Sidney and Sylvia Rosenblum
Reuben and Beth Blumenthal and Family
Jerry and Pearl Mann and Family
Dr. Norman and Judy Rosenblum and Family
Dr. Howard and Miriam Rosenblum and Family

In Memory of Kalman and Helen Winkler
Bruce and Robyn Shoulson and Family
Joseph and Surri Rapaport and Family
Rabbi Jeffrey and Yocheved Bienenfeld and Family

In Memory of Rabbi Harry D. and Bertha Silver
Sam and Ronnee Berger and Family
Jack and Sheri Merkin and Family
Rabbi Shammai Silver

In Memory of Jerry and Sylvia Rosenblum
Dr. Chuck and Nina Cohen and Family
Drs. Jay and Mindy Rosenblum and Family
Dr. Neal and Naomi Rosenblum and Family
Stuart and Estee Shor and Family
Shmiel and Aviva Ramras and Family

BIENENFELD FAMILY
In Loving Memory of Our Beloved Husband, Father and Grandfather
Jerome Bienenfeld, z"l
ירוחם בן יהושע דוד ז"ל
A Generous, Courageous and Proud Jew
To Whom We Owe So Much

Bertha Bienenfeld

Yocheved and Jeffrey Bienenfeld

Leslie and Efrayim Zoldan

Carol and Howard Bienenfeld

Julia and Ira Bienenfeld

Hudi and Howie Frank

Shami and Aaron Ness

Saralea and Eliyahu Dershowitz

Bracha and Chaim Sendic

Dina Bienenfeld

Yaakov Moshe Bienenfeld

...הָקִיצוּ וְרַנְּנוּ שֹׁכְנֵי עָפָר.

(ישעיהו כו:יט)

...Arise and rejoice, you who dwell in dust.

(*Yeshayahu* 26:19)

CONTENTS

THE BOOK OF YEHOSHUA: CONQUEST AND SETTLEMENT

THE BOOK OF SHOFTIM: LEADERSHIP AND SETTLEMENT

PREFACE

וְיֹתֵר מֵהֵמָּה, בְּנִי, הִזָּהֵר עֲשׂוֹת סְפָרִים הַרְבֵּה אֵין קֵץ...

"And more than these, my son, be careful not to write a limitless amount of books..."[1]

Throughout the many months of writing, these words of the wisest of men have haunted me. Indeed, even before embarking on this project, I questioned whether there was a need for such a composition and whether I had anything to add to the increasing number of books on the Bible that flow from the pens of those far more creative and capable than I. My decision to go ahead with this undertaking was spurred by the urgings of my colleagues and students – both young and old – and by the realization that, though what I have to say may not be revolutionary, those interested in developing an approach to the study of our holiest books or those looking for direction in teaching them may benefit from some of the ideas and views I have developed and garnered over the years. This encouraged me to "take the plunge."

In recent years, there has been a clear shift in the traditional curriculum in many day schools, with increased emphasis on biblical text. The study of *Tanach* (Bible – derived from the acronym ***Torah, Nevi'im, Ketuvim***) has

---

1. Kohelet 12:12.

become more "mainstream" within the yeshivah world, with formal classes more commonly part of the curriculum. Such study was routine until about two hundred years ago, when, in reaction to the Haskalah (Enlightenment) movement in Europe, whose scholars emphasized the written text and rejected the oral law, the yeshivot began to discourage and deemphasize the study of *Tanach*. (I recall my beloved rebbe mentioning that, as a young man in Europe, he would "smuggle" the *Tanach* into class, making sure not to be caught studying it because it was considered "*bitul Torah*" [wasting time of Torah study]). Instead, the yeshivot stressed rabbinic literature and insisted that the Bible could not be understood without relying on rabbinic interpretation. This emphasis eventually led to an approach that believed there could be no new insights into the text whatsoever, only insights into previous rabbinic comments, and certainly no novelties that would provide alternative views of the text from those of the earlier scholars.

In recent years, however, traditional students of biblical study have taken to heart the words of the venerated commentator Rabbi Shlomo Yitzchaki (Rashi), who, in commenting upon the midrashic approach to Shemot 6:4, wrote: "…But this analysis [midrash] does not fit into the text for a number of reasons. [Rashi goes on to enumerate the contradictions between the text and the midrash.] So I say, let the text be understood as it is written and the *derash* [midrashic analysis] be learned too (on its level), for, as it is written, 'My word is like fire, says the Lord, and as a hammer shatters stone, it can be divided into many sparks'" (Rashi, Shemot 6:9). This traditional view, that the Midrash was meant to express but one of the many views of Torah – as the sparks are but part of a fire – is what led Rashi to interpret the text as he saw it, even when it contradicted the midrashic approach. This is the approach that almost every commentator took when offering his own insights into the text. This is also the approach of the modern school of traditional exegesis.

The increased interest in an in-depth study of the biblical text is a result of an increase in serious scholarship and in writings that are now available to the ever-growing audience on the Internet, as well as through the traditional print media. This, in turn, has spurred greater demand for such study and, consequently, has encouraged more scholarship and writings on the subject. Synagogue study classes, adult education courses and informal discussion groups, all focused on furthering our understanding of the biblical narrative, have become more and more common. There has been an explosion of serious analysis of the biblical text in the traditional world, and that which was once the pursuit of few has become the passion of many.

And yet, despite these advances, the teaching of *Tanach*, especially in the elementary grades, has changed very little in these years. Our approach to textual analysis and comprehension has remained basically the same as it was. And although understanding the text and the commentary of Rashi are the sine qua non of any effective pedagogical approach within the guidelines of our tradition, the failure to clarify to students, as they mature, the difference between *peshat* (simple textual meaning) and *derash* (rabbinic exegesis) often leads to an ignorance of what is in the Scriptures and what is not. Quite often students, even of middle schools and high schools, will ask in which Torah portion they can find the story of Avraham smashing the idols, or where it's written that Rivkah was three years old when she married Yitzchak. (And these are questions I have been asked by those past the high school level, as well.) This educational failure does not simply contribute to an ignorance of the text but also leads to a lack of awareness of and sensitivity to the brilliance of rabbinic tradition, for the common educational approach rarely illuminates the connection between the text and the midrash. The result is that students generally fail to understand why the Rabbis say what they do or what textual anomaly may have led them to make a certain comment.

Consider, if you will, the standard approach in teaching about the early life of our patriarch Avraham. Every child educated in a yeshivah day school, and in most afternoon schools as well, learns the story about Avraham and how he smashed the idols. Terach, Avaraham's father, was an idol manufacturer and salesman. The midrash relates that one day, when his father was not home, Avraham, the budding monotheist, smashed his father's idols and placed the offending weapon into the hands of the biggest idol. When his father came home, Avraham explained to an enraged Terach that, in a fit of anger, the big idol grabbed a hatchet and smashed the other idols.

"But that is ridiculous," his father said. "Idols cannot argue, or talk or fight!"

"That is true," Avraham replied. "So how can they be gods and how can we worship them?"

When retelling this well-known story to older children, teachers have a wonderful opportunity to direct the students to the final chapter in the book of Yehoshua, where Yehoshua reviews the history of our nation.[2] There he begins with the story of how Terach, the father of Avraham, was an idolater. In fact, the text might even be familiar to the child from the Passover Haggadah, and it would explain to the student the source of the midrash that sees Terach as an idol manufacturer. This, in turn, could be used to explain that God's choice of Avraham, despite his father's profession, led the Rabbis to say that Avraham "smashed" his father's idols and, by doing so, man's belief in the idols. A teacher could then clarify the message to be learned from the midrash, i.e., how great was our patriarch who rejected idolatry despite the societal and familial pressures. It would also afford the student the opportunity of familiarizing himself with a text in the book of Yehoshua that he had not yet learned (or one he had already forgotten). But beyond that, an effective teacher could point out how remarkable is the rabbinic approach of revealing the subtleties of the text in such a fashion.

We certainly teach that idea when dealing with the legalistic parts of the Torah and discussing a *gezeirah shavah* or a *hekesh* (both devices used by the Rabbis to uncover definitions by comparing the similarities in wording from one law to another). All this is missed when we teach the midrash as part of the biblical text or, even worse, trivialize it as being part of the "Avraham mystique." As the child matures intellectually, we should clarify in our teaching the reason that led the Rabbis to say what they did and, by doing so, help students appreciate the textual approach taken by the early rabbinic commentators.

When teaching any midrash, it is the teacher's responsibility to challenge the capable class by asking: "What were *Chazal* (the Rabbis) trying to tell us through this story?" We must let our younger and older students know that there is depth to the words of the midrashim; they must never be regarded as simply entertaining "stories." Regretfully, I have seen the results of those who, upon exposure to the "sophisticated" intellectual world and being unable to relate to the midrashic account or its depiction of any specific individual, find these "stories" to be little more than fairy tales. Tragically, they conclude the same about our holy texts themselves, having been taught to equate the two without understanding the real function of each.

Effective teaching of our holy texts and our *mesorah* (tradition) requires us to involve the student in the story and in the person. A child must be given an

---

2. Yehoshua 24:2.

intellectually honest approach to the biblical text that will serve him well in future years. It is both simplistic and religiously dangerous to leave the student with a third-grade understanding of our scriptures, something that he could abandon when exposed to the "sophisticated" arguments of non-traditional sources. It is therefore crucial – perhaps more than anything else – for an educator to inspire the student and make him or her care about the character, the events and the nation. This is true of the Torah narrative and especially challenging when teaching *Nevi'im*, the biblical section of Prophets.

It is for this reason that this book focuses on the prophetic writings of *nevi'im rishonim* (early prophets), for there especially I believe there is much work to be done in how to approach these narratives. This part of the Bible is taught starting in the third or fourth grades in most day schools, and all too often it is treated as little more than a record of the events that took place during that period of time – from the entrance of the Israelites into the Land of Israel until the destruction of the First Temple. Once the students have grown, they rarely take the opportunity of revisiting these texts and understanding their messages on an adult level. For them, the stories are remembered as they were taught in elementary school – on an elementary level. Rare is the educator who explains to a young class that since these books are part of the *Nevi'im*, the prophetic writings of the *Tanach*, they must carry a prophetic message: a divine theme or word of God important enough to be shared with that current generation, as well as future generations. I have often heard Rabbi Menachem Liebtag of Yeshivat Har Etzion repeat the mantra: "God does not need prophets to teach history – that is what historians are for; God wants prophets to be prophets, to share His word with the people!" It is important to let those words guide us in the study and in the teaching of *Tanach*.

Understanding this simple truth – accepting the fact that the books of the Prophets are not simply a record of historical events – helps us realize how we must uncover the book's theme in order to fully understand the prophetic message found in the choice of stories and in the stories themselves. This requires a broader view of each separate book, with an eye out for repetitive phrases or words that often give us a hint to the theme, as well as searching for parallel events or actions that may subtly direct the reader to compare or contrast the stories and reveal a prophetic message. This cannot be done if the books of the Prophets are studied with each chapter (or story) being treated as an isolated event, or if they are taught without regard to the rest of Scripture, without an "eagle's eye" view of the narrative.

Along these lines, it is also important to understand that the stories included in any particular book do not chronicle *all* of the events that took place at that time. The prophet chose those specific tales that help drive home the divine message he hoped to deliver. This, in fact, helps explain many of the differences between the stories found in the books of Shmuel and Melachim and those included in Divrei Hayamim. If one realizes that these books were written in different generations and were meant as messages especially to the *specific generation in which they were written*, then we can understand the choice of events included in each book. As the great commentator Don Yitzchak Abarbanel has pointed out, it is completely understandable that Divrei Hayamim would have a different focus than Melachim, although they chronicle the same period of time. The book of Divrei Hayamim was written by Ezra and Nechemiah at the beginning of the Second Commonwealth and was addressed to a struggling community hoping to rebuild the glory that once was Israel. The book of Melachim, on the other hand, was written by the prophet Yirmeyahu after the destruction of the First Temple and the exile of the people, so that it addressed a nation thrown into the Diaspora and questioning the infallibility of their "all-powerful" God. One book seeks to comfort and explain the reason for the exile while the other is meant to encourage the establishment of an independent nation and the rebuilding of a destroyed land. It is foolish to believe that the Holy Bible, the greatest of all works, would be carelessly filled with contradictory reports of the same events, especially when the book was taught to a nation that had memorized the chronicles of the past and knew the events that had occurred only one hundred years earlier quite well.

A teacher of these biblical subjects would do well to read the verse in the book of Divrei Hayamim before starting to teach:

וְדִבְרֵי דָּוִיד הַמֶּלֶךְ הָרִאשֹׁנִים וְהָאַחֲרֹנִים הִנָּם כְּתוּבִים עַל-דִּבְרֵי שְׁמוּאֵל הָרֹאֶה, וְעַל-דִּבְרֵי נָתָן הַנָּבִיא וְעַל-דִּבְרֵי גָּד הַחֹזֶה.

> "The earlier and later details of David Hamelech are recorded in the writings of the seer Shmuel, the prophet Natan and the seer Gad."[3]

---

3. I Divrei Hayamim 29:29.

The author of Divrei Hayamim makes clear a little-known and yet enlightening fact: these stories included in the books of the Bible were culled from the writings of the prophets who lived and prophesied during that specific period of time. They are primary sources for what took place then, recorded by those who themselves experienced the events or were contemporaries of those who lived through them. This is true of all of the books of the Prophets.[4] The author was very much an editor who gathered the written records and prophecies of earlier seers (as well as his own) and chose those episodes that best underscored the message he wished to share. Thus, when the Talmud tells us that "Shmuel wrote his book…"[5] it clearly cannot to be taken literally, as Shmuel died before half of the events recorded in the book ever took place! Rather, he was the earliest of the prophets whose writings were included in the book, a book that also included the writings of the prophets Natan and Gad. Likewise, the word "wrote" in this context should sometimes be understood as "compiled" or "edited." The essential point is that these books were based upon first-hand testimony of our holy prophets, and then compiled into one work in order to deliver God's message to the people. It is extremely important and helpful to explain this to anyone studying *Tanach*. Unfortunately, it is almost never done.

In studying and certainly teaching any subject, it is important to create and retain an interest in the subject. That is what will keep you coming back to the study and keep students thirsting for more. This is true whether one is studying privately or teaching either children or adults. There is little an educator appreciates more than that moan of disappointment that escapes from the students when the bell rings to end the class. Leaving them wanting to learn more is a sure sign that we have succeeded in piquing their interest and, by doing so, guaranteeing that they will want to hear "what's next." Generating and retaining a high level of interest in the subject matter in a world of constant distraction is no simple task. But it can be done. The student must see and feel a teacher's passion for the subject.

Unfortunately, teachers often attempt to give students more detail and analysis than they can absorb, thereby obscuring the story line and

---

4. We find a similar comment after reading the stories of Shlomo Hamelech's life: "Other details of Shlomo's reign, both the early and the later periods, can be found in the writings of Natan the prophet, and the prophecies of Achiya of Shilo and the visions of Ye'edo the seer…" (II Divrei Hayamim 9:29). See also II Divrei Hayamim 13:22 and 20:34.
5. Tractate Bava Batra 14b–15a.

causing students to lose interest in the material. The common result is that the students find themselves simply memorizing what seems to them as meaningless detail. Simply put, they lose sight of the forest because of the trees we have placed before them. I do not dare trivialize the words of the *Tanach* by viewing them as only a story. But we can fail to accomplish our primary goal of clarifying the text for the student by over-analyzing each and every verse. We cannot teach an elementary school class all of the commentaries on the text that we, as adults, have learned during our lives. In our excitement to share knowledge, we tend to teach details that are not essential for the basic understanding of the text. If we want to teach the lessons of these stories – if we wish to reveal the underlying prophetic message – we must constantly reinforce the understanding of the text itself. By breaking the flow of the narrative too often we cause our students to lose focus and we may even confuse them. Such an approach can lead to boredom and other undesired consequences, and undermine all of our efforts to inspire and educate.

Furthermore, in attempting to teach "everything," teachers can spend so much time on analysis that they find they have no time to complete the required curriculum. I have often heard students joke to each other of how they learned half of the material in the last month of the school year. And that is the best case scenario. More often than not, the book is not completed at all, leaving the students with gaps in their knowledge and in their understanding of the subject. One cannot fully understand the opening of the second part of the book of Shmuel if one never learned the details surrounding the death of Shaul Hamelech at the end of the first part of the book.

The fact is that every experienced teacher I have spoken to agrees that they are teaching less material and covering less ground than they have in the past (this is true in almost all subjects, secular and religious). There may be many reasons for this phenomenon, but there is no doubt that it is true. This means that it is even more difficult today for the teacher of Prophets to complete the required curriculum.

Some schools, recognizing the lack of time, have redesigned their curriculum, no longer teaching Melachim in the elementary grades. Without commenting on that change, I believe that with the proper approach, it is possible to complete the first book of Melachim in elementary school (and even study well into the second book of Melachim) if teachers remain focused on their goals and follow certain guidelines.

Indeed, one of the reasons I wrote this book is because I believe that we can provide the day school student with a firm background in *Tanach* and implant a love, if not a passion, for our holy book, thereby reversing the pattern of the diminishing material covered in the class. By doing so, we can keep up with the resurgence of *Tanach* study in the adult world and hope to increase it in the future.

To fellow educators: Please understand that this book is not a magical elixir that will provide the specific guidelines every teacher needs for every class. I firmly believe that each unique personality has his or her own approach. We certainly are told to deal with students as individuals, and the same is true of teachers. Each instructor brings to the classroom his or her style of teaching. This is important; it is what defines you as a person and as an educator. I hope that this work will positively impact the educational approach taken by the teacher and provide some enlightening insights that can be shared with the students to further arouse their interest the subject.

It is important to note that this work is not meant for teachers alone. I believe that it will also be helpful to anyone who desires to study the works of our prophets in depth and get a better appreciation of the flow of the narrative. Simple translations of the text do not fully prepare the reader for a complete understanding of the prophetic messages found in the books. Without viewing the text in relationship to the rest of Scripture and to the political and social climate of the time, our basic understanding of the Bible will be deficient. My hope is that through reading these essays, readers will develop their own sensitivity to the text and find parallels to other biblical narratives, thereby deepening not only their knowledge of our holy texts, not only their desire to study them even more, but also their appreciation of these divine works and the brilliance of rabbinic insights into them.

Beyond the traditional rabbinic sources, much of my own study was impacted and indeed transformed by the lectures and writings of Rav Yoel Bin Nun and others of his school, Michlelet Herzog in Har Etzion. Their writings and lectures helped open my eyes to that which always lay before me. I am deeply indebted to them. May they all merit many more years to continue spreading the knowledge and love of *Tanach*, and let them know the blessing that the wellsprings of their teachings spread and feed thirsty generations in the future. [6]

---

6. Based upon a verse in Mishlei 5:16: יפוצו מעינתיך חוצה.

ACKNOWLEDGMENTS

בָּרוּךְ...שֶׁהֶחֱיָנִי וְקִיְמָנִי וְהִגִּיעָנִי לַזְּמַן הַזֶּה.

Before acknowledging the many who influenced and continue to influence my life and, therefore, this work, I must first express my gratitude toward the One to Whom all thanks are due, for having afforded me the privilege of spending my days "in the vineyard of Torah," studying and teaching His divine message. This labor of love was completed only due to Hashem's kindnesses and the blessings that He has bestowed upon me. My love for *Tanach* was nurtured and developed by my loving parents, ע"ה: my mother, who patiently listened to my excited ramblings about the Bible story I had learned that day; and my father, a regular reader of the Torah who encouraged me to be "better" than he, holding me to a higher standard because, as he once explained, I received the education he was never granted. Likewise, I am indebted to my father-in-law, ע"ה, and, תבדל לחיים my mother-in-law, for their affection, concern and encouragement.

I am certainly beholden to the two institutions with which I have been involved for these past thirty years plus: Yeshivat Moriah, the Moriah School of Englewood, and the Young Israel of Fort Lee. I am blessed to be able to teach both the young and excited as well as the mature and knowledgeable. The leadership of both places of Torah kindly granted me a six-month sabbatical during which I wrote the bulk of this book.

My colleagues, both in the rabbinate and in *chinuch*, served as sounding boards and critics of my ideas, while my students in school and my congregants in the synagogue served as the inspiration for many of these thoughts.

My life is ever filled with the love of my wonderful children, Shira and Michael, Tsippi and Michael, Malkie, Yehoshua and Rachel and Ely and the joy that their children bring me each day. Their support and their excitement for this project encouraged me to complete the book when it was difficult to imagine that I could ever finish it.

And finally, nothing that I may have accomplished over the years, whether in the communal rabbinate or in Torah education, would have been possible without Andrea at my side. It is she who sacrificed the time that most couples have to spend together as I worked at two jobs; she who advised, cajoled, criticized and encouraged me and therefore she who must take equal credit for any success I have achieved. It was best expressed by Rabbi Akiva,[1] who stated: שלי ושלכם — שלה היא, the credit for whatever I have achieved and whatever my students have learned from me, belongs to her. That is certainly true of this book as well.

---

1. Tractate Ketubot 63a.

INTRODUCTION

When God decided to destroy the cities of Sodom, Gomorrah and the three other cities in the Dead Sea basin, He insisted on first revealing His plan to Avraham. God explained His decision in the following words:

כִּי יְדַעְתִּיו לְמַעַן אֲשֶׁר יְצַוֶּה אֶת בָּנָיו וְאֶת בֵּיתוֹ אַחֲרָיו וְשָׁמְרוּ דֶּרֶךְ
ד׳ **לַעֲשׂוֹת צְדָקָה וּמִשְׁפָּט**....

"For I have drawn him near so that he will charge his children and family to observe God's path of *doing righteousness and justice*...."[1]

If there were one phrase that could best sum up the purpose of all of biblical literature, I would suggest that it is this one. God's choice of Avraham and his descendants was made for the express purpose of charging them to create a society that would pursue justice and righteousness as would be defined by the laws of the Torah – with the goal that this society would, in turn, lead others to pursue the same ideals.

---

1. Bereishit 18:19. I have purposely translated the Hebrew term ידעתיו as "drawn him near" or even "endeared him to Me," related to the biblical term we find in Bereishit 4:1, והאדם ידע את חוה אשתו, describing the husband-wife relationship. Similarly, ואדעך בשם, which God said to Moses (Shemot 33:17).

It is for this precise reason that God told Avraham His plans for the doomed cities. And our forefather reacted exactly as a "justice-intoxicated" person should, especially one who, beyond simple justice, would also demand "righteousness." The Torah depicts Avraham as engaging God in a debate, attempting to defend the doomed cities by arguing that it would be against God's own standards of justice to destroy the cities.[2] And when he realized that he could not sway God with his justice-based arguments, he appeals to God's divine righteousness and pleads for His mercy.

Although Avraham fails to sway God with his arguments, he does prove himself to be exactly the type of individual that God desired: a person who was not willing to see injustice, even when he believed that it was God Himself who was being unjust. Such a person, God knew, could begin to build a moral world; such an individual, so committed to justice and righteousness, would bequeath this passion to his descendants.

This charge of building a moral, just and compassionate society founded upon the eternal values of the Torah was indeed passed down to the children of Avraham. A cursory glance at the biblical text will show that this is an overriding theme of all the books of Prophets, as through this ideal society the world at large would learn and adopt the Torah's moral values. The prophecies of the *nevi'im acharonim* (later prophets) are replete with warnings to the nation to pursue justice and righteousness, and it is no wonder that the very destruction of Jerusalem, we are told, was brought about by the nation's failure to do just that.[3]

Essential to the creation of such a society was the need to live independently in a land where they could create a world based upon divine values, distanced from the pagan influences that could lead them astray – and by successfully doing so they would become a "light unto the nations." Clearly, such an ideal society could be built only if the nation of Israel were united in its commitment to those values and that common moral code.

In their formative years, while the Israelites were traveling together through the desert, they had little contact with the local tribes and little chance of being influenced by them. But when they approached the inhabited area on the eastern banks of the Jordan, near the nations of Moab, Midian, Edom and Ammon, they indeed were led to sin by the Moabite and Midianite women,

---

2. Bereishit 18:25: השופט כל הארץ לא יעשה משפט, "Will the Judge of the world not act justly?"

3. See Yeshayahu 1:21, and also 1:27 for the formula for Jerusalem's rehabilitation.

surrendering to the pagan influences that invaded their camp.[4] The result of their sin was the loss of some 24,000 Israelites in a God-decreed plague. The episode was to serve Israel as a warning of what could happen once they entered the land and came in contact with the aboriginal peoples who settled the land and their pagan worship. In fact, God charges Israel to remember this punishment, an example of what happens to those who stray from God's path, and the reward, a proof of what awaits those who remain faithful.[5]

The adjustment from a nomadic desert life, in which the nation camped together untouched by foreign ideologies, to an agrarian life where one would be tied to his own estate and have little connection to members of other tribes, would be a challenging one. While the children of Israel traveled through the Sinai wilderness they were told that they should camp "around the Tabernacle."[6] Once they entered the land, the challenge they faced was to see that they still camped together – that they felt part of one nation – and that they still camped "around the Tabernacle" – that their lives were still centered around a commitment to God and His laws.

As previously mentioned, a basic requirement for accomplishing this goal was the need to unite the nation and avoid the anarchistic tendencies of a leaderless society, which are so well described in the concluding chapters of the book of Shoftim. The need for an effective ruler to accomplish these goals and fulfill this mission is clear. The lack of a monarch would not only make Israel vulnerable to enemy invasion but would also prevent the people from remembering that they indeed were one nation with a common past. This, in turn, could blind them to the communal task God gave them. The struggle of each individual tribe to capture and settle the land, and the daily challenges of creating a normal life in a new land, would soon lead the tribes to ignore the general welfare of the nation and focus only on their parochial needs and concerns. The absence of that one leader who could unite the people and redirect their focus, therefore, would limit both their political and religious growth.

Rambam (Maimonides), in his epic legal work, the *Mishneh Torah*, writes: "The Israelites were commanded three things upon entering the land: to appoint a king, defeat Amalek, and build the Holy Temple."[7] A

---

4. Bamidbar 25:1–9.
5. Devarim 4:3–4.
6. Bamidbar 2:2.
7. Rambam, *Mishneh Torah, Hilchot Melachim* 1:1. Rambam is actually echoing the view of R. Yosi quoted in the Talmud, tractate Sanhedrin 20b.

careful reading of the books of the early prophets will show that these three charges actually define the overarching theme of the books and must remain in the mind of the reader in order to understand the events of this period and the prophetic editor's decisions as to which stories were to be included in his work. Simply, these books focus upon *milchamah*, *malchut* and *mikdash* – war, kingship and the Temple: "war" implies the conquest of the land and removal of foreign threats to Israel's independence;[8] "kingship" is the search for and appointment of God's chosen monarch and father of the dynasty that would rule over a united people; and "Temple" means the construction of a permanent physical structure that would centralize the nation's worship of the One God and, thereby, serve as a unifying force within the people. These were the necessary "ingredients" in forming that ideal society that could spread the word of God and build a world of justice and righteousness.

A cursory glance at the books of the early prophets will prove this point:

- The book of Yehoshua centers around the need to conquer the land and remove the enemy: "war."

- The book of Shoftim deals with the failure to remove the enemy and the growing need for a king: "war/kingship."

- The book of Shmuel concerns itself with a failed monarchy that neglected to defeat Amalek and the successful establishment of the Davidic dynasty, resulting in the removal of any external threat to the existence of Israel: "war/kingship."

- The book of Melachim focuses upon the construction of the Temple, the disintegration of the united nation, the corruption of the monarchies and the resulting destruction of the Temple: "kingship/Temple."

Interestingly, these goals of the books of the early prophets are reflected in the structure of biblical verse that discusses the stages that the Israelites must pass before they begin to worship God in a permanent Temple:

---

8. Clearly, the command to destroy Amalek was a separate and specific obligation. I have broadened that command to include the conquest of the land (which was a separate mitzvah as well) and the removal of any threat that would impede the creation of the ideal society.

וַעֲבַרְתֶּם אֶת הַיַּרְדֵּן וִישַׁבְתֶּם בָּאָרֶץ אֲשֶׁר ד' אֱלֹקֵיכֶם מַנְחִיל אֶתְכֶם
וְהֵנִיחַ לָכֶם מִכָּל אֹיְבֵיכֶם מִסָּבִיב וִישַׁבְתֶּם בֶּטַח.

"And you shall cross the Jordan and settle the land that God bequeaths to you, and He will give you rest from your surrounding enemies so that you will live securely."[9]

Note how the individual books of early prophets actually follow the specifics of this verse:

- "And you shall cross the Jordan" – an event discussed in the book of Yehoshua, which goes on to cover the early years of the Israelites in the land

- "and settle the land that God bequeaths to you" – a phrase reflected in Shoftim, where we read of the attempts – successful and unsuccessful – to settle the land and chase away the internal and external enemies

- "and He will give you rest from your surrounding enemies" – refers to the era covered by the book of Shmuel, where we read of the wars of Shaul and David that finally chased away the foreign threats

- "so that you will live securely" – expresses well the early years of the first regents, years depicted in the book of Melachim

It is therefore no surprise that the very next verse in Devarim speaks of the nation bringing their offerings to "the place that God will choose," that is, the Holy Temple. For, after being granted security from enemy attack, as they were at the end of David's reign, they were to build the Temple, as Shlomo did in the book of Melachim.

The reason why the books of the early prophets focus so heavily upon the challenges and demands of kingship, is precisely because kingship was considered so essential for the observance of God's command to the nation and the fulfillment of Avraham's charge to his children: the creation of a just and compassionate society. That idea was best expressed by Rabbi Yosi, who stated that Israel was commanded three laws upon entering the land (war, kingship

---

9. Devarim 12:10.

and Temple), but it is unclear which one took precedence and should be fulfilled first. Rabbi Yosi analyzes the biblical verses and concludes: "They must appoint a king first."

Beyond the textual proofs, we might reach the same conclusion through simple logic: only an accepted king could unite the nation and amass the forces necessary to build a standing army. Such a force would defeat both the internal and external enemies of Israel and remain on guard to protect the population from any foreign assault. Likewise, only a king could have the organization, support and wherewithal to undertake as massive a project as building a center for national worship and uniting the people behind the project and the concept of one religious center.

These books of the early prophets tell the story of Israel through their heroes; that is, we learn the history of our nation through the eyes and experiences of the outstanding personalities of each era. And, although teaching history is not the main purpose of these books, it is essential for anyone studying the books to know the history in order to understand the prophetic message found therein. For this very reason, it is crucial to be able to understand the struggles and challenges that faced these outstanding personalities and identify with their attempts, not always successful, to deal with the problems that confronted them. How well an educator can implant this identification into the heart of a student will often define how successful he or she will be in teaching the material. A student who is connected to what he is learning is a student who will open a text and study on his own. A Torah educator must labor to create individuals who care – not simply people who know.

Ultimately, it is not the knowledge of the specific facts, persons or events that will define success in passing on our *mesorah* (tradition), but the ability to arouse a love, even a passion, in the heart of a student for our past and our heritage – to inspire Avraham's children to embrace the standards of righteousness and justice – that will ultimately decide whether all of our efforts were successful or not.

It is my fervent hope that this work will help do just that, for both the student and the teacher.

THE BOOK OF YEHOSHUA

ספר יהושע

CONQUEST AND SETTLEMENT

OVERVIEW

The first book in the "early prophets," *nevi'im rishonim*, creates its own natural bridge to the previous book of Devarim and to the entire Torah simply because Yehoshua (Joshua) is already known to us as the attendant of Moshe[1] and the commander of the Israelite forces[2] in the desert. We also know that he was designated by God to succeed Moshe,[3] and from the very final verses of the Torah we have learned that he was "a man with spirit"[4] and was "filled with wisdom" so that all of Israel accepted his leadership and listened to his commands.[5]

The opening words of the book take us back to the end of the Torah by stating that "after the death of Moshe God spoke to Yehoshua…." The thematic and linguistic affinity of the book of Yehoshua to the Torah explains why both the Samaritans and the Muslims consider Yehoshua an integral part of the first five books of the Scriptures. Even the Talmud recognizes the similarities and declares: "Had Israel not sinned, she would have received only the Pentateuch and the book of Yehoshua…."[6] It is, therefore, a book whose precise historical period is known, whose main figure has already been introduced to the reader and whose style and substance closely parallels the earlier text. For these reasons, Yehoshua is unique among the books of *Nach*,

---

1. Shemot 33:11.
2. Ibid. 17:9.
3. Bamidbar 27:18–21.
4. Ibid. 27:18.
5. Devarim 34:9.
6. Tractate Nedarim 22b.

forming an almost seamless connection to the books of the Torah. But there are other factors that make this part of the Bible distinctive and special.

The generation of those who conquered the land, the very generation described in the book, proved itself to be quite extraordinary, as did its leader, Yehoshua. With the exception of the sin of Achan (chapter 7), we never find mention of any sin the people committed against God, nor do we find anywhere in this book divine anger directed against the nation. Similarly, we don't read of anger directed by the nation against God or Yehoshua. These same individuals who complained against God and against the leadership of the greatest of prophets, Moshe,[7] during their final year in the desert found nothing to make them complain about God or Yehoshua throughout this time period. Indeed, the book itself testifies that during these years, the people "worshiped God fully and sincerely"[8] and that "Israel served God all the days of Yehoshua."[9]

Given these accolades, we would expect to read the story of Israel's conquest of the entire land and their successful fulfillment of God's expectations of them. We do not. Although we read of Yehoshua's successes in removing the threat of the large armies and military coalitions, we also read of those areas and nations that they failed to conquer. The inability or reluctance of Israel, both in that generation and the following ones, to complete the conquest begun by Yehoshua is a failure that will haunt the people for hundreds of years. When we recall that the very first challenge given to the nation upon entering the land was to remove these foreign influences, we understand why this failure negatively impacted the future of the nation and why it occupies our attention throughout the book of Shoftim. It is a failure that serves as one of the themes of this book and, as we will see, is one of the reasons why the book was written.

The book of Yehoshua itself, as opposed to those that follow, can be easily divided into topics. Rabbi Menachem Leibtag makes a powerful argument when he claims that the book actually follows God's specific two-pronged command to Israel found in Bamidbar:

... כִּי אַתֶּם עֹבְרִים אֶת הַיַּרְדֵּן אֶל אֶרֶץ כְּנָעַן. **וְהוֹרַשְׁתֶּם** אֶת כָּל יֹשְׁבֵי הָאָרֶץ מִפְּנֵיכֶם.... **וְהוֹרַשְׁתֶּם** אֶת הָאָרֶץ וִישַׁבְתֶּם בָּהּ, כִּי לָכֶם נָתַתִּי אֶת הָאָרֶץ **לָרֶשֶׁת** אֹתָהּ.

7. See Bamidbar 20:3; 21:5; 25:1.
8. Yehoshua 24:14.
9. Ibid. 24:31; see also Shoftim 2:7.

"....as you cross the Jordan to the Land of Canaan. You must *chase away* all of its inhabitants.... And you must *conquer* the land and settle it, for I have given you the land to *conquer*."[10]

The repetition of the root word *yarosh* (י-ר-ש), meaning "to conquer" or "chase out," reflects God's first command and Israel's first challenge: to remove the enemy and its influences, clearly referring to the military conquest of the land.

The second part of God's command is found in the verse that follows:

וְהִתְנַחַלְתֶּם אֶת הָאָרֶץ בְּגוֹרָל לְמִשְׁפְּחֹתֵיכֶם, לָרַב תַּרְבּוּ אֶת נַחֲלָתוֹ וְלַמְעַט תַּמְעִיט אֶת נַחֲלָתוֹ...לְמַטּוֹת אֲבֹתֵיכֶם תִּתְנֶחָלוּ.

"You shall *apportion out* the land by lot per family, for the numerous you shall give a larger *portion* and to the few you shall give a smaller *portion*...according to your forefather's tribes shall you *settle* [divide the land]."[11]

In this verse, the repetition of the root word *nachal* (נ-ח-ל), "settlement" or "portion," reflects God's next command and Israel's second challenge: to divide and settle the land. The first chapters of the book of Yehoshua – chapters 1 to 12 – tell the story of Israel's efforts to fulfill God's first command, the military conquest. From chapter 13 onward, the book relates Israel's attempts to meet God's second challenge by telling of the settlement of the land by each tribe.

It is also true that the book can be divided into more specific topics in the following fashion:

The first four chapters deal with the entry into the Land of Israel, including the encouragement given to Yehoshua by the people (chapter 1), the spies sent by Yehoshua (chapter 2), the miraculous crossing of the Jordan (chapter 3) and the setting of the memorial stones at Gilgal and in the Jordan itself.

The next eight chapters focus upon the conquest of the land, including the wars against Jericho and Ai (chapters 6, 7 and 8), the treaty with the Gibeonites and the defeat of the southern tribal alliance (chapters 8 and 10),

10. Bamidbar 33:51–53.
11. Ibid. 33:54.

as well as the defeat of the northern tribal alliance (chapter 11), with a closing summary of Yehoshua's successful campaigns (chapter 12).

The middle chapters (13 to 19) discuss the apportioning of the land to the individual tribes, while the fourth section details the allocation of the Levite cities (as well as the cities of refuge) and the return of the two and a half tribes to the eastern plains of the Jordan River (chapters 20 to 22). Included in this section of the book is the near civil war that broke out with the eastern tribes' construction of an "ornamental" altar, meant to be only a monument but mistaken by the other tribes to be an illegal sacrificial site.

The final two chapters are Yehoshua's final words to the Israelites before his demise, urging them to remain faithful to God and His Torah, their only guarantee of success and growth in the future. He also takes pains to underscore God's righteousness in upholding all of His promises to them regarding their successful conquest of the land and removal of the enemy.

It is interesting to note that the five sections of the book of Yehoshua can be seen as paralleling the Five Books of Moses.[12] The first section of Israel's entry into the land for the first time parallels the book of Bereishit and its description of the entry of our ancestors into the land for the first time. Likewise, the very promises to the forefathers that their descendants will inherit the land, promises repeated numerous times in Bereishit, see their fruition in the first part of the book of Yehoshua.

The actual conquest of the land described in the second part of Yehoshua reminds us of the second book of the Torah, Shemot. In the book of Yehoshua we read the portrayal of a frightened native population, something described in Moshe's song at the Red Sea;[13] we also note the observance of the Paschal sacrifice, which parallels the Israelite observance of the first Passover in Egypt (as well as all of the accompanying laws given in the book of Shemot).[14] We read as well of Yehoshua's encounter with the angel of God, who requires him to remove his shoe when standing upon holy ground, something that brings to mind Moshe's experience at the burning bush – especially as the prophetic author purposely uses the exact words found in the Torah.[15]

---

12. This analysis was done by Rav Yehuda Kiel in the classic *Da'at Mikra* series (Jerusalem: Mossad Harav Kook, 1971–2003). See his introduction to *sefer Yehoshua,* pp. 10–11.
13. Shemot 15:14–16.
14. Ibid. 12:1–20.
15. Ibid. 3:5: של נעליך מעל רגליך כי המקום אשר אתה עומד עליה אדמת קדש הוא, compare to Yehoshua 5:15: של נעלך מעל רגליך כי המקום אשר אתה עומד עליו קדש הוא.

The third section of Yehoshua includes details of those walled cities found within the portions of the various tribes and hearkens back to the end of Vayikra (chapter 25), where all the laws regarding walled cities are given. The fourth section focuses on the Levites and their cities, as well as the cities of refuge, both topics that are discussed in Bamidbar.[16] And, perhaps most obvious, the final section, which relates Yehoshua's final words to the nation, directly parallels the entire book of Devarim in which Moshe does the same.

Beyond these similarities there is one connection between the Five Books of Moses and the book of Yehoshua to which the aforementioned quotation in the Talmudic tractate Nedarim hints:[17] ideally, there should not have been any more books of the Bible beyond the first six. The bulk of the Scriptures was written because the ideal world envisioned by God and given to Israel to create never materialized. The books of the Prophets were written, therefore, as a direct or indirect result of the failure of Israel to carry out its mission. Up until this point, however, the Bible was recording the development of the perfect society. This explains the "sinless" nature of the book of Yehoshua.

When we consider that every other book of the Prophets, both the early and late prophets, often depicts a society deeply affected by sin and misdeed, and that the later prophets were sent to prophesy against the immorality and corruption that existed, we realize the true uniqueness of the book of Yehoshua and the time period in which it takes place. But we also realize that something must have occurred during this era that shattered the perfect world and the ideal society. Some shortcoming that must have laid the groundwork for future mistakes and misdeeds that ultimately led to the collapse of the dream. In the course of analyzing the book, the man and the society, we hope to uncover just what that misstep was and, by doing so, provide an opening for our understanding of the rest of the books of the *nevi'im rishonim*, the early prophets.

---

16. Bamidbar 35.

17. "Had Israel not sinned, she would have received only the Pentateuch and the book of Yehoshua…" (tractate Nedarim 22b).

ANALYSIS

YEHOSHUA THE BOOK

Why was this book written? It is a question that every student of the Bible must ask when studying any biblical book. We ask it before beginning a book because it helps clarify why certain stories or facts were included in the record and why some were not. We must always remember that each book has a specific purpose or purposes. As noted in the foreword, these books were not meant to teach history, although we can learn about our past through them. The prophetic writings are meant to leave a message inspired by God, for the generation in which it was written and for future generations as well. It therefore behooves the reader to consider what message would be crucial for the generation that conquered the land. We must ponder: What might have been bothering the people of Israel that would require a divine response? If we put ourselves in their position, we might well imagine what troubled this remarkable generation as they looked back upon the years of Yehoshua's leadership. And then, when reading the text, we can discover what God's message to them was.

As Yehoshua faced his final days, everything may have appeared to be perfect. After all, the Tabernacle and Holy Ark stood in the town of Shilo, the wars of conquest had ceased and each tribe lived peacefully upon its own territory. But beneath the surface lay the unfortunate truth that belied this seemingly ideal world: God's command had not been followed; the enemy remained in the land while the Israelites remained passive. God's command to eradicate any remnant of idolatry from the land and, together with that, any idolatrous nation from the land is well documented in the Torah. We find the warning given to Moshe in a number of places,[1] and the message is quite clear: Israel must remove the foreign influences from the land so that they remain unaffected by pagan beliefs. Those enemies that remain will become "thorns" in the side of the nation, a source of trouble and eventually the cause for Israel's exile from the land.[2]

The text is also very clear in stating that the land was not completely captured by Yehoshua, but it was never meant to be. Yehoshua was charged with leading the nation into the land and beginning the process of conquest and settlement. The Torah openly states that the settlement of the land would be a slow and gradual process, not one that would be completed in a few years. "I will not chase them away in one year…. Little by little shall I chase them away from you, until you increase and inherit the land."[3] It was never God's intent to have Yehoshua complete the task of conquering every part of the Land of Israel, only that he would lead the nation into the land, apportion out the land to each respective tribe and oversee the beginning of the settlement.

The rest of the conquest was to be completed by the people of that generation as well as those living in future generations. It would be a gradual process taking some years that would eventually see the Israelites take over the entire land by converting the pagan population or removing them from the area. In fact, the book of Yehoshua takes pains in detailing precisely which parts of the land had been captured and which parts of the land remained to be conquered. Furthermore, this charge, which was given by God before the Israelites entered the land, was reiterated by Yehoshua before his death. He told those who would survive him that the challenge of total conquest still remained before them. Yehoshua reminded the people before his death that God had defeated the nations and conquered the land as He had promised,

---

1. Shemot 23:24, 29–31 and 34:12–13, 15–16; Bamidbar 33:52–53, 55.
2. Bamidbar 33:56.
3. Shemot 23:29–30.

and He will continue to do so if they listen to His commands.[4] It is actually this final address of Yehoshua that provides us with the key to understanding the purpose of this book.

As Yehoshua prepared to leave his nation, the people looked back and may very well have believed that God had failed them. After all, Yehoshua was old, as he himself confesses,[5] and no longer capable of leading any military force. Yet it was clear to all that much of the territory still remained in the hands of the enemy. Whatever happened, the nation may have thought, to God's promise of removing the native population and eradicating the enemy? Hadn't God guaranteed their victory in His words: "God will chase all of these nations away from you...wherever your foot treads shall belong to you...";[6] Why had God failed them? they pondered. Yehoshua answered them directly, and in doing so, explained for future generations the purpose of his book. In chapter 23, Yehoshua speaks to the nation and echoes the words of his immortal teacher, words found in the book of Devarim. Yehoshua insists that God had not failed them at all. He had conquered every nation as He had promised. No tribe or alliance was able to successfully stand up to Israel, exactly as God had guaranteed. The enemies that still surrounded them were the result of *their* failure and not God's.

Yehoshua looked back upon his life and reflected upon the fact that since he "retired" from active service to his village of Timnat Serach, the bulk of the tribes had failed to continue the conquest. They remained content living in those portions that had been taken by Yehoshua and the national army, reluctant to take up arms as individual tribes to remove the enemy completely. The people may have recalled God's promise, but they forgot (or ignored) the condition upon which the promise was made: "If you observe these commandments that I give you today...then God will conquer all of these nations....";[7] God required Israel to fight, and He would then help them to victory. He clearly stated: "Wherever your foot treads will belong to you," indicating that Israel had to make the first move; they had to march into battle. God would fight on their *side*, but not in their *stead*. To a disillusioned and aging generation who saw their dream unfulfilled, and to future generations who suffered

---

4. Yehoshua 23:3–5.
5. Ibid. 23:2.
6. Devarim 11:23–24.
7. Ibid. 11:22–23.

from the years of inaction, Yehoshua left the clear message of his book: Don't blame God! The fault is yours!

YEHOSHUA THE MAN[8]

E very student of the Bible knows that Yehoshua succeeded Moshe as leader of the people, and most know as well that Yehoshua was Moshe's attendant. The choice of the new leader seems to be an obvious and natural one. After all, we read of Yehoshua serving his teacher and his nation as leader of the armed forces in their war against Amalek, as the one who accompanied Moshe partly up Mount Sinai,[9] as the defender of his master's honor when two elders began to prophesy[10] and as one of the two spies who, after traversing the Land of Canaan, brought back a positive report about the land and its conquest.[11] Given his steadfast support of Moshe and his apparent courage in the face of popular resistance, it is wholly logical that he was chosen to lead the nation into the Land of Israel.

And yet, upon close analysis, that choice might not be so obvious. A review of those episodes found in the Torah that describe Yehoshua and his actions may give us pause and have us wonder why he was chosen and why he was such a successful leader.

The People's Hesitancy

The opening chapter of the book depicts the first weeks after the death of Moshe, the first weeks of Yehoshua's leadership. What becomes clear with a careful reading of the text is that there seems to be an atmosphere of insecurity and hesitation within the nation and among its leaders. All of this is certainly understandable. Moshe was the only leader these people had ever known, and although they might have argued with him, they knew very well that he was carrying God's word and had successfully led them due to God's presence and inspiration.

---

8. I am indebted to Rabbi Hayyim Angel upon whose studies much of this approach to the book of Yehoshua is based.
9. Shemot 24:13.
10. Bamidbar 11:28.
11. Ibid. 14:6–7.

Would the same be true with Yehoshua? they wondered. And so we read of the encouraging words given the new leader: "Be strong and courageous,"[12] God tells Yehoshua, repeating the same charge again just one verse later. And in case Yehoshua did not "get" the message, God repeats it yet a third time: "Behold I have charged you: be strong and courageous!"[13] These same words were addressed to Yehoshua by Moshe[14] as God had commanded him,[15] and then by God himself,[16] when the Israelites were still in the desert. We fully understand the support and encouragement that Yehoshua received from his mentor and certainly value the warning he received from God through these words. But when the heads of three tribes issue the same words to their new leader,[17] we must see a clear pattern emerging. After all, could we ever imagine the people saying these words to Moshe while he led the nation? Clearly, there is a mood of tentativeness and insecurity about Yehoshua's leadership abilities.

And for good reason. When we study the early actions of Yehoshua, those episodes in the Torah where he takes an active role, we can well understand the people's insecurity.

Yehoshua's History

The first mention of Yehoshua in the Torah is as commander of the Israelite forces that attempted to defend themselves from the surprise attack of the Amalekites. Moshe turns to Yehoshua and tells him to choose men and go to war against Amalek.[18] The reader has no idea who this "Yehoshua" is. In fact, the Torah does not even bother to tell us his father's name, something we would expect it to do! He is just "Yehoshua." Remarkably, although we are soon told that his father's name was Nun,[19] the Torah never reveals any other detail of his ancestry, as it does when relating the stories of Noah, Avraham

---

12. Yehoshua 1:6: I have translated the term *ve'ematz* according to the opinion of the Gra, who states that the term *chazak* refers to a physical strength, while *amatz* refers to the "strength of the heart," i.e., "courage."
13. Yehoshua 1:9.
14. Devarim 31:7.
15. Ibid. 3:28.
16. Ibid. 31:23.
17. Ibid. 1:19.
18. Shemot 17:9.
19. Ibid. 33:11.

and Moshe. This is even more puzzling given the fact that Yehoshua had an impressive ancestry, for he was the grandson of the head of the tribe of Efraim, Elishama ben Amihud![20] To us, the readers, Yehoshua remains an enigma, a puzzle waiting for us to solve by discovering the character and essence of the man through his own deeds and his own accomplishments and not through his ancestry.

It is true that he was Moshe's attendant but perhaps that was not the most important factor in making him God's choice for the next leader of Israel. In this first encounter with Yehoshua, we see him as a military leader but one sharing leadership with Moshe. He fights the battle, but it is Moshe's outstretched arms, supported by Aharon and Hur, that guarantee the victory. Notably, however, Yehoshua's future leadership role is hinted to at this juncture. When God pledges to war eternally against Amalek, he also commands Moshe to inscribe the dastardly deed of Amalek in "the book," and "place it in the ears of Yehoshua,"[21] a phrase foreshadowing Yehoshua's future role as leader of Israel.

Nonetheless, although Yehoshua shows talent as a military leader and is an accomplished student of the master teacher himself, qualities that are invaluable for successful leadership of the nation of Israel, we still are less than confident of his leadership qualities. What gives us pause – and perhaps what caused the hesitations and insecurity of the nation at that time – were the intangibles necessary for leadership, especially the ability to know and relate to different people and personalities. How would Yehoshua deal with individuals? How would he cope during times of crisis? What were his "people skills?" When we analyze his actions at different occasions, we are far from impressed.

When we read of Yehoshua at Mount Sinai, we see that he ascends part of the way with his master[22] and awaits Moshe's descent from the mountain.[23] During Moshe's absence from camp, it is not Yehoshua who replaces him but rather Aharon and Hur who become the acting leaders.[24] Far from taking a leadership role, Yehoshua is relegated to simply being the "attendant" of Moshe who, as the Torah describes him following the episode, "does

---

20. I Divrei Hayamim 7:26–27.
21. Shemot 17:13; see also Rashi, ibid.
22. Shemot 24:13.
23. Ibid 31:11.
24. Ibid 24:14.

not depart from the tent."[25] If he is being "groomed," either by God or by Moshe, to be the successor, why is he missing from this crucial event in Israel's history?

Remarkably, it is at this precise time that the people demand a visible and tangible replacement for – or representation of, or go-between with – God. As a result, they commit the sin of worshiping the golden calf. The Torah depicts a near-riot among the people, and the commentaries suggest that actual murder took place with the killing of Hur.[26] More shocking to the reader is the fact that this act of perfidy by the nation took place only a few weeks after the Ten Commandments were pronounced at Mount Sinai! And all this occurred as a result of Moshe's absence. It was a time that clearly cried out for a strong voice and firm leadership, which was missing.

So where was Yehoshua? He was not there; he was not involved at all and, in fact, remained totally unaware of what events were unfolding back in the camp. Yehoshua stood beyond the fray, up on the mountain, waiting for the return of Moshe. We might suggest that, perhaps at this stage of his development, Yehoshua had to remain attached to his teacher and mentor, learning from the master and never "departing from the tent." Or we can surmise that, at this point, Yehoshua lacked the necessary leadership qualities, and his youth and inexperience made it impossible for him to be considered a replacement, albeit temporary, for Moshe. Either way, no real leadership qualities are reflected in this episode, qualities that should have been evident in the future leader of Israel.

Furthermore, the very first time Yehoshua is heard speaking is when Moshe descended the mountain and heard the shouts of wild celebration coming from the camp. Yehoshua offered his explanation for the shouts, and he was wrong! "There is the sound of war in the camp,"[27] he told Moshe. The venerable leader responded that there was no war in the camp, for neither the shouts of victory nor the cries of defeat were to be heard. The young general thought in terms of war; the experienced guide knew better. The youthful charge revealed a lack of understanding of human nature; he spoke as one who "would not depart from the tent,"[28] while the master detected the reality of the situation even before seeing it.

---

25. Ibid 33:11.
26. Midrash Tanchuma, *Ki Tissa*, note 20.
27. Shemot 32:17.
28. Ibid. 33:11.

The second time the Torah records Yehoshua's opinion is in the book of Bamidbar, when Moshe appointed seventy elders to assist him. At that time, two elders who were not among those chosen to share the burden of leadership, Eldad and Medad, remained in the camp, while the others had gathered around the *ohel mo'ed*, the "tent of gathering." When word came to Moshe that these two elders had begun to prophesy in the camp, Yehoshua offered his unsolicited opinion as to what should be done: "My master Moshe," he said, "lock them up!"[29] And once again, Yehoshua "got it wrong." Moshe corrected his charge and told him that he was in no way jealous of the two elders. On the contrary, he went on to explain, he wished that all of Israel would merit God's spirit as these two had.

Yehoshua misread the people again. It seems that he once again failed to have his hand on the "pulse" of the populace. Our Rabbis, ever sensitive to these nuances, comment: Yehoshua said two things before Moshe that were not proper in his [Moshe's] eyes: one when appointing the judges and one in the episode of the golden calf...."[30] They end their comments with the observation: Moshe said, "One who will lead six-hundred-thousand cannot differentiate between the cries of his people?" The Rabbis see these shortcomings in the youthful Yehoshua. Can we not now begin to understand the tentativeness with which the nation greets Yehoshua's ascension to leadership?

The third time we hear from Yehoshua is during the infamous sin of the spies. In the well-known story, Moshe sent twelve spies to reconnoiter the land before the Israelite invasion. Ten of the spies returned with a report that the nations living on the land were far too powerful to ever conquer, throwing the nation into a panic. The people wailed and complained all night that they would be slaughtered. God's punishment fated them to die out in the desert over the remaining thirty-eight years, and only those beneath the age of twenty at the time of the sin would ultimately enter the land.

Yehoshua, together with Kalev, refused to join the majority and proclaimed that, with God's help, they would conquer the land and defeat their enemies. But a closer study of the events reveals that it was not Yehoshua who argued fruitlessly against his fellow spies, but Kalev. Yehoshua, who gave Moshe unsolicited advice in the past, remains mysteriously silent at a time when his voice was urgently needed. It was Kalev who quieted the murmuring crowd, Kalev who assured them of victory and Kalev who courageously supported

29. Bamidbar 11:28.
30. Kohelet Rabbah, ch. 9.

Moshe. Yehoshua first opens his mouth only after his colleague had spoken out and only after the people proclaim their intention to change leaders and return to Egypt! At a time when we would have expected to hear the voice of a future leader, we hear only silence from him.[31]

To be fair, as many have commented, Yehoshua may have very well felt that, as the closest student and attendant of Moshe, his opinion would only serve to undermine Kalev's argument. Nonetheless, forty years later, as the nation looked at their new leader and recalled his initial silence, can we blame them for their hesitations? Here then we have the next leader of Israel who is wrong when he speaks and wrong when he doesn't!

If we need any more reason to explain the nation's insecurity at the choice of their new leader, we need go no further than Yehoshua's teacher. The Torah, while relating to us the names of the twelve spies, adds the parenthetical statement "And Moshe called Hoshea, 'Yehoshua.'"[32] Throughout the book of Shemot the Torah refers to Yehoshua by that moniker, without mentioning anything about his original name, Hoshea, and without revealing that Moshe had changed his name to Yehoshua. Our Rabbis comment on the inclusion of this fact in this story rather than earlier in the Torah. They explain that the change of name was directly connected to the episode of the spies because Moshe gave his student a blessing right before sending him out on this mission, stating: "May God save you from [involvement in] the plot of the spies."[33] It appears that rabbinic tradition was also sensitive to the question of Yehoshua's ability to stand firm in face of popular opposition, of whether he had the moral strength necessary to be God's chosen leader. Their comment indicates that perhaps, without Moshe's blessing, he would not have had that strength. The Rabbis thus subtly express their opinion of Yehoshua, at least in his early years, and give credence to the tentative reaction of the people to Yehoshua's appointment.

Given all of these good reasons for the people's insecurity and doubts, and understanding the less-than-overwhelming impression of Yehoshua's leadership capabilities that we get from these events, we must ask: How did he become the hugely successful leader, a man who led the conquest of the land,

---

31. There are even those who claim that Yehoshua himself was initially supportive of the majority, as the text states: "But the men who entered the land with him [Kalev] said: We cannot defeat the nation, for it is stronger than we," implying that everyone besides Kalev, Yehoshua included, claimed that they could not defeat the enemy. I believe that is a forced reading, clearly contradicted by the subsequent events.
32. Bamidbar 13:16.
33. Tractate Sotah 34b; see also Rashi, Bamidbar 13:16.

who kept the tribes united as one and who inspired the people to remain faithful to God throughout his tenure at the helm of the nation? How did he, by the time of his death, become the only person in the entire Bible – besides his teacher and King David – to merit the title "the servant of God?"[34] The answer is somewhat surprising.

Yehoshua the Leader

The Sun versus the Moon

When Moshe was told that he would not be leading the Israelites into the land, he requested that God choose a successor so that there will be no time when Israel would be leaderless. God responds by telling Moshe to take Yehoshua, "a man of spirit," and share his own glory with his student. This mandate from Moshe would sanction Yehoshua with the authority he required and grant him acceptance from the people. The Talmudic authorities pick up on one crucial letter (the letter מ in מהודך) that, they say, explains the difference between Moshe and Yehoshua: "'And you shall place of your glory upon him'[35] –'*of* your glory' but not *all* of your glory. The elders of that generation said: 'Moshe's presence [lit. face] was like the sun; Yehoshua's presence is like the moon; woe to us from that shame, woe to us from that embarrassment.'" [36]

There was a clear diminishing of the greatness and the glory of leadership when Yehoshua took over. How could there not be? Moshe was the man of whom the Torah states in the final verses: "And there arose no other prophet in Israel like Moshe."[37] Who, therefore, could compare to him? And, the Rabbis of the Talmud suggest, the leadership of that time felt that diminished presence and were very well aware of Yehoshua's comparative limitations. Yet, as we have pointed out, there are no complaints against him throughout the book. There is no hint of rebellion and no suggestion of finding a replacement for Yehoshua. Even following their disastrous defeat in the battle of Ai, a setback that cost the lives of thirty-six fighters, the nation does not complain or turn their backs on the new leader.

---

34. Yehoshua 24:29; Shoftim 2:8.
35. Bamidbar 27:20.
36. Tractate Bava Batra 75a.
37. Devarim 34:10.

One Shoe or Two?

The Malbim[38] comments that the success of Yehoshua may very well have been due to the fact that he was *not* Moshe, the perfect, almost superhuman, leader. The Malbim expands on a seemingly minor occurrence, common to both Moshe and Yehoshua, and finds in the difference between the two events a key to understanding the differences between the two leaders – and the key to Yehoshua's success.

When God appeared to Moshe for the first time, Moshe was standing at the "mountain of God," at Horeb (Mount Sinai), and God told Moshe "Remove your shoes from your feet, for the place upon which you stand is holy ground."[39] When God appeared to Yehoshua before the battle of Jericho, he similarly told Yehoshua: "Remove your shoe from your foot, for the place upon which you stand is holy."[40] The difference between the singular (shoe/foot) and the plural (shoes/feet), says the Malbim, is significant.

Shoe removal is significant in Jewish tradition and symbolizes two things: sanctity and mourning. The removal of shoes is meant to remove us from the mundane world of every day, to either elevate us or lower us. On Yom Kippur, a day of heightened holiness and spirituality, the Jew removes his shoes as he is elevated above this world to almost angelic heights. On Tisha B'Av, the national day of mourning, the Jew removes his shoes because he has fallen to subhuman existence, wallowing in the tragedies of his history on that day.

When they stood upon holy ground, both Moshe and Yehoshua were told to remove their shoes. Moshe, who reaches almost to the level of the divine, was totally removed from the mundane and removed both shoes. Yehoshua, on the other hand, though elevated in spirituality, kept one shoe on, firmly planted in the reality of this world. Understanding this symbolism, we can suggest that Moshe was almost beyond human comprehension and, as a result, very difficult to identify with or relate to. Yehoshua was an exceptional person who remained a person, very human and easy to identify with. He was prophetic, yet real; Godly, yet human. The people saw his shortcomings, his weaknesses, and they saw him struggle with them. They could identify with that struggle for they struggled as well. The words of the Talmud explain this well: Moshe was like the sun, Yehoshua was like the moon. A person can gaze

---

38. The biblical commentator R. Meir Leibush ben Yechiel Michoel, 1809–1879.
39. Shemot 3:5.
40. Yehoshua 5:15.

at the moon and appreciate it, but the sun will only blind those who stare at it. Yehoshua was more reachable than Moshe and, perhaps, could understand the failings of the people better than the almost sinless Moshe could. Yehoshua's greatness as a leader was to be found in his humanness.

We might even suggest that Yehoshua was popular and accepted because his very authority differed from that of his teacher. Whereas Moshe's pronouncements bore the ultimate authority coming, as they did, directly from God, Yehoshua's authority was derived from the people themselves. Note how God Himself envisaged this type of leadership when first investing Yehoshua with this position of authority: "And before Elazar the priest shall he stand, and he will ask for him [the decision of] the *urim* before God; at his [Elazar's] word shall he and the people go and come as well as the entire congregation [leadership]."[41]

Yehoshua's popularity may well have been based on the fact that he was not the autocrat that Moshe had to be, but from the very beginning shared the leadership responsibilities with others. Similarly, as opposed to Moshe, his investment with the position of leadership took place in the presence of the high priest and the elders, symbolizing the people's involvement in directing the nation.

Basing ourselves upon this approach of the Malbim, we can better understand Yehoshua's very human behavior during these crucial episodes. Perhaps the very human Yehoshua was strangely silent when he returned from spying the land because he had been frightened by the "giants" he saw there. And yet he *does* overcome that fear and he *does* join Kalev in defending Moshe and insisting that the people must enter and conquer the land. We watch as Yehoshua develops his character by overcoming his natural reticence; through faith and belief in God, we see him growing into his role as leader of the nation. Note, for example, that when the Israelites cross the Jordan and enter the land, it was the priests who lead the nation across, not Yehoshua. Likewise, when the nation gathered at Mount Gerizim, reenacting the Sinaitic experience, Yehoshua, as opposed to Moshe at Mount Sinai, was marginal to the story.[42]

All of these actions, or non-actions, reflect Yehoshua's natural humility and his early training not to "depart from the tent." But when called upon to be the leader, Yehoshua never hesitates or shirks his responsibility. It is he who

41. Bamidbar 27:21.
42. See Yehoshua, ch. 8.

prepares the people and the army for their entry into the land, he who gives the military directives before the battle of Jericho and he who leads the army to victory over the Canaanite alliances. Despite his tendency to shun the spotlight, Yehoshua is the unquestioned leader of the nation, at times marching in front, at times remaining in the background. The reader might be amazed at the dramatic contrast that takes place within the first ten chapters of the book. Yehoshua, who is told over and over again in the opening chapter "be strong and courageous," is the one who, when warring with the kings of the South, told his people "be strong and courageous."[43] He, who once needed encouragement, now gave it. Yehoshua the man had become Yehoshua the leader.

The Challenge

Yehoshua had to do more than keep the nation united, organize an army and conquer a land. Yehoshua had to move an entire society from a nomadic lifestyle to an agrarian economy; from living as tribes traveling together and camping aside each other to being independent, self-sufficient yet united mini-states; from a supernatural existence in the desert to a normal, natural life in their own land. Yehoshua had to wean them off a total dependency upon God's miracles to a life of military and political responsibility common to all sovereign nations. Perhaps most crucially, Yehoshua had to impress upon the nation their continued obligations to God and His Torah. He had to teach them to sense God's presence and active involvement in their lives despite the absence of the daily reminders of God's existence that were present in the desert.

And he succeeds to a most remarkable degree!

Meeting the Challenge

Teaching the newly arrived nation to recognize God's hand in their successes and their victories was not a simple task, and it is God Himself who offers the first lesson. In a shocking development, the Israelite army is defeated in its second battle, actually the very first one they themselves were to fight. The first victory over Jericho came as a result of God's miracles and not Israel's military prowess. In fact, the Israelites did not even need to raise a sword. The

43. Yehoshua 10:25.

walls that crumbled killed the local population, and the army simply marched in and laid claim to the city. In the next battle for the small city of Ai, the Israelite forces are routed, forced to flee and suffer thirty-six casualties.

Naturally, when they return to camp Yehoshua tears his clothing and beseeches God to tell him why such a tragedy occurred. God responds by informing Yehoshua that the Israelites had sinned, as one of their number had taken from the spoils of Jericho. We are taken aback by the severity of the punishment for a sin committed by only one of the people. Is this why dozens had to die? Was this a "serious" enough sin to delay the conquest of the land and to send the Israelites into a panic? Why does the text claim the *Israelites* sinned when only one of them did? The answers to these questions will reveal to us the lesson God was teaching the nation and help us understand the episode more fully.[44]

Before the battle of Jericho, Yehoshua warned the people, as God had commanded him, not to take any spoils from the city. Jericho was to remain untouched, "a *cherem* to God,"[45] never to be rebuilt. The stricture against benefiting from the booty can be easily understood by a common expression: "to the victor belong the spoils." God hoped to impress upon the Israelites that the "victor" both in this first battle and, truthfully, in all subsequent ones, was *not* the Israelite army but God. The spoils, therefore, belonged to God, not to them. This was God's way of impressing on them the lesson that their success came from Him, certainly when they could see open miracles and even when no hand of God was apparent. This is why the Israelites pledge no benefit from their victory over the king of Arad,[46] why Shmuel warns Shaul to take no spoils from his war against Amalek[47] and why David dedicates all of the spoils from his wars to God.[48] It was essential for leaders to drive home the same lesson – that God was behind each and every victory.

If we recall the laws of the first fruits (*bikkurim*), and firstborn sons (*bechor adam*) and firstborn animals (*bechor beheimah*) that belong to God, we better understand the significance of the *first* conquest and why the spoils of Jericho were to remain untouched.[49]

---

44. I am beholden to Rabbi Menachem Liebtag for these insights.
45. Yehoshua 6:17.
46. Bamidbar 21:2.
47. I Shmuel 15:3.
48. II Shmuel 8:11.
49. This idea of the sanctity of the first also helps us understand God's declaration to Pharaoh (Shemot 4:22): "Israel is my firstborn son."

But they didn't remain untouched.

The sin of Achan, who trespassed the ban and took the booty, was more than a crime of greed. God saw it as a rejection of the lesson being taught. The theft of the property was a statement that victory *did* belong to the Israelites. It was a rebellious act which implied that they, at least partially, deserved to share in the wealth, for they too were victors. It was a reflection of the people's blindness to God's involvement in their lives. This was this sin that brought such loss and sorrow to the nation, for the punishment would teach them the necessary lesson of God's involvement in their undertakings. And to a nation who before the war with Ai were so confident of victory that they recommended to Yehoshua not to "tire the army" and send instead only a small force – such a reminder was crucial. The actual sin may have been Achan's alone, but the sinful attitude was shared by the people, who shared in the punishment as well. The lesson was learned well.

Similarly, as the book of Yehoshua closes, we read of a massive gathering of the nation in the city of Shechem.[50] There, Yehoshua reviews the history of the people, emphasizing the numerous kindnesses God granted them. Beginning with the admission that their forefather Avraham was not native to the land, having been born and raised "across the river,"[51] Yehoshua tells them of how God promised this land to Avraham and how, after generations and enslavement, God miraculously brought them to the land and conquered it for them.

He then exhorts them: "And if you find it wrong to worship God, choose today whom you will worship: either the gods that your ancestors from across the river worshiped or the gods of the Emorites among whom you dwell; but as for me and my family – we will worship God!"[52] The people naturally respond that they would never leave God to worship idols. But more remarkable than the response of the nation is the "choice" that Yehoshua gives the people. The commentaries are shocked at the seeming choice, when it is clear from the Torah that the covenant with God is immutable.[53] Many quote the verses in Yechezkel – "It shall not be…as you say: 'Let us be like all the nations…worshiping wood and stone.' I swear, proclaims God, that I will rule

---

50. See the final section of this chapter for an explanation of when this gathering may actually have taken place.
51. Yehoshua 24:2.
52. Ibid. 24:15.
53. Devarim 29:14.

over you with a strong hand, outstretched arm and spilt wrath"[54] – as clear proof for the fact that Israel had *no* real choice!

Rashi's answer is illuminating for us and supportive of this very point.[55] The classic commentator states that the prophet was warning Israel of his time that they could not claim that their acceptance of the Torah and the covenant in the time of Moshe was invalid since they did so only to enter the land. After all, the prophet reminded them, you accepted the Torah *willingly* and by choice in the time of Yehoshua.

The approach reflects the difference between the leadership required from Moshe and that required from Yehoshua. Moshe was obligated to impress upon the recently enslaved nation their responsibilities and obligations as God's "priestly nation and holy people."[56] They had no real free choice since they had been chosen by God and, therefore, were obligated to listen. In effect, God imposed His rule upon them, making Israel a passive partner in the covenant,[57] much as they were passive recipients of God's life-giving miracles in Egypt and in the desert. Yehoshua, however, dealt with a newly independent nation who had conquered their promised land by dint of their prowess in war and God's assistance. This generation was weaning itself away from the supernatural existence to a natural, more normal, one. They were no longer passive recipients; they were now active participants. How fitting, therefore, that Yehoshua saw to it that the covenant entered into in the time of Moshe, a one-sided covenant, would be reformulated and refreshed, this time with human initiative and not simply as divine imperative. As Rashi implies, this was a more binding covenant for it was entered into with pure free will. Ultimately, Yehoshua had succeeded in meeting the challenge of sensitizing his people to the presence of God in their lives, inspiring them to love Him and, consequently, to accept their obligations and responsibilities to Him joyously and willingly.

---

54. Yechezkel 20:32–33.

55. Rashi, Yechezkel 20:32, quoted in *Mosaf Rashi*, Rashi's additional comments culled from his writings.

56. Shemot 19:6.

57. Being a passive partner to a covenant is not a unique phenomenon. The first covenant with Avraham, the "covenant of the pieces" (*brit bein habetarim*) was made while Avraham was in a deep slumber (Bereishit 15:12). He subsequently accepted the covenant willingly in the "covenant of circumcision" (*brit milah)* when he performed the circumcision and committed his descendants to do the same (ibid. 17:23).

Moving the Tabernacle

Yehoshua's challenge to settle the tribes into their portion and yet keep them as one was equally daunting. Yehoshua was able to complete the first part of his mission, that of conquering the land, with the help of God. It was a straightforward operation of military conquest that, accompanied by God's miracles, was successfully accomplished with little resistance from the people. Settling the land, however, was something that required a complete change in the lifestyle of the nation. For the first time in their lives, these people were going to be living separately and independently of each other and yet were expected to retain close ties as a united nation. When they lived in the desert, the tribes camped near each other and traveled together. Now they were to separate from each other, yet conquering the remaining native population as independent tribes living separately was a task that most of the tribes were reluctant to undertake.

This becomes clear to us when reading the text. After detailing the different portions of land doled out to each tribe, the author tells us that the people gathered at Shilo where they erected a more permanent structure for their Tabernacle.[58] Until that time, the Tabernacle constructed in the desert had remained with the people in Gilgal, the place of Israel's encampment during their wars of conquest. The reason why Yehoshua chose to move the Tabernacle is never revealed in the text, but it is fairly clear to the careful reader.

The wars of conquest had ended.[59] Yehoshua's stint as military leader was effectively over. The land had been apportioned, and some of the tribes had settled in their territories and begun their campaigns to chase away the native population. Yet the majority of the tribes had not yet settled their territories; seven tribes remained in Gilgal, apparently content to live there off of the spoils of war.[60] Their daily life at Gilgal was not much different than their years in the desert when they camped together and lived off of the manna. It was a life of relative ease, especially as these tribes were able to ignore their responsibility of removing the enemy, working the land and building an economy.

---

58. Tractate Zevachim 112b. The Rabbis explain that the structure at Shilo was built of stone rather than the simple wooden frame draped by different skins that characterized the original Tabernacle.
59. As stated in Yehoshua 18:1, as well as 11:23 and 14:15.
60. Ibid. 22:5.

Yehoshua therefore moves the Tabernacle from the lower plains of Jericho, where Gilgal stood, to the mountainous region of Samaria, north of Beit El, where Shilo stood. In doing so, Yehoshua was indicating that life had changed for Israel. No longer were they to rely solely on God's beneficence, but they now had to take an active role in shaping their own future. No longer would the center of the people's life, the Tabernacle, be found in an isolated encampment of a wandering nation, but rather it would be in the midst of the land where the population had to settle and grow. He hoped that the transfer of the Tabernacle – the people's focal point and the very symbol of the unity of the nation – to the center of the country would remind the tribal leadership of their obligation to conquer their territories and encourage the population to settle their land. For that same reason Yehoshua built a more permanent structure for the Tabernacle, indicating to the nation that their nomadic lifestyle had ended.

Yehoshua urged the remaining tribes to fulfill their mission with more than exhortations and warnings.[61] He moved the Holy Ark and the religious center to the middle of the country and, by doing so, taught the reluctant tribes that they had reached their destination, their promised land. Israel's wandering days had ended; the nation had finally come home.

In Conclusion

The ending of the book of Yehoshua is not necessarily in chronological order. This pattern of ending a book with a chapter that underscores the book's theme or connection to the following book is consistent throughout the books of the early prophets. As we will see, the books of Shoftim and Shmuel likewise conclude with chapters telling of earlier events and not the final episodes of the time period.

Interestingly, the same may very well be true of the Torah, the Five Books of Moses. Although the final verses tell of the death of Moshe and the rise of Yehoshua to the leadership of the nation, thereby creating a perfect bridge to the book of Yehoshua, the earlier chapter[62] that relates Moshe's blessings to the individual tribes is not chronologically set, according to some commentaries. They explain that these blessings could not have been given where the Torah indicated, as the earlier chapter describes how Moshe was commanded to go

---

61. See Yehoshua 18:3–7 for his words to these tribes.
62. Devarim 33.

up to Mount Nebo to die. No longer in the camp with the people, Moshe could not have given a blessing to them. According to this view, these blessings were given earlier, when we are told that Moshe "went and spoke all these words to the Israelites."[63] If we accept this approach, then the final words of Moshe to the nation would be found at the end of chapter 32 of Devarim, words of harsh admonition but also of a promised final redemption.

The book of Yehoshua as well may actually end before the final chapter; that is, the concluding events of Yehoshua's era are to be found in chapter 23 and not 24. Although commentators such as Radak (David Kimchi) and Abarbanel approach the text as written – i.e., chapter 24 tells of the final gathering of the people before Yehoshua's death – others argue that this is hardly logical. They contend that Yehoshua had already committed the nation by covenant not to worship idols in the previous chapter. Why bring them to Shechem to repeat this very same thing, especially since bringing the entire nation, or even just the leaders and representatives, all the way to Shechem was a massive undertaking? The tribes were already settled in their respective territories, and their armies were protecting the populace from possible attack by surrounding, hostile natives. To spread the word for a gathering of this size – to get such a massive amount of people together just for Yehoshua to repeat a message he had recently delivered to them – makes little sense. The proponents of this approach suggest that this gathering actually took place much earlier, at the end of the years of conquest, when Yehoshua was bidding a farewell to the army and stepping down from his position as military leader. At that time, the nation had already been gathered in Shechem to pronounce the blessings and curses at Mount Gerizim and Mount Ebal as the Torah commanded.[64] Following that ritual, after writing the words of the Torah on stone and before the tribes were to retire to their own portions, Yehoshua gathered them and reminded them of their obligations to God.

If this approach is correct it would mean that the previous chapter, chapter 23, was chronologically the final one, which is why it begins with the words "And Yehoshua was old and getting on in years," the precise phrase used to describe the final days of Avraham[65] and David.[66] It would also mean that Yehoshua's final words to the nation were the words of harsh admonition found

63. Ibid. 31:1.
64. Ibid. 11:29 and 27:12.
65. Bereishit 24:1.
66. "And King David was old, getting on in years" (Melachim 1:1).

in chapter 23. Although this might sound puzzling to the modern reader, it is a pattern established by the forefathers, who likewise shared both blessings and admonitions right before they died.[67]

More likely, however, is that Yehoshua was following the precedent set by his mentor so many years before. Just as Moshe leaves the people with a warning of what would occur should they abandon God and His Torah, so does Yehoshua remind the people of their obligations to God and the consequences that would befall them should they ignore those responsibilities. But this is certainly not the way an author would want to end his book, which may explain why the events of Shechem from years earlier were placed in the final chapter as a closing episode.

In retrospect we can look at the period of Yehoshua's leadership as one of great accomplishment and growth. Yehoshua, like Moshe, serves as both prophet and "king."[68] He is to be the last single, unifying leader that Israel will have until the ascension of Shaul, the first king of Israel, some 350 years later. Nonetheless, there existed beneath the surface the roots of the problems that would haunt Israel throughout the difficult period of the judges. The struggle of the nation to find the one, unifying leader who could serve as a king is the subject of our next chapter.

---

67. See Yaakov's blessings in Bereishit 49 and Shmuel's words in I Shmuel 12.
68. "King" is used as an expression of a single recognized leader, something that, as we will see, was crucial to the success of the Israelite mission. In keeping with this thought, many explain the verse in Devarim 33:5, "And there was a king in Jeshurun when the nation's leaders gathered," as referring to Moshe.

THE BOOK
OF SHOFTIM

ספר
שופטים

LEADERSHIP
AND
SETTLEMENT

OVERVIEW

T he book of Shoftim highlights those events that impacted the growth and development of the nation of Israel following the death of Yehoshua. This work, attributed by tradition to the prophet Shmuel,[1] covers the longest time period of any of the books of the Prophets with the exception of the book of Melachim: over 350 years. These were especially difficult years, a time when the Israelite nation struggled with its own identity and with its very survival. We learn of individual leaders, primarily military heroes, who stepped up to save and subsequently lead the people at crucial times. By detailing the stories of these leaders, the book also informs us of the enemies of Israel, some from within its borders and some from without, who threatened the very existence of the nascent nation of Israel.

The book opens after the death of Yehoshua, when there is a clear vacuum in the leadership of the nation. God calls upon the tribe of Yehudah to lead the army against the enemy. We read of their victory over the local Canaanites and the act of heroism of Otniel, the man who would eventually become the first *shofet*, or judge, and how he helps his brother Kalev conquer and settle the area of Hebron. Likewise, we read of the conquests of the tribe of Yosef (Efraim) and its success in capturing some of the land apportioned to the tribe. The bulk of the opening chapter, however, focuses upon the failure of the tribes to fulfill the charge given to them by Yehoshua before his death: to conquer and settle their land and chase out the local idolaters.

---

1. Tractate Bava Batra 14b.

The book then gives the reader the reason for the difficulties Israel will face throughout the book: that very failure to chase out the enemies as they had been commanded[2] angers God, Who has them suffer under the oppressive rule of the surrounding nations. Their pattern of (mis)behavior throughout this time period is revealed in succinct detail by the author: Israel sins, God places them under the enemy's rule, they cry out to God, God responds with a savior, and, upon the death of their savior, Israel reverts again to her sinful behavior. The individual who serves as the instrument of God to relieve the nation of their suffering is referred to as a "*shofet*," generally translated as "judge." But these leaders were more often than not military leaders who donned the mantle of leadership in times of chaos and national need.

And so we read of Otniel and Ehud and Shamgar who save the people from Aram and Moab and the Philistines. We learn of Devorah and Barak, of Gid'on and Yiftach who battle the Canaanites and the Midianites and the Ammonites. We are also told of the lesser known leaders, Tola, Yair, Ivtzan, Elon and Avdon. The final judge, and best known, was Shimshon, whose troubling story we will discuss in detail. And after each battle and each struggle, after every miraculous victory and divinely inspired feat, the nation, despite God's repeated warnings and threats, reverts to idolatry and slowly begins to disintegrate, losing its collective memory of God's mission to become a holy nation and even losing a sense of nationhood. The final chapters describe quite clearly the state of anarchy that existed in Israel during that time period and the tragic consequences that would follow.

The book of Shoftim should not be seen, however, as a mere record of events. As we will see, there are important lessons and underlying themes that will help us put these events in perspective and give us a better understanding of what lesson or message the prophetic author hoped to share with future generations. If we remember that this book details the struggles of conquest and kingship, of removing the existential threats and finding a God-chosen founder of Israel's dynasty, we will comprehend the events and the decisions with greater insight and understanding.

---

2. Bamidbar 33:58–59.

ANALYSIS

Uncovering the Theme

It is important to realize that when analyzing the works of the early prophets, the *nevi'im rishonim,* it is most helpful to give careful attention to the opening and closing chapters. The opening chapters always serve as a bridge from the past book. But what is also true is that they can introduce a major theme that will be the focus of the rest of the book. Likewise, the closing chapters tend to prepare us for the next book while often expressing the theme of the book just completed. In fact, as we will continue to see, none of the closing chapters of any of the books are in chronological order. The final chapters of the books of Yehoshua (as we have shown), Shoftim and Shmuel are all "add-ons," depicting events that actually took place earlier. They were chosen as closing chapters precisely because the events that they describe drive home the theme of the entire book and serve as a bridge to the next book. The book of Shoftim is no exception to this rule: studying the opening and closing chapters as well as the story of the last judge of the book reveals the prophetic message hidden within all the events covered by the book.

The book of Shoftim depicts life in ancient Israel over a span of three hundred fifty years. It is difficult to present any single overview that could accurately describe such a long period of time, but there is one underlying struggle that characterizes the stories found in this *sefer* (book) and that entire period of time: the battle to find a leader who would create a sense of nation among the tribes – or, more correctly, the inability to find such a ruler who could unite the tribes and create one nation.

The Israelites had successfully settled in the land, but failed to settle the land; that is, they did not complete the mission God gave them of conquering all of Eretz Yisrael and removing the idolatrous nations from their midst.[1] This is precisely why the final chapter of the book of Yehoshua was chosen as the coda for the book, even though it very well might not reflect the final words of Yehoshua to the people. Nonetheless, the chapter was chosen in order to serve as a bridge to the book of Shoftim precisely because Yehoshua challenges the people to complete the process of conquering the land and removing the idolatrous influences from their midst, the very challenge that serves as the focal point of the book of Shoftim. The connection between the two books is therefore quite clear: the final speeches delivered by Yehoshua to the nation warn them to meet this challenge[2] and the opening chapters of Shoftim describe the nation's refusal to heed those warnings. The inability of the Israelites to remove the foreign influences haunts them throughout the book of Shoftim, and is reflected in the opening chapters that deal with that very failure and its consequences.[3]

This inability, or reluctance, of Israel to remove the idol worshipers from the land led to much suffering under the oppressive hand of the local enemies, both from within Israel's borders and from without. And the anguish endured by the Israelites was only aggravated by their inability to unite as one nation and defend themselves from these threats. The military leaders, or judges, who arose to relieve the suffering and save Israel from their oppressors, were also given the opportunity to meet the challenges of bringing Israel closer to each other and closer to God and thereby to facilitate the fulfillment of the command to appoint a monarch and build the Holy Temple.[4]

---

1. Ibid. 33:52–53, 55–56; see also Psalms 106:34.
2. Yehoshua 23:12–13; 24:14–15.
3. Shoftim 2:1–3.
4. Rambam in *Hilchot Melachim* 1:1 writes that the Israelites were given three tasks to fulfill upon entering (and conquering) the land: choose a king, defeat the Amalekites and build the Holy Temple. These tasks are the focus of all of *nevi'im rishonim*. See the introduction to this work.

A United Nation?

One of the oft-forgotten truths of this time period is that these "judges" were only local chieftains who, inspired by God, were able to throw off the yoke of foreign domination for a number of years. These were not national heroes, though some may have been known outside of their own tribes. These *shoftim* led armies from their own, and at times neighboring, tribes and fought to remove the enemy that threatened their particular geographic region. For this reason, for example, Devorah and Barak (chapters 4 and 5) were able to remove the threat of Yavin, Sisera and the Canaanites, but were unable to involve the surrounding tribes who were not directly threatened.[5] Likewise, Yiftach and his local militia (chapter 11) fought the immediate threat of Ammon who bordered on the area of Gilead and the tribe Menashe, but the tribes on the western side of the Jordan were uninvolved in the war. This pattern is followed throughout the book.

In order to understand the lessons of the *sefer*, one must understand the limitations of the term *shofet*, "judge," and why these men were not given the title of *melech*, "king."[6] Significantly, it was this very inability of the tribes to unite as one nation that made it impossible for them to choose a king. In effect, therefore, the absence of unity resulted in the failure to choose or even request a king, while the failure to choose a king resulted in an inability of the tribes to unite. As we shall see, this is one of the overriding themes of the book of Shoftim.[7]

What Went Wrong?

When one takes an overview of the era of the judges we find that it begins with great promise. The opening stories tell us of the fulfillment by some of the tribes of God's command to conquer the land and remove the idolaters. We read the story of Kalev, the hero we recall from the story of the spies of Moshe. It is a story that probably took place soon after the death of Yehoshua (and perhaps even before), but it is included in the book of Shoftim as it too

---

5. Shoftim 5:14–18, 23. Note Devorah's praise for those who joined and criticism of those who did not.
6. See the Abarbanel's introduction to the book of Shoftim for his list of similarities and contrasts between kings and judges.
7. The final words of the book echo this theme: בימים ההם אין מלך בישראל, איש הישר בעיניו יעשה, "In those days, there was no king in Israel; every man did what was right in his own eyes." See also Shoftim 17:6, 18:1 and 19:1.

is a story of conquest of the land accomplished by individual (or tribal) initiative and not by a national army (as in the book of Yehoshua).

This is a basic fact that is often not considered. Yehoshua's mission was not to conquer the entire land and chase out all of the enemies, thereby leaving the tribes to merely settle the land. Yehoshua led the organized army of a united nation in battle against the major powers and alliances in Canaan. As the book of Yehoshua records, Yehoshua defeated the powers and the military alliances in central Israel, in the northern plains and in the south. But he then leaves the conquest of the smaller, local militias up to each and every tribe.[8] This is the challenge he presents to Israel at the end of his life.[9] The book of Shoftim commences by explaining how the tribe of Yehudah takes up this challenge, as do some of the other tribes.

But the author then goes on to reveal the failure of most of the tribes to face this challenge, and includes the story of the prophet (an "angel of God") who berates the people for ignoring God's will. This event took place after the death of Yehoshua, for as the text reveals soon afterwards,[10] the nation remained faithful to God throughout Yehoshua's life and throughout the next generation; they were not then considered a sinful nation. The episode of the prophet-angel at the beginning of Shoftim foreshadows the eventual spiritual collapse of a leaderless nation.

Important to recognize as well is the pattern of sin, suffering, repentance and redemption that was to characterize the time of the judges. It is a pattern established by a fickle people who, perhaps fearful of the surrounding nations, perhaps influenced by them, turn to idolatry and the false beliefs of the neighboring lands; and it is behavior reinforced by the lack of a spiritual leader, or even a military one, who could bring the nation back to the worship of God. This too underscores a basic truth of the time: the lack of leadership impacted both the security of the people and their spirituality. Their fear of the enemy led them away from fealty to their God.[11]

---

8. See Yehoshua 13:2–6 and 23:3–13; note the declaration that God *had* fulfilled His promise to chase away the nations, but the rest is up to the individual tribes. Also Shoftim 1:27–36, specifying how the tribes failed to fulfill God's command to conquer their land; and Shoftim 2:1–3, where God's messenger (angel) berates the people for this failure.

9. Yehoshua 23:4–13.

10. Shoftim 2:1, echoing the verse from Yehoshua 24:31.

11. We find this behavior repeated during the beginning of the Second Commonwealth, during the time of Ezra and Nechemiah, when the leadership intermarried with the local nations because they feared those nations and hoped to solidify a political alliance and peaceful relations by doing so.

Interestingly, this behavior was not meant as a rejection of the God of Israel. The accepted belief was that God was indeed the Deity of Israel. The people were challenged, however, by the revolutionary idea of monotheism, specifically the notion that there was *no other god* (even of the other nations). Worshiping the gods of other nations was simply a device used by Israel to prevent the enemy from overwhelming them, believing that by worshiping the other gods, they would avoid their "wrath" and these gods would not help their enemies defeat them. It was this false belief that led to the pattern we find throughout the book: Israel is unfaithful, God sends an enemy to oppress them, the nation repents and cries out to God for help, God sends a "savior" who defeats the enemy and all is well for a period of some years (usually, but not always, forty).

This pattern is introduced with the verse describing precisely what we see in many of the subsequent stories:

וַיָּקָם דּוֹר אַחֵר אַחֲרֵיהֶם, אֲשֶׁר לֹא יָדְעוּ אֶת ד'...

> "A new generation arose after them [the elders] that did not know God..."[12]

The ignorance of God and His laws was, as mentioned, one of the weaknesses of the Israelite nation at that time, and understanding that will help us better comprehend the troubling events of the final chapters of the book as well as the connection of the book of Shoftim to the next book, the book of Shmuel.

The Decline of Leadership

The period of the judges, as the judges themselves, was meant to prepare Israel for an eventual monarchy. By removing the immediate threat to his people, the judge could accomplish two main objectives: to unite the people and impress upon them their responsibility one to the other, and to bring the nation closer to the worship of their God and the eventual construction of the permanent Temple. By gathering armies from different tribes, fighting forces who would confront the common enemy, the judge would impress upon the people their collective fate; and by attributing the victory to God, the judge

---

12. Shoftim 2:10.

could educate the nation as to their common destiny. This, indeed, is the task of Israel's future monarch: to unite the people into one nation and to serve as God's "representative" to the people. The success of any particular judge, therefore, could be measured by his success in accomplishing these two goals, thereby better preparing Israel for the monarchy.

As we study the book of Shoftim, we see how the level of leadership goes through a clear decline as the years pass. The first "major leader,"[13] Devorah, is a prophetess and a judge who receives a direct word from God to war against the Canaanites. Following the battle, she sings praises to God, clearly attributing the miraculous victory to Him. She even attempts to unite the nation behind her in a battle against the Canaanites and actually succeeds in attracting various tribes to join and unite against the enemy. Perhaps more so than any other leader, Devorah incorporates those traits necessary for an Israelite monarch: bringing about both tribal unity and recognition of God as the true victor in Israel's wars. Although the prophetess is not fully successful in her attempts to unite the tribes,[14] she does show the way for other leaders to follow.

The next leader, Gid'on, is visited by an angel and, like Devorah, receives the divine command to rescue His nation. Though a doubter at first,[15] Gid'on merges his mission of defending Israel with that of bringing them back to the worship of the true God by destroying the local idol (indeed, he is subsequently know as Yeruba'al, "he who fought Ba'al").

Militarily, he successfully gathers the tribes of Asher, Zevulun and Naftali to his army from the tribe of Menasheh and defeats the Midianites. Gid'on is so well respected by the people of his time that, with their support, he is able to punish those towns whose residents refused to help him in the battle. In fact, Gid'on is so popular after his victory that he is offered the throne. Additionally, his defeat of the far larger Midianite army – indeed, the very act of reducing his own army at God's command to a scant three-hundred fighters – made clear to the people that this victory was nothing short of a miracle. And although we read of no victory song to God as his predecessor had composed, Gid'on's very refusal to take the throne, with the explanation

---

13. For our purposes I define "major leader" as a judge whose story is related in more than one chapter.
14. In her song of victory, Devorah praises those tribes who joined the battle and strongly criticizes those who remained deaf to her pleas to create a national army; see Shoftim 5:14–18.
15. Even after the sign given to him by the angel, Gidon needs constant reassurances and multiple signs that God is with him.

"God will rule over you," gives us ample proof that Gid'on hoped to impress upon the Israelites that the victory belonged to God, Who was their true leader.

Here, then, was a leader who was able to unite part of the nation and represent God, as was his duty. And yet, ironically, the man who began his mission for God by first destroying the idol in his city lays the groundwork for renewed idolatry by leaving behind a golden ephod he fashioned, which becomes a focus of idol worship for the people. Rather than bring the nation closer to God by having them recognize God's hand in the victory, he draws them closer to idolatry and a denial of the one God.

The subsequent leaders pale in comparison to these first two. Avimelech, a son of Gid'on from a "minor" wife, cares only about power and his desire to establish a kingship. Indeed, his very name, Avimelech, "my father is king" (or "was king," or "should have been king") reflects his true intentions.[16] He begins his campaign by murdering his seventy brothers, thus removing any other possible heir of his father or contender for the "throne." Truthfully, it is even questionable whether or not he can be considered a *shofet*, as the text never applies that term to him. Indeed, many do not include him as one of the judges of Israel. He receives no communication from God and never wars against any threatening enemy, and yet he demands kingship. He is successful in gathering many to his side and building a strong army, yet he proceeds to use that army to divide his people and war with them. He has a certain charisma that allows him to attract a following, yet he is as far as one could be from God and His divine morality. It is no wonder and no coincidence that the name of God is never mentioned throughout the story of Avimelech.

The next leader is Yiftach, a man who lacks even the proud lineage of his predecessor, Avimelech. Being of questionable heritage, he was rejected by his own family and forced to flee his home. Eventually he gathers a band of malcontents[17] and forms a small army.[18] Through desperation, the elders of Gilead urge him to take on the threat of the king of Ammon, which he does only on the condition that they retain him as their leader after the battle as well. He is a leader chosen not by God, but by the people; and not out of preference, but out of desperation.

---

16. Significant too is the fact that "Avimelech" was the title of the Philistine monarch.

17. ויתלקטו אל יפתח אנשים רקים, "And 'empty' men gathered around Yiftach" (Shoftim 11:3).

18. Compare to the story of David: I Shmuel 22:2.

After a failed attempt to avoid war, Yiftach, though never commanded by God to go to war, prays fervently to God and defeats the enemy. His moving words to the king of Midian defending Israel's right to her land are evidence of Yiftach's strong connection to his nation. But his subsequent war against those Ephramites who claimed a desire to be part of the war and yet failed to join Yiftach's forces (much as Gid'on had punished those who refused to help him), led to the death of some 42,000 from Israel. Even after what should have been a unifying victory, the Israelite tribes failed to behave as one people and reassert their nationhood. Instead they fell into petty dispute and civil war.

Lastly, the tragic story of the daughter of Yiftach, the acceptance of (possible) human sacrifice,[19] is testimony to the misconceptions regarding the worship of God that abounded during this time and certainly reflects his failure to be the leader that would bring the people closer to the authentic and proper worship of God. Ultimately, therefore, Yiftach failed to effectively unite the people or to serve as a true agent of the Divine.

And this brings us to the final leader in the book of Shoftim – Shimshon *Hagibor*.

The Symbol of the Failed Leadership

Of all the fascinating characters we meet in this book, none is more contradictory or problematic than the personality of Shimshon, or Samson. And yet, only by studying his story and properly understanding what these strange events were meant to portray can we fully understand the message of the entire book.

At the very opening of the story, we are presented with one who was to be the "savior" of Israel. He was an individual chosen by God for greatness; he would be granted superhuman strength and endowed by his Heavenly Father with a holy mission: "And he shall begin to save Israel from the [oppressive] hand of the Philistines."[20] Here was a leader chosen before his birth to loosen the oppressive hold of the enemy, and one who was to be so dedicated to his divine mission that he had to assume the strictures of the Nazirite from his

---

19. Shoftim 11:31. Although Yiftach uses the term *v'ha'alitihu olah*, "I will offer it as a sacrifice," most commentaries explain that Yiftach's daughter was actually not sacrificed but was isolated from human contact and thus dedicated to God.
20. Shoftim 13:5.

very birth – indeed, from his conception. He was, in fact, the only personality in all of *Tanach* ever identified as a *nazir*, one whose life is restricted by the prohibitions against wine, intoxicating beverages, haircutting and contact with the dead.[21] The *nazir* takes on a life of limited physical pleasure in an attempt to lead a more spiritual life, one in which he can draw closer to God. The very word "*nazir*" finds its roots in the Hebrew term meaning to separate, distance and even isolate oneself.[22]

Now, given this promising beginning, one would expect a story of both glorious military victories and spiritual enlightenment. We look forward to learning of a leader who through the power of his spirituality would lead the people back to God, and through his simple physical prowess and presence would direct a united army to victory over their oppressors. And yet we find neither. By the time his story closes, we find the hero not a victor but a prisoner; not a seer but one who is blind – he is the leader whose own people hand him over to the enemy. Shimshon was charged to live the ascetic life of a Nazirite and yet he led a most hedonistic, pleasure-oriented life. He was to be a military leader and yet he never led an army. In the end, Shimshon appears as a tragic figure that chooses death with the enemy over life with his people.

So who was this man and what message does his story leave for us at the end of the book of Shoftim?

In the Beginning....

As we've mentioned, the account of Shimshon's life begins even before his birth, with an encounter between an angel and the soon-to-be-parents, Mano'ach and his unnamed wife. The angel appears to the barren woman and foretells the birth of a son. This auspicious beginning clearly echoes the story of the birth of our patriarch Yitzchak, whose birth was foretold to his parents, Avraham and Sarah, by three visiting angels disguised as men.

Yet, upon reflection, the contrast is more illuminating than the similarities. In the Bereishit story, the angels appear to the husband, while the wife

---

21. The rabbis of the Mishnah (Nazir 9:5) debate whether the prophet Shmuel was a *nazir* or not; the text, however, makes no direct mention of whether or not he was. Likewise, the Talmud describes Shimshon's Naziritism as being unique (*nezirut Shimshon*) in a number of ways, but this does not change the nature of a *nazir*, one of being more attached to the spiritual.

22. See Rashi, Vayikra 22:2.

remains in the background. Indeed, her absence is sensed by the angels, who ask Avraham "Where is your wife Sarah?"[23] only to be told that she is inside, in the tent. The angel of the Shimshon story, however, appears to the woman, who is outside, in the fields, while the husband, it seems, remains inside, at home.[24] In this story, the angel never asks the woman where her husband is and, in fact, seems completely unconcerned with Mano'ach, never even mentioning his name or referring to him. Even after Mano'ach asks God to send the "man of God" back for a return visit to clarify His message, the angel still appears only to the woman, and it is she who must then fetch her husband.[25]

Unquestionably, it is the unnamed wife who is to carry out God's message. It is she who would be in charge of bringing up this special son, she who would observe the strictures of *nezirut* throughout her pregnancy and therefore she to whom the angel appears. In the patriarchal story, it is the barren woman who laughs in disbelief,[26] while in the Shimshon story the woman does not doubt the veracity of the angel's word; on the contrary, she believes fully, while her husband seems to question her report, requesting the angel's return. Remarkably, when he realizes that this visitor was an angel, Mano'ach actually fears that they will die for having "seen" God,[27] and it is the wife who insists that they are in no danger. This choice of the mother to be the recipient of God's word is wholly fitting, not only because she would be in charge of raising the child during his youth, nor simply because she too was charged to observe the Nazirite proscriptions, but because the prophetic author foreshadows the life of that son, a life that indeed would be deeply impacted and shaped by the different women with which he was involved.

The story of the birth of Shimshon also reveals much about the society at that time; it reflects an insensitivity to the Divine that results in ignorance of God's expectations. This "blindness" to God is expressed at the very outset of the narrative, especially when we compare it to the story of Yitzchak's birth. Whereas Avraham recognizes that the "men" who come to him with a message from God are angels, Mano'ach is unable to see this "man of God" for what he is. Even after receiving the message from the angel, Mano'ach has

---

23. Bereishit 18:9.
24. Shoftim 13:9–10.
25. Note the text's inclusion of the phrase "and Mano'ach followed his wife" (Shoftim 13:11).
26. Bereishit 18:12–15.
27. "We shall surely die for we have seen God" (Shoftim 13:22); note too the similar reaction of Gidon when he first encounters the angel (ibid. 6:25).

no idea who he is and invites him to partake of a meal with him. And when the angel goes up to heaven together with the "flames of the altar," Mano'ach still seems to have his doubts. It is only when the "man" never again appears that Mano'ach realizes they had seen a heavenly being.

In this lack of sensitivity to the Divine word, we hear echoes of the description of the generation of Eli and Shmuel: "God's word was rare in those days; prophecy was not widespread."[28] Not only was prophecy rare, but even the simple awareness of God's involvement in the destiny of Israel was lacking as well. It is a condition that gets progressively worse throughout the era of the judges.

What's in a Name?

With this in mind, we turn to the naming of Shimshon, as the parents' choice of name for this miracle child is also interesting and revealing. Names are of extreme importance in the *Tanach*. Not only when God Himself gives the name (e.g., Yitzchak, Yishmael, Yisrael), but even when a name is given by the parent, it often reflects the mindset of the parents at the time of the birth (e.g., Levi, Yosef, Gershom, Ichavod). Furthermore, names can even hint to the mission God had for them or the life they would live (e.g., Shlomo).[29] One would have imagined that after an unexpected pregnancy and a birth predicted by a heavenly angel, the name of this promised child of Mano'ach would reflect the joy and gratitude of the parents. Our matriarchs do this a number of times,[30] as does Chanah, the mother of the prophet Shmuel. We would have expected a name such as Shmuel (שמואל) or Shimon (שמעון), reflecting God's involvement in the birth. Perhaps Shmaya (שמעיה) or Elishama (אלישמע) should have been given, both biblical names indicating that God had heard their prayers. Instead he is given the name Shimshon (שמשון), which sounds more like a salute to the sun (*shemesh*, שמש) or to the nearby city Beit Shemesh.

Yet, understanding the ignorance of the time and the behavior of Mano'ach, should we be surprised in the choice of his name? Not really. After all, nowhere do we read that either Mano'ach or his wife ever prayed to God for a child. We read only that the angel came to this barren woman and told her the good

---

28. I Shmuel 3:1.
29. See I Divrei Hayamim 22:9.
30. See Bereishit 29:32–35, as well as 30:6–8, 18–20, 23–24.

tidings. Compare this to the stories of other barren women: Sarah, Rivkah, Rachel and Chanah, all of whom pleaded with God and/or their husbands to bless them with a child. But this was not true with Shimshon's mother. We read of no prayers to God at all, no pleas by the wife to her husband for a child, no entreaties by Mano'ach to God for an heir. There is very little "communication" with God about their problem – and very little gratitude expressed to Him.

Ironically, when Mano'ach asks the angel to "stay for dinner" he is told that, if he is going to make an offering, then he should make one to God. It was then, and only then, that Mano'ach offers a sacrifice to God,[31] and yet, as the verse continues to state, Mano'ach still did not realize that he was speaking to an angel. He goes on to ask this "man of God" what his name is so that they could "honor" him when his prediction came true. Nonetheless, even after the birth of Shimshon, we read of no sacrifice, no prayer, no open expression of thanks or gratitude to God. Mano'ach chooses to honor the man but not God – never, it seems, recognizing God's hand in this birth. As we have seen, the child would not even carry a name that hints to the grate-fulness of the once-barren parents. Once again, the author grants us a subtle glimpse into the weakened spiritual level of the nation of Israel and, through understanding that, we can better understand why and how the tragedy of Shimshon unfolded.

The Problem with Women

The first recorded event in Shimshon's life is the demand he makes of his parents to take a Philistine wife for himself, much to the chagrin of both his mother and father. The arguments of his parents against marrying a non-Israelite, indeed a woman whose nation was oppressing Israel, carry no weight. The reader is understandably taken aback by this turn of events. Was this the "savior" of Israel? Is this the divinely inspired leader who would defeat Israel's enemy? Would we expect a Nazirite to be tempted by physical attraction and perform what might be considered a traitorous act against his people and his God?

The text understands our surprise and, in a crucially important verse, immediately states: "His father and mother did not know that this had come from God, for he searched for an excuse [to attack] the Philistines, and the

---

31. Shoftim 13:19. One can also explain the verse as saying that the angel was the one to offer the sacrifice.

Philistines ruled Israel at that time."[32] We should not be shocked or disappointed. The text reassures us that Shimshon was merely carrying out God's plan, for by marrying a Philistine, he now had an excuse to attack the enemy. So explains the Talmud Yerushalmi[33] and most of the commentators, who understand the pronoun "he" as referring to Shimshon – that is, Shimshon needed a Philistine wife so that he could use that relationship, or his involvement with her family and community, as a pretext for attacking the Philistines.

This approach is hardly satisfying. After all, do we ever find any other plan of God that requires transgressing a most basic Torah command – a command that Yehoshua specifically warned Israel to observe[34] – in order to create a justification to attack the enemies of Israel? Does God look for such a strategy to help any other *shofet* battle against the enemy? Is not the oppression of His people enough reason to fight the enemy? That is why He designated Shimshon before his birth! That was the very mission Shimshon was given! That was the purpose for which he was born!

Perhaps, we would suggest, that verse does not refer to Shimshon as the one who sought an excuse in order to attack the Philistines and, thereby, fulfill the mission given to him by God. The just-quoted verse might be saying: "…for *He* searched for an excuse [to get Shimshon to attack] the Philistines…," that is, God sought a strategy that would encourage Shimshon to engage the enemy. And if we accept this as a possible approach, we better understand the final part of that sentence as a subtle criticism of Shimshon: "…*even though* the Philistines ruled Israel at that time." God searched for a ploy, a device, to get Shimshon to carry out his mission, that which was told to his parents even before his birth: to save the nation of Israel. Shimshon revealed no strong desire to help his people, even though they were ruled and subjugated by the Philistines for forty years, and the only way God could get Shimshon involved is by making the struggle a personal one. And this was part of the Shimshon tragedy.

Nor is this an exaggeration. When reading the story of Shimshon, one realizes that there was absolutely no victory or even an act of bravery that Shimshon performed on behalf of Israel. Shimshon never led an Israelite army; he never fought a battle because his nation was threatened or suffering. We

---

32. Judges 14:4.
33. Sotah, ch. 1, halachah 8; see also Talmud Bavli, Sotah 9b.
34. Yehoshua 23:7, 12–13.

never even see Shimshon aiding a distressed countryman. Shimshon fought only when *he* was threatened, or angry or wanted revenge. Whether we accept the traditional explanation of the verse or prefer this alternate understanding, what is clear is that Shimshon, for whatever reason, does not raise an army, or even attempt to do so, from his tribe or surrounding ones, to face the threat to Israel. It appears that he was a leader who had very little connection to his own people, little identification with their suffering and, therefore, little influence upon them.

And, indeed, Shimshon goes on to alienate himself from his nation by marrying the foreign woman. When his Philistine wife divulges the solution to the riddle to the Philistines, he loses a wager he had made with them and angrily kills thirty Philistines, taking their clothing to pay off his wager. Subsequently, when his father-in-law takes away his wife, Shimshon takes revenge against all of the Philistines by burning down their fields, using three-hundred foxes with torches tied to their tails. When the Philistines kill his wife and father-in-law in revenge, Shimshon proceeds to kill yet more of the enemy. The Philistines then hunt down Shimshon, and he is handed over to the enemy by Judeans, his own countrymen, who are upset with this "hero" for having angered the very people who ruled over them. Shimshon, of course, snaps the ropes that bind him and kills one thousand Philistines.

Note, however, that each act of strength and bravery was performed for a personal reason. Note too how the (three thousand!) Judeans blame Shimshon for stirring up trouble with the Philistines and therefore willingly hand him over to their foe. Similarly, when Shimshon visits a harlot in the Philistine city of Gaza and the enemy hopes to capture him there, he moves the gates of the city up from the valley and is able to insure his own escape. Shimshon escapes, but his people remain subjugated. Once again, Shimshon uses his overwhelming strength to benefit only himself.

So is this the promised leader who was to save Israel?

Where Was God?

It is after Shimshon killed the one thousand Philistines that we read of his only prayer to God, besides the final words he cries before his death. Shimshon recognizes that God had granted him the strength to defeat the Philistines and now begs Him for water. When God responds, Shimshon, in gratitude (it seems), renames the place Ein Hakoreh, "the spring of he who called out [to God]." We should be fascinated by the fact that, here too, no mention of God is made. He renames the well but does not use God's name.

We must be stricken by the contrast to the story of Hagar, Avraham's handmaiden, who when visited by God in the desert renames the spring where she had that vision Be'er Lachai Ro'i, the "Well of the Living God Who Appeared to Me," recognizing God's involvement in her life.[35] But the same cannot be said regarding Shimshon. When he renames the spring where God responded to his pleas, he keeps the focus upon himself, the "*koreh*," the "caller" to God. It becomes the spring of the caller, not the spring of He who answered. Even when recognizing God's help, Shimshon manages to avoid making direct reference to Him!

And finally, we get to the well-known story of Shimshon and Delilah. Once again, Shimshon is involved with a foreign woman who attempts to entrap him. Enticed, seduced by the Philistine, Shimshon seems to be very comfortable with his powers and appears to have "adopted" them as his own, conveniently forgetting that they were granted to him by God for the purpose of saving Israel. After all, Shimshon must have figured out that Delilah was "out to get him." She had tried to weaken him three times, testing Shimshon's claims of what would take away his superhuman strength. She tied him with damp ropes, with new ropes and she then she wove his hair into the loom – but all for naught.

By this time Shimshon knew that she was trying to take away his strength, and yet he still reveals his secret. Is it not logical to propose that perhaps Shimshon did not believe that he would lose his strength this time either? Or perhaps he was weary of his mission and hoped to remove the "burden" of that responsibility? If we suggest that Shimshon may have now believed that the strength was his and not God's, or that he had no desire to have that strength, can we not conclude that Shimshon had forgotten about his divine mission and his debt to God or, worse still, perhaps even rejected them?

---

35. Bereishit 16:14.

Where Were the People?

The story of Shimshon is very much the story of Israel, and that is why it is so important to understand. If we are disappointed by Shimshon's choices and behavior, we must equally realize that he was a product of his time, and in some ways he failed to fulfill his mission due to the people and not only himself. Our Rabbis proclaim: "יפתח בדורו כשמואל בדורו, Yiftach in his generation [must be regarded as highly] as Shmuel in his generation."[36] Every leader must be respected fully, and no one may refuse to show honor to his leader by comparing him to a past leader and finding him lacking. This statement reflects the simple truth, according to our Rabbis, that every leader reflects his generation. If leadership falls short of our expectation, it is no doubt because the people fall short as well. So if the leader is lacking, they suggest, it is because that generation is not worthy of any better.

Consider, therefore, the following: God's choice of Shimshon was known to the local population. His acts of strength helped spread his fame – certainly within his own tribe of Dan, and within the nearby tribe of Yehudah as well. The nation was subjugated to the Philistines for many years and God sent a savior. Shimshon performed acts of strength and bravery,[37] thereby spreading his fame throughout the area. One must imagine that rumors of the visiting angel, of his miraculous birth, of his unique lifestyle, must have been known to more than a few. And yet, the people fail to rally behind their leader. They lack the faith in God or in each other to bond together behind their hero and fight the enemy. If Shimshon "went it alone" must we blame only him? Was it not also the fault of a nation who, though suffering under the rule of a foreign power, refused even to attempt to support their God-chosen hero? Did Shimshon fail to lead or did the people fail to follow?

The tragedy of Shimshon underscores the theme that echoes throughout the book. Throughout the period of the judges, there was a failure of leadership, a failure of "followship" and, at times, a failure of both. The result was predictable. The people are unable to form a united front or even think of themselves as one nation. They stray further and further from God and His laws until they hardly resemble the "kingdom of priests and holy nation"[38] God wanted them to become when He placed them in the land.

36. Devarim 19:17; see also Rashi, ibid.
37. See Shoftim 13:25, *Metzudat David*, Radak and Ralbag.
38. Shemot 19:6.

In Conclusion

The prophetic author presses home these very themes by closing the book with the two episodes: *pesel Michah*, the image of Michah; and *pilegesh b'Giv'ah*, the concubine of Giv'ah. These closing chapters are the only ones besides the first chapters that relate stories in which we read of no leader, no *shofet*. Indeed, these troubling chapters really require a separate study and in-depth analysis, something that is beyond the parameters of this chapter. What seems clear, and what rabbinic sources also indicate, is that the events found in these chapters occurred at the beginning of the period of the judges[39] yet were added in this place because of their connection to the story of Shimshon.[40] However, as we will see, they also serve as a fitting bookend, dramatizing as they do the failures of Israel throughout the time of the judges.

Chapters 17 and 18 relate the story of the idolatry that was openly practiced throughout the years that the Mishkan, the Tabernacle, stood in Shilo. The chapters begin with the words בימים ההם אין מלך בישראל, "At that time there was no king in Israel,"[41] a rather revealing phrase that explains the underlying reason for the events that follow. In these first two chapters we read of an individual named Michayhu (or Michah) who confesses to his mother that he stole her money, and she, after blessing him in the name of God, explains that the money was earmarked for God. She subsequently takes the money and makes an idol or image to worship and keeps it in her son's house.

Eventually, Michah appoints one of his sons to serve as "priest" for the idol but then replaces him when a young Levite passes through and is given the job. Michah is now confident that God approves of his actions and will bless him now that he has a priest from the tribe of Levi.[42] At this point, we learn of the dissatisfaction of the tribe of Dan with their God-given portion and their search for (and eventual conquest of) another portion found in the far north in the locale of the city Layish. As the story reveals, these Danites steal the idol and its priest and bring them to Layish, eventually establishing a Temple of worship to the idol, with the young Levite, Yehonatan, and his sons as priests to their god.

---

39. *Seder Olam Rabbah*, ch. 20; see Rashi, Radak and Ralbag.
40. Tractate Sanhedrin 103b.
41. Shoftim 17:6.
42. Ibid. 17:13.

Clearly, this is a story of theft, of violence and of idolatry. The ignorance of acceptable Israelite practice and Torah law, as well as the inroads made by the surrounding pagan religions, is evident both in the behavior of the individual and the actions of an entire tribe. The religious "collapse" detailed in this chapter is reflected not simply in the idolatry that was adopted by the entire tribe but also by the unauthorized invasion and capture of Layish. The tribe of Dan chose to ignore the challenge of conquering and settling the portion granted them by God and instead attacked a people described as quiet, secure and not part of any military alliance.[43] Their actions change the story from one of individual corruption to one of communal corruption. But as the author consistently reminds us, "at that time there was no king," and without a monarch there would be no enforcement of the Torah's laws or any unifying power that would define proper practice and educate the populace.[44]

The second story is a horrible tale of immorality, murder and war, frighteningly reminiscent of the story of Sodom and Gomorrah,[45] the ultimate symbols of immorality and corruption. This story also begins with that repetitive phrase "at that time there was no king in Israel," and the story ends, as does the book, with the exact same words. Here, the horrific acts of "inhospitality," of kidnap and of rape reflect a society immersed in immorality and violence. On the other hand, the shocked reaction of the tribes to those acts and their desire for swift retaliation make it impossible to generalize about the society as a whole. What is clear, however, is that the refusal of the leaders of Binyamin to punish the evildoers – their insistence on protecting the criminals – speaks volumes, not simply about the lack of justice that prevailed within that tribe, but also about the fierce independence, almost a detachment, that Binyamin felt from the rest of Israel.

This final episode of the book, which spawns a civil war between the tribes and almost leads to the disappearance of one, underscores the lack of unity among the tribes that characterized much of the period of the judges, as we've seen. By repeating the mantra about the lack of a king at the beginning and the end of the first story,[46] as well as at the opening and closing of the final

---

43. Ibid 18:7.
44. See Shoftim 21:25, comments of Radak and Mahari Karah.
45. Not only the plot but even the language is strikingly similar to the Bereishit story, especially Shoftim 19:20–22.
46. Shoftim 18:1.

chapters,[47] the author is leaving a clear message: The horrible events of this section were the result of the lack of a monarchy, which engendered a climate of anarchy, disunity and ignorance of God's laws. Were the proper person occupying the throne, the prophetic author is telling us, these events could have been averted. And if we understand that the king's mission was to bring the nation closer to God and to each other, this phrase is most fitting.

We see, then, that the era of the judges as depicted in the book of Shoftim was one of instability, regarding both religious commitment, political independence and national identity. Following the passing of the charismatic and powerful leaders Moshe and Yehoshua, the tribes became more insular, focusing upon their own specific needs rather than the good of the entire people. No longer fighting together, no longer camped as one, the tribes lost touch with each other and with those things that united them. Eventually, each tribe developed its own character, its own speech pattern[48] and even its own mode of worship.

The Mishkan at Shilo did little to centralize the worship of God, and it does not seem to have played a major role in the religious life of the people. In fact, the Tabernacle at Shilo receives almost no mention at all throughout the book of Shoftim. Indeed, as the last chapters relate, there was even a "competing" temple where certain tribes came to worship.[49]

It was a time that cried out for a national leader who could unite the disparate interests and focus upon the common goals, thereby creating a national consensus, a united political entity. The tribal leader, or judge, who ruled a limited area for a limited time, had the potential of unifying the surrounding tribes in order to face a common enemy and through his influence bringing the people back to the proper worship of their God. In doing so, the judge would be preparing the people for the eventual king of Israel, by uniting them and refocusing their attention on national, rather than local, concerns. Unfortunately, very few of these leaders were able to accomplish this, and as a result, years and years would have to pass by before a king would rule over Israel.

The author reveals these truths most clearly at the end of the book, especially in the story of Shimshon and in the events of the final chapters. It

---

47. Ibid. 19:1; 20:25.

48. Ibid. 12:6.

49. Ibid. 18:31. According to rabbinic tradition, the temple of Michah was erected at the very beginning of the period of the judges and lasted until the days of Shmuel.

would appear that the nation of Israel still had to mature before the people would learn to look beyond the local tribe and feel part of an independent nation. It would take a national threat to the entire nation. It would take the capture of their Holy Ark. And it would take the remarkable personality of the prophet Shmuel.

THE BOOK OF
I SHMUEL

ספר
שמואל א

THE SEARCH
FOR
KINGSHIP

OVERVIEW

The "books" of I Shmuel and II Shmuel are, in reality, but one book. It is comprised of fifty-five chapters and covers the history of the Jewish nation from the ascendancy of the prophet Shmuel until the final years of the reign of King David, about eighty years later. The Septuagint considered the book of Shmuel and the book of Melachim as one large unit, called "The book of Royal Dynasties," while the rabbis of the Talmud considered the two books as independent works that were written by different authors.[1] For the sake of convenience and easier referencing, the early Church fathers later divided the book of Shmuel into two books, a division that is commonly used today. The first part of the book, known as Samuel I (or I Shmuel or *Shmuel Aleph*), tells the story of the birth and ascendancy of the prophet Shmuel and ends with the death of the first Israelite king, Shaul; the second part, Samuel II (or II Shmuel or *Shmuel Beit*), focuses entirely on the rise and reign of King David.

The book begins where the book of Shoftim left off, depicting a nation unprepared for a monarchy but in desperate need of one. Once again the closing chapters of the previous book serve as a bridge to the beginning of the book of Shmuel. At the end of the book of Shoftim we read of the people's seeming lack of regard for the Tabernacle, which is why it is not mentioned at all throughout the book of Shoftim; we also see the corruption of the ritual service with the episode of the idol of Michah, where the people went so far

---

1. Tractate Bava Batra 14b.

as establishing an alternative center and mode of worship.

This same atmosphere is reflected in the opening chapters of the book of Shmuel. The high priest, Eli, is the acknowledged leader at the time, but he is advanced in years; his sons, who control the ritual worship at the Tabernacle in Shilo, are corrupt and immoral. But the signs are there that this will soon change, for at the very outset of the book the reader is presented with a contrast of families. We first learn the story of the righteous Elkanah and his saintly but barren wife Chanah, and then we read of the sinful behavior and immoral actions of the priestly family of Eli.[2] The opening chapters tell us of the miraculous birth of Shmuel to Chanah and of her oath to offer her only son as a servant of God, working in His holy Mishkan. Following the magnificent ode of thanksgiving to God composed by Chanah, the book details the corruption of Eli's sons and the punishment that awaits Eli for his failure to properly reprimand them, a punishment told to Shmuel in his first prophetic revelation. While corruption of ritual service continues, Shmuel grows in his service to God, and his reputation as God's prophet spreads throughout the nation.

The author of this work goes on to detail the battle against the Philistines in which the Holy Ark – improperly brought to the battlefield – is captured and the sons of Eli, who brought the Ark to war, are killed. The high priest himself loses his life upon hearing the tragic news, and the city of Shilo is sacked and destroyed.[3] The book relates what happens to the Philistines while the Ark is in their possession, the plagues and punishments that visit them, and how the Ark is finally returned to Israel.

By this time, Shmuel is the acknowledged leader of the people; we read of how he brings the nation back to the proper worship of God. They regard him as their leader in more than just religious matters, so that when they are threatened by the Philistines, once more it is Shmuel to whom they go for help. He leads them in prayer to God, and the Israelites are successful in chasing the Philistines out of parts of the land. Following their victory, the people argue for a king, a request that troubles both God and Shmuel. Nonetheless

---

2. The Rabbis point to the stark contrast between the two families: whereas the behavior of the priestly family led the people to avoid traveling to the Tabernacle and worshiping there, Elkanah and his family made a conscious effort to encourage the pilgrimage, choosing different routes each year in order to expose, and thereby educate, more people to the practice of worshiping in Shilo at the Mishkan. See Midrash Shmuel 1:1 and 1:5.

3. Although the destruction of Shilo is not found in the book of Shmuel, it is clearly referred to in Tehillim 78:60 and Yirmeyahu 26:6.

their request is granted, with God informing Shmuel of His choice of Shaul to be Israel's first monarch. The public anointing of Shaul and his subsequent military campaign against the Amonite regent, Nachash, unite the people behind their new king, and they all now regard Shaul as the man they had requested to lead the nation against their enemies.

Things change soon afterward as the story of King Shaul reaches its turning point. After another impressive victory, this time over the Philistines, Shaul is told that the time has come to destroy the nation of Amalek. God and His nation had waited hundreds of years to fulfill this biblical command,[4] yet Shaul fails to carry out God's precise directive; he allows the army to take the spoils and spares the life of the Amalekite king. By doing so, Shaul unwittingly proves himself to be unequal to the task and position he was given, and thereby forfeits his right to the throne. God had chosen another to be the progenitor of the Israelite dynasty, and He tells a disappointed Shmuel to go to the house of Yishai, where he anoints the youngest son, David, to be the future king of Israel.

The rest of I Shmuel is a story of friction, jealousy and struggle between the emotionally unstable and politically weakened Shaul and the hugely popular and militarily successful David. We read the story of David's defeat of Golyat, his ongoing victories over the Philistine enemy and his marriage into the royal family, which makes him a legitimate heir to the throne. In jealous rages, Shaul attempts to kill David a number of times, and the rest of the first book of Shmuel is a record of David's efforts to escape and survive in this hostile environment. By the time I Shmuel closes, David finds himself seeking refuge with the Philistine enemy while Shaul finds himself abandoned by God as he dies on Mount Gilboa in battle with the Philistines. Important to note is that in this final battle, Shaul's sons are also killed, leaving Israel leaderless once again and setting the stage for David's ascension to the throne.

The second part of the book of Shmuel documents the rise of David to the throne of Yehudah and his eventual elevation to the kingship of the entire nation. His successful conquest of Jerusalem and defeat of Israel's enemies increase his popularity among the masses. His conscious efforts to present himself as ruler of a united nation rather than of one tribe, and his acts of humility before God, stand in clear contrast to the failed leadership and national disunity that characterized the period of the judges.

---

4. Devarim 25:19.

The second half of the II Shmuel is preoccupied by the story of David and Bat-Sheva and the consequences thereof, including the rape of Tamar, David's daughter,[5] the murder of David's firstborn, Amnon, and the rebellion of his oldest surviving son, Avshalom. The tragic events that overwhelm David in his latter years serve as a backdrop to understanding this remarkable personality, who throughout his torment never questions or abandons God. Indeed, much of the story reflects David's acceptance of God's justice and clear admission of his own shortcomings.

Overall, the book of Shmuel is the story of a failed kingship followed by one of a successful kingship, a reign that established the dynasty of Israel for all time. It is, perhaps, primarily a study of what makes a successful kingship and what would cause one's rule to fail. It is this contrast that reflects the underlying reason behind the book: to establish the legitimacy of the Davidic dynasty. As the book itself relates, this was not a simple task, as the acceptance of David and his descendants as the rulers of Israel was challenged for many years, even after the death of David. It was only with the disappearance of the northern kingdom and its rulers that there was complete acceptance of David's legitimacy, and by the time of the Second Temple, it was no longer questioned.

Many serious questions challenge a proper understanding of the book. In our analysis we will try to uncover the reason behind Shmuel's (and God's) reluctance to appoint a king, the puzzling choice of Shaul to be the first king, the reign of Shaul versus the reign of David and the numerous challenges to David's reign.

---

5. Or, perhaps, stepdaughter; the commentators are divided on this issue.

ANALYSIS

The book of Shoftim, as we have seen, describes a nation that was in desperate need of a king. The book of Shmuel, on the other hand, describes the challenge of finding that unique individual who could retain the proper balance necessary for a Torah-ordained monarchy, and the process of molding such an individual into the type of leader God demanded. This God-chosen king had to be one who understood that his primary task was to be a servant – to serve God and to serve the people. The Israelite monarch needed to be not only a judicial, political and military leader, but he also had to serve as a conduit to God, leading the people to believe in and remain faithful to the One above. Simply put, the king had to be seen as the reflection of God and not as His replacement.

Could such a person be found? Could a king, the most powerful individual in the nation, strike the delicate balance necessary to rule with authority and yet recognize and let his people know that God is the ultimate authority?

Finding and shaping such a personality is part of what the book of Shmuel is about, and it is something that will be discussed further on. What we first must do is study the opening and closing chapters of the book, for they help us see the connection to the previous and subsequent books and reveal to us the prophetic message as well.

The Beginning...

The opening chapters illuminate life in Israel at that time, painting a picture of Israelite society and defining the great challenges it faced. These first chapters describe a nation of Israel that lacked a clear direction due to the absence of an effective leader. The corruption of the sons of the high priest and their father's reluctance to discipline them, as detailed in the opening chapters, lowered the regard for the Tabernacle in the eyes of the people and, as a result, weakened the state of divine worship. Through such behavior, the priestly family also forfeited any possibility of being regarded as potential leaders in the eyes of the people and in the eyes of God.

Prophecy had all but disappeared, a fact pointedly emphasized at the beginning of chapter 3 of the book,[1] and there were no longer local military heroes who could serve in leadership roles, as was true during the period of the judges. In fact, we are informed that Israel was in such a weakened military state that the Philistines had made serious inroads in occupying parts of the Land of Israel, thereby threatening the very independence of the nation.[2] In summation, there was no priestly leadership, no military leadership and no prophetic leadership. Clearly, Israel had lost sight of its mission, and for the first time it lived in its land with no one individual capable of directing the people back onto the proper road.

Following the story of the birth of Shmuel and the depiction of the corruption of Eli's sons, the text relates the story of the capture of the Holy Ark (in chapter 4), a dramatic revelation to Israel (and to the reader) of the unfortunate state in which they existed. It was the sons of the high priest, the very individuals who undermined the ritual service to God,[3] who led the army into war, although Levites and priests were prohibited from serving in the army.[4] They brought the Holy Ark to the battlefield, even though it was always to remain in the Tabernacle,[5] thinking that its presence alone would

---

1. I Shmuel 3:1.
2. The battles against the Philistines all take place in areas around Afek, Mitzpah and the heartland of Israel but never in the coastal plains of Philistia. By the end of the book, Shaul's final battle is fought on Mount Gilboa and his body hanged on the walls of Bet She'an close to the Jordan Valley!
3. I Shmuel 2:12–17.
4. Bamidbar 1:45–47.
5. Some commentators argue that this was an ark that was meant to be taken to war (see Radak, I Shmuel 4:4), yet the text indicates that this was the Ark that was *not* to be brought to the battlefield; see also Rashi, Devarim 10:1.

guarantee victory. The fact that the pagan enemy believed the same thing[6] indicates that Israel had no better understanding of their religion than did the Philistines!

With the defeat of Israel, the death of these two priests and the capture of the Holy Ark, God hoped to teach the nation that their success as a people depended upon their allegiance to Him and the fulfillment of their divine mission, and not on any "magical" power of the Ark. Furthermore, the defeat should have clearly illustrated to the people how far they had drifted from their mission and their God, as the very symbol of their "invincibility" and unique monotheistic worship was stolen from them.

As we see from these episodes, the nation desperately thirsted for effective leadership. It was a vacuum that had to be filled in order for Israel to fulfill her destiny. There was a need for an inspiring teacher, a selfless role model, a righteous prophet. Into this vacuum stepped the remarkable Shmuel, a man who, as the Talmud points out, was compared – indeed, equated – to two of Israel's greatest leaders, Moshe and Aharon.[7] It is Shmuel who successfully unites the people; it is Shmuel who leads the nation back to the proper worship of God; it is Shmuel who anoints the first (and second) king of Israel. And yet, despite the long wait and clear need for a king, when the choice is finally made, it is a reluctant choice: God is reluctant, the prophet is reluctant and the chosen monarch is likewise reluctant. To understand why, we must first take a broader look at the book of Shmuel, to better appreciate the structure of the book and to understand the requirements that had to precede the appointment of the king.

Once again it is important to remind the reader that the goal of the book of Shmuel is not simply to relate the events of the period of Shmuel and David. As mentioned in the introduction, each of the books of *Tanach* contains an underlying theme than runs throughout the book and reveals the prophetic message of the work. Our task is to uncover that message, that theme. When we address that challenge, we will find, as we did when analyzing the book of Shoftim, that the opening and closing chapters of the books are crucial, as they often serve as a bridge to the next – or previous – book and, at times, subtly reveal the message the prophet hopes to share with us. So that is where we will begin.

The book of Shmuel (and, of course, I refer to both I Shmuel and II Shmuel) opens with the depiction of a family. It is an outstanding family and an

---

6. I Shmuel 4:7–8.
7. Tehillim 99:6; see tractate Berachot 31b.

important family. But its story is not the only focus of the prophetic author. Rather, the story of this family is used to provide a glimpse into the sorry state of ritual worship in Israel. So what we would first believe is a simple portrayal of the family of Shmuel – the man who would appear to be the focus of the book – is actually an introduction to the description of the widespread corruption of the ritual service in the Tabernacle at Shilo, corruption perpetrated by the very priests who were supposed to guard the its sanctity.

Following the pattern established in the previous books, the opening stories of I Shmuel form a logical bridge to the end of the book of Shoftim, where we read the episode of Michah's idol and the foreign worship that was spread to the tribes. There we saw clearly how widespread and pervasive the ignorance of God and His proper worship was. But this closing to the book also forms a fitting bookend to its opening, as it portrays how the failure of the tribes to root out the pagan forms of idolatry (as detailed in the beginning of the book of Shoftim) deeply impacted the nation's ability to fulfill its God-given destiny.

Truthfully, the fact that an individual member of a monotheistic and image-rejecting nation could fashion an idol is not overly shocking. Nor should we be surprised that one Levite, although trained to serve in the true Tabernacle, would choose to lead the service to a graven image. After all, private failings of individuals do not, necessarily, reflect the general attitudes of an entire nation. But, that this illegitimate mode of worship was adopted by other members of the monotheistic nation, the fact that it replaced the service in the national religious center and was so attractive that it is stolen by the leaders of an entire tribe to be their form of worship[8] – that indeed is troubling, for it underscores the Israelite nation's complete ignorance of the worship of the God of Israel, at least proper worship, as God had defined it.[9] And that is one of the points the author tries to convey regarding this "lost" generation.

---

8. See Shoftim 18:19, 30 where the tribe of Dan establishes this false worship in their newly conquered portion.

9. It is important at this point, I believe, to clarify the concept of *avodah zarah*, usually understood as "idolatry." The literal definition of the term, however, is "foreign worship" and not "worship of a foreign god," which would be called "*avodat zar.*" The point is that one would be guilty of *avodah zarah* even when worshiping the One God, if the mode of worship is "foreign." God limits not only *whom* we may worship but also *how* we may worship. Throughout the Bible we read condemnations of those who worshiped the One God, but did so in an improper fashion. Most common was *bamah* worship, sacrifices that were made to God but offered outside of the Holy Temple (see Vayikra 17:1–9 for the specific prohibition), which was practiced and condemned throughout the book of Melachim.

This idea is carried into the book of Shmuel through the depiction of the corrupted ritual service in the time of Eli. And this idea is touched upon once again at the very end of the book.

…And the End

The final chapters of the book of Shmuel, like the final chapters of the book of Shoftim, are not in chronological order. There are a number of telling reasons as to why we make this assumption:

1. Chapter 22 of II Shmuel speaks of the punishment visited on the descendants of Shaul for his mistreatment of the Gibeonites. It would appear that in his zeal to remove all forms of idolatry and foreign influences, Shaul sought to remove the Gibeonites as well and, by doing so, break the covenant and alliance that was entered into by Yehoshua and the elders. It is hardly reasonable to believe that God would choose to punish a sin that occurred some thirty-five to forty years earlier and cause innocents to suffer: people who were not even alive when Shaul's campaign took place. Why would He have waited so long and allowed the sin to remain unpunished for almost half a century? It is far more logical, therefore, to date this event at the beginning of David's reign, when the same Gibeonites who were wronged by Shaul were still alive and desirous of exacting revenge.

2. Likewise, we are told that, at the end of the aforementioned episode, David reinterred the bodies of Shaul and Yonatan in the family plot, in Tzela. Here too, it is difficult to imagine that David would have waited so long after the tragic death of the former king and crown prince, his own father-in-law and brother-in-law (as well as closest friend), before giving the royal family a proper and permanent burial.

3. In chapter 24 we read of the three-day plague that afflicts all of Israel and causes thousands of deaths. The plague was the result of a direct census of the people taken by King David, who confesses his sin to God. Offering David God's choice of punishment was the prophet Gad who functioned during the first part of David's kingship, while the prophet Natan served God and Israel during the latter years of David's reign. This too seems to indicate that these

events took place at an earlier date.

4. In chapter 21 we unexpectedly start reading of the Philistines, the enemy who had already been defeated by David in chapter 5. Since that chapter we have read nothing of the Philistines, aside from a reminder of their defeat found at the outset of chapter 8. They have effectively been removed from the book of Shmuel, with no mention of them at all. This sudden reappearance of the Philistines with the record of the different battles fought against them clearly hearkens back to previous battles at an earlier time; none of these battles would have taken place during the final days of David.

5. We cannot fail to notice the unique pattern of facts and events chronicled in the final chapters.[10] Chapter 21 consists of the story of a sin committed by a king (Shaul) for which others (his descendants) would suffer and for which only a king (David) could atone. The chapter ends with a list of the heroic officers who served David during his reign. Chapter 22 is the epic song of praise to God, while chapter 23 begins with yet another song of praise and continues with another list of the brave officers who served King David throughout his rule. The final chapter tells us of the sin of a king (David) for which others (his people) would suffer and for which only a king (David) could atone. To clarify the point being made, let us look at the ending of the book of Shmuel in chart form:

a	chapter 21 (1–14)	Royal sin, punishment and atonement	A
b	Chapter 21 (15–22)	David's heroic officers	B
c	Chapter 22	David's song of praise	C
d	Chapter 23 (1–7)	David's song of praise	C
e	Chapter 21 (15–22)	David's heroic officers	B
f	Chapter 21 (1–14)	Royal sin, punishment and atonement	A

This type of sequence, ABCCBA, a "chiastic" structure, is often used to indicate a separate and independent section of a book.

For all of these reasons, it seems clear that these final chapters form a separate unit that includes events that took place sometime during the reign of David but *not* in the very final years. The question we must answer is: Why?

---

10. This final point is based upon the lectures of Rabbi David Silber.

Why then are they there? Why were they not placed in chronological order at the time that they occurred, earlier in the book?

As we have seen in previous books, the author-editor consciously creates a "bridge" to connect this book to the next book, the book of Melachim, and by so doing highlights the contrast between the end of the book of Shmuel and the opening of the book of Shmuel. First, we note the bridge that these chapters create. The opening of the book of Melachim deals with the establishment and strengthening of the reign of King Shlomo. We read of how King David quelled the controversy regarding Shlomo's succession to the throne by having him publicly anointed and by insisting that Shlomo begin his reign during David's own lifetime.

David's final words of advice to Shlomo focused upon practical steps the new king should take in order to stabilize the government. These included ridding himself of those who threatened his hold upon the throne and thereby threatened the very stability of the kingdom. Specifically, Shlomo was told to monitor the behavior of Yoav and Shim'i: Yoav, the faithful general who backed Adoniyahu's bid for the throne, and Shim'i, who cursed David but was spared death when the king pardoned him. Both would be quick to try and weaken a young king's hold upon the throne. David also instructed the young man to show favor to those who would bolster his claim to the throne and strengthen the alliances with those who support him. By doing so, Shlomo could firmly establish his rule over the people despite the fact that he was not the oldest son and was, indeed, rather young in age.[11] All this was necessary to unite the nation behind him so that he would finally be able to build the Beit Hamikdash, the Holy Temple.

These final chapters of the book of Shmuel deal with the sins of kings and their atonement for those sins, the faithfulness and bravery of the king's men as well as praise for God, who is credited for the king's military victories. Each of these topics forms a logical segue into the book of Melachim and the preparation of Shlomo to assume the throne of Israel. However, it is perhaps the final story of the book of Shmuel that creates the most powerful connection to the theme and focus of the book of Melachim.

As the divinely ordained plague decimated the population of Israel, King David cried out to God for mercy, arguing that he alone should be pun-

---

11. Although the text never gives the precise age of Shlomo, King David declares: "My son Shlomo is young and tender…" (I Divrei Hayamim 22:5). The Rabbis disagree as to his precise age at that time, with estimates that he was as young as twelve (see Rashi, ibid.).

ished as he alone sinned. Moved by David's prayers, the prophet Gad told
him to construct an altar on the top of the hill overlooking the City of David, in the field of Aravna the Jebusite. In an episode reminiscent of Avraham's purchase of the field of Machpelah in Hebron,[12] we read of David's
insistence on paying full price for the field and all that was necessary for the
offering. David erected an altar on that spot and offered various sacrifices
to God, who responded by ending the plague and the death. With this, the
book of Shmuel ends. What connection to the book of Melachim does that
story offer?

King Shlomo's ascension to the throne was an act of historical importance
not only because it was a relatively smooth transfer of power, nor because it
provided Israel with its first dynasty and therefore the guarantee of political
continuity and governmental stability. After establishing a firm grip upon the
throne, Shlomo's first and most essential task was to build the Holy Temple.
And although this charge is not mentioned at all in the book of Melachim
and only mentioned in passing in the book of Shmuel,[13] it is clear from Divrei Hayamim that it was regarded as Shlomo's most important task.[14] In fact,
after solidifying his hold upon the throne, Shlomo does indeed begin the
massive undertaking of the construction of the Temple. And where is that
Temple built? Once again, the specific place is not mentioned in the book
of Melachim but is found in Divrei Hayamim. There we find the following
verse: "And Shlomo began to build the House of God in Jerusalem on Mount
Moriah as was shown to his father David, [the place] that David prepared in
the threshing floor of Aravna the Jebusite."[15]

Fascinatingly, that which so many assume is a rabbinic tradition or midrash is actually found clearly in the text. Mount Moriah, the very place
where Avraham bound Yitzchak,[16] was the place where the Temple stood –
and that very place was purchased by King David from Aravna at the end
of the book of Shmuel! This explains the author's departure from recording
events in chronological order, for the closing story sets the scene for the next
book, which details that massive undertaking shouldered by King Shlomo:
the construction of the Beit Hamikdash. In this way, the book of Shmuel

---

12. Bereishit 23.
13. II Shmuel 7:13.
14. I Divrei Hayamim 22:5–19; 28:2–10.
15. II Divrei Hayamim 3:1.
16. Bereishit 22:2.

leads smoothly into the book of Melachim, not only in the chronology of events – i.e., the reign of David that precedes the reign of his son – but also in their underlying themes of kingship that must inspire worship; monarchy that had to lead the nation to the *mikdash*, the Holy Temple.

But the book of Shmuel is also a contained unit in which these themes can be uncovered by a close study of the opening and closing of the book. As we've seen, the opening chapter of the book centers about the story of Shmuel's family and his miraculous birth to the once-barren Chanah. This miracle is the cause for one of the most moving poems in all of *Tanach*, the Song of Chanah.[17] In the opening verses of the second chapter of Shmuel, when Chanah offers words of praise and gratitude to the merciful and all-powerful God, she finishes her prayer with the prophetic words: "He will give strength to His king and raise the power of His anointed one."[18] Even before there is a king – before David, before Shaul – Chanah spoke of God's king, God's "anointed one." She prayed for the success of monarchs who had not yet been anointed, and would be by her son, the not-yet-but-soon-to-be prophet. In doing so, Chanah reflects the thirst the nation had for stable and God-ordained leadership, and she expresses a major theme of the book as well: the establishment of an Israelite monarchy.

Remarkably, when reading these words, we also hear echoes of yet another moving ode. As we read the prophetic words of Chanah, do we not also hear the words of King David's poem in the closing chapters of the book? "He is a tower of strength for His king and does kindness to His anointed one…"[19] Thus, one theme of the book opens and closes the work, serving as "bookends" and tying together the different events of the book.

Meluchah and *Mikdash*[20]

Interestingly, we can find in the book of Shmuel another subtle yet fascinating hint to the themes of kingship and the building of the Holy Temple. After depicting the flagging spiritual intensity of the Israelites of Eli's times, the book of Shmuel goes on to depict the corruption of Eli's sons, Chofni and Pinchas. As mentioned earlier, their fraudulent use of their high positions for

17. I gratefully acknowledge the studies of Rabbi Nathaniel Helfgot for the following insights.
18. I Shmuel 2:10.
19. II Shmuel 22:51.
20. "Kingship and the Holy Temple."

their own selfish gain further distanced the masses from worshiping in the Tabernacle, thereby contributing to the lack of unity among the people. In chapter 4, we read of the terrible defeat inflicted on the nation by the Philistines. After the Israelites had lost the first battle, these two sons in an act of sacrilege accompany the Holy Ark, the *aron*, into the battlefield. The story describes the capture of the Ark and its subsequent "wanderings" from Philistine city to Philistine city, eventually back to an Israelite city and then to yet another Israelite city.

In effect, the Holy Ark goes into "exile," never again to rest within the Tabernacle, the Mishkan, which had been destroyed with the Philistine sack of the city Shilo.[21] And then, in the final chapter of the book, we learn of the purchase of the field ("threshing floor") of Aravna the Jebusite which, as we have seen, becomes the final destination and permanent resting place for the Holy Ark. The book of Shmuel that began with exile of the Ark thus ends with the purchase of the Ark's permanent resting place.

Certainly, this is a fitting close to the story and theme of the book. Remarkably, this "Holy Temple" theme becomes even more evident when we realize that the very name of the owner of the field, Aravna (ארונה), is actually a combination of the two words "Aron Hashem," the Ark of God (ארון ה'), when using the final letter (*hey*) as a shortened form of God's name![22]

In conclusion, the author sends a message to those studying the book that there is a connection between the opening and closing chapters. By doing so, he hopes to make the theme of the book clear: it was time for a monarch who would stir the people to greater devotion to God and to their nation. The king was a necessary cog between "conquest" and "worship"; between settling the land and formalizing the devotion to God in a permanent religious center. The Torah makes it clear that Temple worship was to be delayed until military security could be established in the land. Before

---

21. See Yirmeyahu 7:12, 14; 26:6; Tehillim 78:60.
22. Aravna's name appears as "Arnon" in II Divrei Hayamim 3:2, while the first time it is mentioned in Shmuel 24:18 it is spelled "Arniyah" and pronounced Aravna. I believe that this is no coincidence. The author of the book of Shmuel wanted to underscore this connection to the *aron*, the Ark, and therefore spelled the name Aravna with a *vav* the next seven times it appears, in order to include the word *aron* within his name. By doing so, he is able to connect this final story to the events found in the opening chapters of the book, when the Ark was captured by the Philistines.

God would "dwell" securely, the nation of Israel had to.[23]

The prophet Shmuel prepared the ground for kingship though his inspirational leadership and unswerving commitment to God. What was needed now was a king who would succeed in strengthening the people's allegiance to the monarch and to God, so that the entire nation would unite as one in undertaking the ambitious project of building a Holy Temple. The book of Shmuel records what kind of individual would ultimately succeed as king and what type would fail through the stories of Shaul and David: a failed kingship and one that would establish Israel's eternal dynasty.

So What Is Wrong with a King?

The story of Israel's first king is, seemingly, a story of lost opportunity, of wasted potential. It is a saga of a man chosen by God, humble, modest and committed to his God and his nation, who nonetheless fails to establish the much-needed dynasty that would guarantee a stable government. The fault, if there is one to be found, is not Shaul's alone. In order to understand this failure and find out what went wrong and why, we must look beneath the surface of the text and clarify what exactly "kingship" was meant to be in Israel and how the first monarch and the people fell short of God's expectations.

HaRav Yosef Dov Soloveitchik defines the role of an Israelite king in the following manner: "Monarchy...was permitted not to create symbols of national glory or to forge empires. A king was expected to fulfill a specific...

---

23. Devarim 11:10–11. Our Rabbis saw in the juxtaposition of verses the necessity to arrive at a state of rest and peace (*menuchah*) before the Temple could be built. This is also made quite clear by David himself, who urges the people to start planning the construction because "Behold, God is with you and has given you rest from your surrounding enemies…therefore arise and build God's Temple…" (I Divrei Hayamim 22:18–19). Indeed this is the very reason given to the prophet Natan as to why King David was not permitted to build the Temple. In II Shmuel 7:10, God explains that Israel was still not securely settled in her land. David correctly understood that as a great warrior, he had a different challenge to meet: conquering all of Israel's enemies and thereby making it possible to construct the Temple. Indeed, the very opening words of II Shmuel, chapter 7 ("When David sat upon his throne in his palace and God had given him respite from his surrounding enemies") explain why David thought that the time had come to build the Temple and why he made the request of God. Ultimately, it was not David who was unworthy of building the Temple, but rather the conditions for the construction that were not right. The well-known reason often given for God's refusal to allow David to build the Temple ("for you spilled much blood") is never mentioned in the book of Shmuel. We find it in I Divrei Hayamim 22:8 and 28:3 as the explanation given by David himself to his son and then to the people.

assignment. Shaul was anointed to repulse Philistine attacks; David's goal was to unify the loosely federated tribes into a single nation and to complete the conquest of the Holy Land. Shlomo's mission was to build the Temple...."[24]

Interestingly, Rabbi Soloveitchik also contends that Israelite kingship had to be requested by the people and not imposed upon them. Indeed, following a great victory over the invading Philistines, the leadership and people of Israel turn to their leader and request a king.

This is not the first time that Israel desired a king. In the book of Shoftim, Gid'on is also asked by the people to serve as their king following his great victory over the Midianites. In the book of Shmuel, however, the request is not made to the conquering hero himself. In truth, it would seem that this latter appeal was far more thoughtful than the previous one, as it was based upon the clear recognition by Israel's leaders of their need for a king. It was the expression of a sincere desire to establish, once and for all, an Israelite monarchy, rather than a demand to appoint a specific individual who gained popularity among the people. Their request was, likewise, properly addressed to the prophet Shmuel in the hope that he may get God's approval to the people's appeal.[25] And yet, despite what appears to be a proper and logical request, one conforming to the Torah's own dictates, both God and Shmuel are upset at the request and view it in a negative light.

Shmuel's opposition to the people's request is both ironic and problematic. It is ironic because the one person most instrumental in preparing the nation for a monarch was Shmuel himself. There had been no king, indeed no one national leader, since the death of Yehoshua, primarily because the people were scattered in different parts of the land and tended to be rather provincial and close-minded, unable to look beyond their own immediate and local needs. They saw themselves as members of specific tribes more than as members of God's chosen nation. As a result, they placed their own parochial concerns above those of the nation.

As we discussed when studying the book of Shoftim, the ultimate success of any particular judge was not simply if he or she was able to save the nation from the immediate military threat, but whether the judge was able to unite the people and teach them that any military victory belonged to God,

---

24. Abraham R. Besdin, *Reflections of the Rav* (New York: Ktav Publishing House, 1993), chapter 12: "Who Is Fit to Lead the Jewish People," p. 131.
25. Clearly delineated in Devarim 17:15: "You shall place upon yourselves a king *whom the Lord your God chooses....*"

and not to the judge or the army. The earlier judges were often successful in uniting surrounding tribes into an effective fighting force, but the later judges were not. The lack of unity and purpose that grew and intensified throughout the time period of the judges threatened to tear apart the nation, as the final story of the book of Shoftim proves. There had to be a dramatic change in the attitude of the people in order for the nation to survive. There had to be an outstanding personality who could change their attitude and alter the course of events that threatened the very existence of the nation of Israel. There was. His name was Shmuel.

Shmuel was both prophet and judge. His miraculous birth to the barren Chanah was not predicted by God or heralded as the birth of the savior of Israel, as was true of Shimshon, and yet he did save Israel. In contrast to the Shimshon saga, Shmuel was not charged to be the instrument of God; rather, he was offered to be one. He was never meant to be a military hero and indeed never actively fought in any war, and yet he inspired a united army to victory. As a member of the Levite tribe, he had no allegiance to any specific geographic area of the country, as the Levites had no one portion allotted to their tribe, living instead in cities scattered among the other tribes.[26] As such, no one tribe could claim him as their "favorite son," and he was perceived as everyone's leader, regarded as one who belonged to *all* the people, to the entire nation of Israel.

The prophet further encourages such a view by serving as a "circuit" judge. In contrast to the prophetess Devorah, who sat beneath her tree and judged those who came to her,[27] Shmuel insisted on going to the people and judging them in their own towns,[28] rather than having them come to him. The result was that many more people got to see him, to know him and to regard him as their spiritual guide. Following the Philistine sacking of the city of Shilo, the destruction of the Tabernacle and the exile of the Holy Ark, Shmuel becomes the focus of the people. He prays for them, sacrifices for them, exhorts them to repent and return to God, and even leads them into war.[29] Israel now had one acknowledged leader and began to think in terms of the nation rather than the tribe.

It was only logical, therefore, that the nation would now turn to him and ask for one political leader, chosen by God, to rule over their one

26. See Bamidbar 35:1–8; Devarim 10:9; 18:2; Yehoshua 13:14; 18:7.
27. Shoftim 4:3.
28. I Shmuel 7:16–17.
29. Ibid. 7:3–11.

nation. This was not a rejection of Shmuel's leadership. The people themselves explain why they were requesting a king: "You have grown old and,
behold, your children have not followed your ways."[30] The only reason for
their request was that they desired a continuity of leadership. A religious
leader, a prophet or a scholar, was not a position bequeathed to one's heirs.
Were a prophet to become the national leader, there would be uncertainty
and argument each time the prophet died. And yet, had Shmuel's sons
been worthy, the people would have accepted them as their future leaders and not have requested a king. They would have been satisfied in the
knowledge that there would be a peaceful transition of power to the next
generation and the creation of relative political stability, if only for one
more generation.

This then was their underlying reason for requesting a king. By becoming
the focus of all of Israel, by treating the nation as one, Shmuel had succeeded
in uniting them as no leader since Yehoshua had. By doing so, he had unwittingly given the people a taste of normalcy and awakened within them a
thirst for political stability. The result was their request of Shmuel to appoint
a king.

Beyond the irony in Shmuel's reaction to the request, Shmuel's objection
to the appointment of the king was also problematic because the people
were doing no more than what the Torah instructed them to do![31] The
Israelites were given specific instructions regarding the king, details as to
what commandments he alone was obligated to follow, and the permissibil-
ity – indeed, according to many commentaries, the command – to appoint
a king. In fact, Rambam includes the appointment of a king as one of the
three commandments incumbent upon Israel from when they entered the
land.[32]

Furthermore, the king was given specific commandments to carry out for
the people. He was designated to read the Torah in the Holy Temple, in a
public gathering on the holiday of Sukkot, every first year of the *shemittah*

---

30. Ibid. 8:5.
31. Devarim 17:15.
32. Rambam, *Hilchot Melachim* 1:1. Although there is an argument in the Talmud (Sanhedrin
20b) between R. Nehorai, who explained that there was no command to appoint a king,
merely an anticipation that we would do so, and R. Yehudah, who claims that, indeed, it is
a commandment, Rambam sides with R. Yehudah; other commentaries, including Ibn Ezra,
Ramban and Abarbanel, agree with R. Nehorai.

(Sabbatical) cycle.[33] If there were a general objection to the institution of the monarchy, why would the Torah give a king special commandments to perform for the nation? So the question is obvious: Why did Shmuel object to the request? And, more troubling, why did God show displeasure? Simply put: What is wrong with a king?

Timing Is Everything

The commentaries disagree as to the precise reason for both God's and Shmuel's discomfort with Israel's request. Many point to the text itself ("they have not rejected you [Shmuel], but they have rejected Me from ruling over them")[34] as proof that the very request for a king was sinful, for it implied that they were rejecting God as the true King of Israel.

The Rabbis of the Talmud see the sin of the Israelites in the language of the request. The Talmud says[35] that the leadership asked properly when they merely requested a king ("Give us a king to judge [or lead] us"[36]), but the common people wrongly added the words "as all the other nations,"[37] implying that their king would be the same as those of other nations. By doing so, the nation was clearly ignoring the many commandments that would be incumbent upon an Israelite king, commandments that would make him and the Israelite monarchy unique. Therefore, when God subsequently says that the people have rejected Him, He refers to the rejection of His commandments that were meant to guide the king and limit his power.

By implication, the Israelites were claiming that they did not want their king to have any limitation to his power,[38] certainly a direct contradiction of the Torah's demands.[39] What is also clear is that the people failed to understand the revolutionary concept put forth by the Torah that the king was to be

33. The mitzvah of *hakhel*, "gathering," is the next-to-last mitzvah in the Torah and is found in Devarim 31:12. Although the king is not specified, the Talmud (Sotah 41a) declares that the commandment is addressed to him, one who was able to "congregate" the entire nation. The Rabbis also comment that the book of Kohelet refers to King Shlomo as *kohelet* (קהלת), the "congregator," because as king he gathered the people for the mitzvah of *hakhel,* הקהל.
34. I Shmuel 8:7.
35. Tractate Sanhedrin 20b.
36. I Shmuel 8:5.
37. Ibid.
38. See Ralbag, I Shmuel 8:4.
39. Devarim 17:16–20.

subservient to the law and not above it. He would not be a "god" but would serve the One God.

Although these approaches seem to resolve the question, they do leave us less than satisfied, for our basic question remains: Didn't the Torah itself command the people to appoint a king upon entering the land? "When you arrive in the land...and say: 'I shall appoint a king as leader like all of the surrounding nations.' *You shall certainly appoint a king over you,* one of God's choosing...."[40]

Furthermore, we must be troubled by another challenge to these approaches: If their request was sinful, if they had indicated a desire to rebel against God, to reject Him, why would God have granted their request?

In attempting to resolve this question commentators have suggested that the Torah's proclamation was not a command but rather a statement meant simply to grant permission to the Israelites to have a monarch. That is, *if* the nation desired a king then they *may* appoint one. This approach too is dissatisfying, for it ignores the double language used – which, loosely translated, would mean "you shall *certainly* place a king over yourself," a language that hardly implies a mere suggestion or a granting of permission, something that Rambam likewise understood.[41] Additionally, the very fact that they approached the prophet Shmuel with this request indicates that they desired God's approval; in effect, they understood that the king had to be as the Torah demands: "of God's choosing."[42] This clearly contradicts the idea that they wanted to appoint one who would be above God's laws, a king who would have limitless power. Why would they have approached their beloved prophet Shmuel, the representative of God Himself, to ask him to help them reject God and find a new leader?

If we need any more proof that God did not oppose the concept of monarchy, we need merely to remember what happened after God rejected Shaul. Shaul's failure as king could have sounded the death knell for an Israelite monarchy. After removing Shaul, God had every right to deny any request for another king. The experiment failed; the trial was over; the people would have to accept that they were not to have a monarchy. And yet, immediately after rejecting Shaul, God tells Shmuel to anoint David to be Shaul's successor. Now, the people did not reject Shaul; the people had no problem with Shaul,

40. Ibid. 17:15.
41. See note 32.
42. Devarim 17:15.

and they did *not* request another king. And yet, God commands Shmuel to anoint another king. The institution of monarchy was not doomed. God Himself desired a successor to the throne! God, it seemed, agreed that it was good for the nation to have a king. And so we return to our original question: Why does God oppose the people's request of Shmuel to appoint a king?

To resolve this problem, we should turn our attention to the text itself and find out what it was about the people's request that disturbed both God and His prophet.

As chapter 7 begins, Israel is still under the grasp of their intractable enemy, the Philistines. It is they who had years earlier captured the Holy Ark,[43] and they who had destroyed the Tabernacle and the entire city of Shilo, the religious center of Israel. The Ark had been miraculously returned to Israel, but the enemy still controlled much of the land. Shmuel leads a movement of repentance and return to God by calling upon the nation to rid themselves of any forms of idolatry. As the Israelites gather to Mizpah at Shmuel's behest for a massive communal sacrifice and prayer, the Philistines suspect that the gathering is also meant as an attempt to gather an army and prepare for war. As the enemy, in response, amasses its forces against Israel, the Israelites, in great fear, urge Shmuel to cry out to God for them. After the people fast, pray and offer sacrifices, God responds to their supplications and throws the enemy into a panic and confusion. Israel inflicts a telling defeat on the Philistines, pushing them away from the heartland of Israel toward their own settlements on the coast.

The victory was so complete, the text reveals, that for the rest of Shmuel's life, the Philistines would never again pose so great a threat. This remarkable victory led to the return of many Israelite cities, and as a result of the fear of Israel's newly revealed power, it also led to peaceful relations with the remaining Emorites who lived on the coast. It is no wonder that Shmuel erects a thanksgiving monument to God following the battle.

In summation, Israel had, after many years, returned to a pure worship of God; immediately afterwards, it successfully pushed the enemy away from its land. God's hand in these events was not difficult to see. Their victory came after their repentance and as a result of their prayer and sacrifice, led and inspired by God's prophet. Shmuel drives home that point by erecting the monument and declaring: "God has helped us until here [or now]." The

---

43. The exact timing is unknown. The chapter opens with the statement that, after the return of the Ark to Israel, the nation followed the ways of God for twenty years. Whether the events that follow took place after the twenty years or during them is a matter of conjecture.

lesson for Israel should have been clear: there was no need for an Ark, no need for chariots or weapons, no need for a large army. The lesson was the same as that taught to Israel in the time of Yehoshua and one that would yet be repeated to future generations: victory belonged to God, and allegiance to God and His Torah was their only guarantee of success on the battlefield.

But what was Israel's reaction? We read of no holiday to God, no thanksgiving sacrifice, nothing at all to indicate that the people had learned this lesson. It was Shmuel who erected the monument of thanksgiving and not the people. In fact, the only reaction from the people that we read of following the battle is their request for a king, whom they desired for a specific purpose: one who would, as they said, "fight our battles."[44]

The failure of the Israelites to see God as the source of their help and their victory indicated that they were not ready for a king, at least not one that would rule as God had desired. After all, the king was to bring the people closer to God. He was to be, as mentioned earlier, a reflection of God and not His replacement. God did not wish to appoint a person who, in effect, would be a "competitor." It was a very fine line for the people to tread, and it required a certain sophistication and spiritual stature to guarantee that the nation would not fall victim to hero worship, something that could lead to the deification of the monarch and actual worship of the king himself. Israel, by her reaction to the victory, proved that she was not yet ready for such a king. In hindsight, we realize that God (and Shmuel) was not upset by the request itself but by the timing of that request.

"It is not you whom they reject," God told Shmuel, "but Me."[45] God indicated to Shmuel that he was not to be the political leader of the nation at any rate, and the people's desire for a temporal leader was not to be seen as a rejection of Shmuel's moral leadership. Rather, God explained, the nation's request for a king to fight for them that came immediately following a miraculous victory wrought by God, was a rejection of the concept that God was the true victor. It reflected their inability to see God's intense involvement in Israel's history and how deeply He impacted their lives.

This approach explains why God acceded to the request even though He disagreed with it. He knew that it was a mistake and would eventually lead to tragedy, but it was not sinful, per se. It was not a rejection of God, but an ignorance of His hand in their history. God therefore surrendered to the

---

44. I Shmuel 8:20.
45. Ibid. 8:7.

request because He will not force a person to sin, but He will allow one to be tempted to sin.[46] This, then, helps us understand this troublesome passage, and it also sheds light on the expectations God has of the people and the king in a Torah-ordained monarchy.

But Why Shaul?

God's choice of Shaul is a curious one. We read of no barren mother, we know of no prophetic message to the parents of the impending birth and we learn nothing of his early life or any outstanding qualities that would have him qualify to be Israel's first monarch. And yet all of these curiosities are not, of themselves, overly surprising or puzzling. After all, Moshe was not born to a barren mother, no prophetic message was received before David's birth and we know very little of Avraham's early years. We can assume that Shaul was a special enough personality to have been designated by God for this position even if the Bible chooses to leave out details about him and his life.

The phrase used to describe his physical stature, "[head and] shoulders above the rest of the nation,"[47] is meant also, I believe, to describe his moral character. Certainly, the description of Shaul as בחור וטוב ואין איש מבני ישראל טוב ממנו, "young and good, with no one in Israel surpassing him,"[48] is testimony enough to his sterling character and suitability for kingship.

What is particularly curious about the choice of Shaul is his tribal affiliation: Shaul hails from the tribe of Binyamin. Binyamin is the youngest of Yaakov's sons; certainly we would expect that one of the older sons would merit the monarchy. Furthermore, when we last read of the tribe of Binyamin, it had nearly been eradicated in the civil war that closed the book of Shoftim! We could well imagine that there must have been some deep-seated resentment by the populace against the tribe that had caused such terrible bloodshed and loss of life! Yet this would be the tribe to merit the Israelite monarchy?

Finally, when Yaakov blesses his children, as we read at the end of Bereishit, he tells Yehudah: "The [ruling] staff will never leave Yehudah nor will leaders [depart] from among his descendants,"[49] which rabbinic scholars

---

46. See Rashi, Bamidbar 13:2.
47. I Shmuel 9:2.
48. Ibid.
49. Bereishit 49:10; this interpretation follows the traditional explanation of the verse. See tractate Sanhedrin 5a, and Rashi and Ramban, ibid.

have interpreted as meaning that the king would always come from the tribe of Yehudah! Even Shaul himself is shocked at his choice and tells Shmuel: "But I am a Benjaminite, the smallest [alternatively, least important] of the tribes of Israel!" How then can we understand God's choice of Shaul from Binyamin? The answer can be found in understanding the symbolism of the choice of tribes, and in realizing what Binyamin's role was among the tribes.

And Why the Tribe of Binyamin?

The tribe of Binyamin had a crucial role to play in Israel's destiny. Binyamin as an individual was unique amongst the brothers of Yosef. Binyamin was not involved in the sale of his brother; Binyamin did not lie to his father; Binyamin never knew of the dastardly deed and so never "covered up" for the brothers. It was Binyamin who brought about the rapprochement between Yosef, sold as a slave, and Yehudah, who initiated the sale. In order to save Binyamin, Yehudah offered to replace him and remain a slave to Yosef, and it is then that Yosef broke down and revealed his true identity. It was, therefore, through Binyamin that the long-awaited reunion between Yosef and his brothers took place. Binyamin was the catalyst.

As a result of this, Binyamin became the symbol of harmony and unity. His very birth, though tinged with tragedy, brought about a certain unity, as the death of his mother Rachel in childbirth put an end to the jealous divisions between her and her sister Leah. In effect, Binyamin brought about the fruition of the yet-to-be-delivered prophecy of Yechezkel: "I shall take the branch of Yosef…and place it together with the branch of Yehudah and make them into one branch…."[50] How interesting that the ancestral estate of the tribe of Binyamin was specifically situated between those of Yehudah and Yosef (Efraim). Binyamin, the tribe who received the honorific "beloved of God"[51] in Moshe's blessing, was indeed deserving of that title as the peacemaker and unifier of the brothers and of the tribes. It is no wonder, therefore, that the portion of Binyamin was chosen to house the dwelling place of God's presence, the Holy Temple, for as the Temple was to unify the nation, so too was the tribe of Binyamin.

This understanding can help us find an approach that will answer our

50. Yechezkel 37:19.
51. Devarim 33:12.

question. Consider: God knew that the nation was not yet ready for a dynastic ruler. As we pointed out, they lacked the understanding that the king could not replace God. But they also lacked true internal unity. Their desire for one king was based upon the common fear of an external enemy and not a true feeling of oneness with each other. God therefore ordained that a man from the tribe of unity, the tribe of Binyamin, would first rule over Israel and create one fully united nation, something Shaul succeeded grandly in doing through his victory over Nachash, the king of the Amonites. It is a truth that we might miss when studying the events of chapter 11, if we ignore the previous events in the early prophets, but it is a truth that helps us understand this choice of Shaul to serve as Israel's first king.

At this point, it is important to consider the entire story of the attack of Nachash and Shaul's overwhelming victory over the Amonites. There are questions that must be answered regarding this entire episode. Why, after all, do the Amonites attack the small town of Yavesh Gil'ad? Certainly, it was a tempting target: it was isolated, a border town in the eastern part of the Israelite kingdom, and it was weak, lacking an independent army. But that does not fully explain the reason for the attack. We should be troubled by Nachash's insistence on warring with the small city, refusing their surrender unless they would forever wear a "badge of shame," a gouged right eye. The story is even more puzzling, for Nachash even grants them permission to gather an army so that they can fight him! Why would he do so? What was the thought process of this king? Why would he refuse surrender and prefer war instead? The answer will provide us with an interesting insight and greater appreciation of King Shaul's remarkable success in uniting the people.

The neighboring states had little to fear from a divided Israel. For centuries, the separate tribes posed no threat to the area and, as the book of Shoftim documents, were often dominated by surrounding nations. However, a united Israel serving one king was seen as a great threat. But before such a king could establish full control, with a national army and widespread support, he was quite vulnerable.[52] The king of the Amonites was well aware of the history of his neighbor and knew of the events surrounding the civil war against Binyamin. As the book of Shoftim reveals, there was but one town that did not send their men to battle against the Benjaminites, only one city that would not get involved in the civil war and, as a result, was also attacked by the other

---

52. A similar story is found in II Shmuel 5 when the Philistines attack David upon his ascension to the throne of a united people.

tribes. It was, in fact, the only city outside of the portion of Binyamin that was almost completely destroyed: the city of Yavesh Gil'ad![53]

The king of Ammon, therefore, was challenging the newly established unity of the tribes under the reign of Shaul. Would Israel respond if a king from Binyamin were to try and raise a national army to defend Yavesh, or would they most probably see this as an alliance from the past: the tribe of Binyamin aiding their one and only ally in the civil war? Would this not challenge the supposed unity of the nation and, as Nachash hoped, bring the short-lived monarchy to an end? This, then, was indeed the plan. The nation of Ammon insisted on a war because they expected the new Israelite king to fail in his attempts to organize an army; they assumed that the people would regard Shaul as no more than another tribal leader concerned with his own tribe and its debt to a despised city.

Shaul's success in gathering an army under these circumstances, therefore, was even more remarkable. It is wholly understandable why the people, following the victory, asked Shmuel to re-anoint Shaul. Now that all the people were united behind their new king they could truly celebrate his ascension to the throne.

This also explains why, at this juncture, Shmuel bade farewell to the nation[54] as he stepped down from the political leadership of the people. He did not step down when Shaul was first anointed – but only now, after the victory and the people's celebration of their new king, did Shmuel feel confident enough to leave his position, for he realized that there was a new, popular and effective leader in Israel. The mantle of leadership has been passed down to the next generation: Israel's first king. It is certainly ironic that Shmuel's temporal leadership ends because his sons were not fitting successors,[55] much as Shmuel himself receives the mantle of leadership from Eli because Eli's sons were also not fitting. Neither great leader could create a dynasty and provide the desperately needed political stability. Neither, in fact, could Shaul.

Though descended from a non-Judean tribe, Shaul would be given the opportunity to create a ruling family, but he would fail to do so. Nonetheless, Shaul did succeed in creating a cohesive nation from what was a loose confederation of tribes concerned with their own local agenda and not a

---

53. Shoftim 21:8.
54. I Shmuel 12.
55. The people state, "Your sons have not followed in your ways," a far less critical description than that of the text: "They took bribes and perverted justice." See I Shmuel 8:3–4.

national one. By doing so, Shaul successfully laid the groundwork for the establishment of the Davidic dynasty. He was a crucial cog in the wheel of Jewish history and in providing for the eternal dynasty. Why Shaul failed to create that dynasty himself is a subject worth our attention.

What Went Wrong?

Shaul eventually falls from God's favor. The beginning of that downfall occurs before a crucial battle against the Philistines. As depicted in chapter 13, Shaul had gathered a small force of three thousand fighters, apparently not intending to start a war with the more numerous and more powerful Philistine army.[56] However, Shaul's son Yonatan then assassinated the Philistine governor in the town of Geva, raising the flag of rebellion. Shaul attempts to gather a fighting force capable of facing the enemy who had gathered for war, and manages to attract some men to Gilgal. However, upon seeing the size and might of the Philistine army, many Israelites flee across the Jordan or go into hiding in caves.

It was a time of fear and desperation. In order to raise the confidence of the nation and emphasize God's saving power, Shmuel had told Shaul to wait seven days for him to arrive and offer the sacrifice to God. By having the prophet, the clear messenger of God, offer this sacrifice, Shmuel hoped to drive home the point that God would be fighting for His nation and that victory was His. Given Shmuel's (and God's) feelings about the people's reason for choosing a king, this lesson was an important one to drive home to the nation.

But as Shaul's army kept slipping away (only six hundred remained), Shaul displayed a complete lack of confidence in God. He feared that he would be left with no army with which to fight the enemy, who by now numbered thirty thousand chariots alone and innumerable foot soldiers. As a result, Shaul decided to ignore Shmuel's command and offer the sacrifice himself, in the absence of God's prophet. Shmuel arrived as the offering was completed, and he told Shaul that he had behaved foolishly, and that as a result Shaul would not establish a permanent dynasty – that God would now find a leader more attuned to God's word.

---

56. See I Shmuel 13:2, where we learn that Shaul sent most of the fighters back home and retained only a small force of three thousand men precisely to teach Israel the lesson of God's involvement in their victory. A similar tactic was used in Gid'on's battle against the Midianites.

Upon studying this story, we must ask: What was Shaul's sin? What did he do that was so terrible? And why did Shaul, through this one highly understandable act, forfeit his opportunity to create the permanent Israelite dynasty?[57]

Understanding Shaul's Mistakes

When carefully analyzing this story, we can see how Shaul failed both as a military leader and as a king of Israel. As a military leader, the very purpose for which the Israelites demanded a king, he displays fear and panic at a time that cried for confidence and courage. When the people run to hide and the soldiers begin to desert, it is the commander in chief who must rally his army to confidently face the enemy. Instead of rallying his troops, Shaul watches helplessly as his army dissipates. Instead of encouraging them with stories of God's miraculous victories over Israel's enemies, he remains passive. As their military leader, admired as the hero who defeated Israel's enemies, Shaul had the opportunity of instilling pride and courage into the hearts of his countrymen. Yet, he behaves in a way that simply adds to their feeling of doom and dread.

Shaul also failed as a king of Israel. As an Israelite king, it was his task to publicly remind the people that the impending victory would come as a result of God's involvement in Israel's destiny. It was God's victory, not Shaul's! The previous victory over the Philistines (chapter 7) was preceded by a sacrifice offered by Shmuel, which was also accompanied by the prayers of the people, national fasting and a communal act of repentance, all inspired by the words of the prophet. The result was a stunning victory, which Shmuel marked by erecting a monument to God. And yet here, we read none of this. Shaul usurped the function of the prophet and misused the concept of sacrifice. Instead of leading the people in prayer and repentance to God, Shaul went through the superficial motions of worship, as if God would somehow be "appeased" by sacrifice alone.

Let us recall the two most basic functions of a king: to unite the nation and bring them closer to God. Shaul succeeded admirably in his first function. But as we have pointed out previously, it was vital for the king of Israel to realize that he served both God and Israel and insure that he never became the object

---

57. I Shmuel 13:14.

of worship. The king must inspire the nation to worship God and not frighten them into worshiping the king. Failing to do this meant failing as a king.

The same mistake is repeated in a second episode during which Shmuel repeats his prophecy of the collapse of Shaul's monarchy.[58] The repetition of this same blunder reveals a basic flaw in Shaul's personality and in his very understanding of the nature of his kingship, dooming any possibility of a successful ending to his reign.

Now that Israel had relative security and stability, Shaul receives God's command to destroy the nation of Amalek, thereby fulfilling the Torah obligation.[59] Included in this charge was the command to spare nothing and no one. As in Yehoshua's battle against Jericho, there was to be no personal or national enrichment through this victory. Shaul goes on the campaign and successfully defeats Amalek. However, he pointedly spares the life of the king, Agag,[60] and allows his soldiers to take booty, the best of the cattle. God appears to Shmuel that night and angrily denounces Shaul, telling the prophet that He regretted His decision to appoint Shaul as king.

When confronted with the charges, Shaul attempts to excuse himself, saying that he indeed had fulfilled God's command, and the decision to allow the soldiers to take the animals was only so that they could offer thanksgiving sacrifices to God![61] In response, Shmuel shares with Shaul one of the basic beliefs of Judaism: God has no desire for sacrifices if they are meant to replace obedience to God. He then informs Shaul of God's decision to replace him with another who would better follow God's wishes.

This second lapse of Shaul allows us to better understand why God regarded him as unsuitable for the kingship of Israel. Firstly, Shaul never really overcomes his original feelings that he was not worthy of the position. He was by

---

58. I Shmuel 15:26, 28. This quotation differs somewhat from the original prediction that Shaul's kingdom would collapse; see I Shmuel 13:13. We might explain that at first Shmuel predicted only that Shaul would not succeed in building a dynasty, while after the second lapse, Shmuel said that Shaul's reign itself would be cut short; see Radak, I Shmuel 15:28.

59. Devarim 25:19.

60. The sparing of Agag is not insignificant. Agag was the head of a nation known to prey on the weak and defenseless. Shaul's misguided mercies reflect a moral confusion that led our Rabbis to say: "He who shows mercy to the guilty will eventually act cruelly to the innocent" (Midrash Tanchuma, Parashat Metzora, siman 1). Shaul indeed does just that when he later wipes out all of the innocent priests living in Nob.

61. Rabbi Soloveitchik comments that King Shaul conceded that he was a follower – not a ruler.

nature quite modest, an admirable trait in any human being.[62] But in order to rule effectively it is necessary to overcome the natural reticence that modesty engenders. A leader must have the courage and confidence to make the correct decisions even when they may be unpopular ones. Shaul gave in to the soldiers' demand for booty because he was reluctant to stand up to them and prohibit an act that was forbidden by God. By surrendering to the will of the masses in contravention of God's command, Shaul failed in his duty to bring the people closer to God. His failure proved that he was not fit to lead God's nation.

Secondly, as we learned in our study of the book of Yehoshua, the taking of booty was an act done by the victor: "To the victor belong the spoils." But, at crucial times, God chose to remind the people that it is He who is the true victor and, consequently, forbade them from taking the spoils. This was true of the battle against the attacking Canaanites, when the Israelites voluntarily pledged to avoid any gain from their victory, recognizing by themselves that the victory would be God's,[63] and it was repeated at the battle of Jericho,[64] when God commanded that no spoils be taken, thereby reminding the nation that God was the victor, they were not. Shaul's agreement to allow the taking of booty from the Amalekites was reflective of his belief that he shared in the victory and was at least partially responsible for the enemy's defeat. By acting in such a fashion, he was doing exactly what an Israelite king may not do: he was *replacing* God, claiming that victory was *his,* when he should have been teaching the people that victory came from God.

This was precisely what God and Shmuel feared when they reluctantly agreed to anoint a king. Recall our original point: the people had just won the victory over the Philistines as a result of their passionate prayers to God, yet failed to realize that God brought them the victory. They requested a king who would "fight our battles." God's hope was that the proper king would be able to teach them that it was God fighting their battles all of the time.

---

62. The text reveals Shaul's modesty a number of times: in I Shmuel 9:21 we learn of his original reluctance to accept the kingship; in ibid. 10:16 we are told of his failure to reveal, even to close family, that the prophet had anointed him king and in ibid. 10:22 we read how he hid away from the nation at the very public ceremony where he was to be anointed.

63. Bamidbar 21:2. This was the very first attack of a Canaanite city against the Israelites in the last year of their sojourn in the desert. It was seen as a prelude to the invasion of the land, hence the importance of the battle in the eyes of the Israelites.

64. Yehoshua 6:19. As the first conquest in Canaan this was considered such an important victory of God that He even prohibits ever rebuilding the city, decreeing, rather, that it serve as an eternal reminder that God conquered the land for Israel; see ibid. 6:26.

He desired a fitting leader who would be able to reflect God in the eyes of the people, helping them realize that their success against the enemy would depend directly upon their faithfulness to God and His commands. Shaul's decision to ignore the dictates of God may very well have revealed his growing belief that victory belonged to him as well. Shaul began to assert his royal power, but in the wrong sphere. The leader who could not stand up to his men chose to stand up to God.

Although this may seem to be an overly critical analysis of Shaul's actions, if we study the text we will find proofs that, I believe, express the precise point that we just made. While chasing the Philistines out of the land after a glorious victory, Shaul makes a decision to attack the retreating army at night, while they were resting. Although this suggestion was acceptable to his officers, Shaul doesn't think to ask God until the priest comes to him and suggests that they do so.[65] Only when God fails to answer does Shaul seek out God's help to find the guilty party who broke the oath. Shaul feels confident enough not to bother asking God about his crucial decisions, and this was the case earlier in the battle as well, when he adjured his men not to eat anything all day. This rash oath caused the masses to sin, as the ravenous army hurriedly slaughtered animals that night without following God's ordained law.[66]

Yonatan, Shaul's son who was the key to the victory, did not hear the oath, and Shaul was ready to put him to death for having eaten some honey. The people eventually saved Yonatan's life, refusing to allow Shaul to kill the one person who brought them victory. Yet throughout, Shaul never looked to God and never asked God to forgive his son's unintentional trespass. It is the people who prevented the near travesty that almost came about as a result of Shaul's independent actions and rash pronouncement. God is all but missing from the story.

65. I Shmuel 14:36.
66. Shaul corrected their sin and set up a rock upon which to slaughter the animals. The text then states that Shaul built an altar to God, which Ralbag and others explain as a monument to God for the victory, much as Moshe built one after his victory over Amalek. It is difficult to accept that in the midst of Shaul's pursuit of the Philistines, a pursuit that Shaul hoped to continue that very night, he would have stopped to build an altar rather than wait until after the battle to do so, as others did. The altar seemed to have been part of the repair of the people's sin, granting them a place to slaughter the animals for their meat. Yet even if we accept the explanation of Ralbag and others, it seems that even this act of thanksgiving was brought about only through the act of the people and was not initiated by Shaul himself. In fact, Radak suggests that the very rock that Shaul used to slaughter the animals for the people was then used as the first stone for the altar. See I Shmuel 14: 35.

We sense the same shortcoming in the next chapter as well. Following the battle against Amalek, God appeared to Shmuel and told him of His decision to reject Shaul as king. The next day, Shmuel searched for Shaul to tell him of God's word. He arrived at camp to find that Shaul was gone. When he asked where he went, Shmuel was told that Shaul had gone to Carmel "and behold he is erecting *for himself* a monument."[67] Shaul was erecting a victory monument, but not to God.

In fact, following none of his victories do we read that Shaul thanked God or recognized His hand in the victory. Whereas Shmuel built a monument following the victory over the Philistines, calling it Even Ha'Ezer, with the explanation that "God has helped us [chase away the enemy] until here,"[68] and while David challenged Golyat with the words "I come in the name of the Lord of Hosts,"[69] and "all will know that God controls battles and He will give you into our hands,"[70] Shaul did no such thing. Throughout the book of Shmuel we never find Shaul offering even one thanksgiving sacrifice. Not after he was chosen to be king nor after his ascension to the throne; not after his public coronation nor after his military victories! In fact, nowhere throughout the reign of Shaul do we read anything about the Tabernacle or the Ark or the altar. No visits to the place of the Tabernacle, no worship at the Holy Ark (which we know stood in Kiryat Ye'arim, not far from Shaul's own home),[71] no sacrifices at the national altar. It is significant that the one mention of a thanksgiving offering following a victory comes only after Shaul confessed his sin to Shmuel, when he realized that he had ignored God's command and God's hand in the victory. It is then that he pleaded with Shmuel, "Forgive my sin, return with me and I shall worship God,"[72] a request that seems more an attempt to "save face" in front of his nation than a desire to recognize God as his savior.

If these examples are not convincing enough, then the biblical text certainly is. Upon his ascension to the throne, King David calls for the leaders to join him in bringing the Holy Ark to Jerusalem. In doing so, he offers the

---

67. I Shmuel 15:12; commentators suggest that this was a monument of victory dedicated to God, yet the wording (מציב לו יד) implies that the monument was for himself, not God.

68. I Shmuel 7:12.

69. Ibid. 17:45.

70. Ibid. 17:47.

71. I Shmuel 7:2.

72. Ibid. 15:25.

following reason for moving the Ark closer to the population centers of the nation: "For we did not seek it out [the Ark] in the days of Shaul, "[73] clearly implying the weak state of public worship during Shaul's reign.

In Conclusion

As humble and promising as were his beginnings, Shaul's ending was swift and tragic. The king who rid the land of sorcerers and necromancers is forced to search for one in a desperate attempt to receive the word of God, an act that the Torah prohibits.[74] Shaul, whose story began with an unsuccessful search for his father's donkeys, ends with his unsuccessful search for God. The hero who defeated the Philistines twice but never fully subdued them is killed on the battlefield by that same enemy, as are his sons, the heirs to his throne. Shaul did not live up to his great promise because, as he grew more and more confident, he seemed to have grown more and more independent of God and His directives.

It is this that led to his downfall, for he failed in the very challenge that must be faced by every Israelite king: the challenge to place God and His commandments ahead of himself and his own desires. The sad truth is that before God removed His favor from Shaul, Shaul had drifted away from God; before God abandoned Shaul, Shaul had abandoned God.

---

73. I Divrei Hayamim 13:3.
74. Vayikra 20:21; Devarim 18:11.

THE BOOK
OF II SHMUEL

ספר
שמואל ב

THE IDEAL
MONARCH

OVERVIEW

The second part of the book of Shmuel – II Shmuel – could rightfully be referred to as the book of David, for although we have been introduced to this remarkable personality in the first part of Shmuel, the bulk of David's story is related in II Shmuel. In fact, there is not one chapter in the entire book of II Shmuel in which David's name is not mentioned. King David was not only the first successful king of Israel, he was not only the first royal father of a king, he was not simply the conqueror of Jerusalem, nor was he merely a unifier of the tribes – David was the founder of the Israelite dynasty. He was the progenitor of kings who would rule for over four hundred years and the father of any future legitimate monarch, including the ruler in messianic times.

It is difficult to overstate the importance of this one individual to the history of the Jewish nation. And yet, in a very real sense, David is "everyman." He was not born to greatness. His birth was not remarkable in any way. He was not born to a barren woman, as were Yitzchak, Yaakov, Yosef and Shmuel; his birth was not predicted by a prophet, as were the births of Yitzchak, Yishmael and Shimshon. His childhood does not seem out of the ordinary, nor do we read of any outstanding event in his early life that would presage his future role. He was not born to a royal family or a priestly family. He was a simple shepherd – like Avraham, Yaakov and Moshe. And yet, one could argue that the impact of this multi-dimensional personality on our nation – the effect that this musician, poet, warrior, judge and king had on Israel – was second only to Moshe himself. It is through the study of II Shmuel that we get a glimpse into who this leader was and how he grew into greatness.

ANALYSIS

THE MAN WHO WOULD BE KING

The story of David is so well known and extensively written about that one is hard-pressed to present any new information about this outstanding figure. And yet, as in previous studies, there is much revealed to us within the text that helps us understand the story, the time period and the person, and gives us a greater appreciation of the man who established Israel's eternal dynasty. David, like Shaul, was chosen by God, Who revealed that choice to Shmuel. And, as is also true of the story of Shaul, Shmuel was never told the name of God's choice. Rather, he was told to go the Bethlehem, to the family of Yishai, from whom God had chosen a successor to Shaul.

David, though physically attractive,[1] was not as impressive a figure as Shaul.[2] And this is just one of the differences that the text subtly reveals as

---

1. He is described as "a young lad, with ruddy complexion [or red hair], with attractive eyes and good-looking" (I Shmuel 16:12).
2. Physical attractiveness was actually considered an important factor in choosing a king. Shaul was described as being "head and shoulders above the nation" (I Shmuel 9:2) and David as "good-looking." Avshalom, a contender to the throne, was described as the most attractive one in the nation to whom none in Israel could compare, "from foot to head he had no blemish" (II Shmuel 14:25), and Adoniyahu, who also claimed the throne, was described as being "very good-looking" (I Melachim 1:6).

it contrasts the personalities of the first two Israelite monarchs. When the prophet arrived at the home of Yishai, God made it clear to Shmuel – who was sure that the eldest son, Eliav, was the chosen one due to his impressive stature – that physical appearance is how man chooses, but "God looks into the heart."[3] This is a none-too-subtle reference to God's disappointment in Shaul, who, though physically attractive, failed to live up to God's expectations. God reminded Shmuel not to judge by appearance alone. In a number of ways, the scripture depicts David as the "anti-Shaul," as he succeeded where Shaul failed and displayed strength where Shaul showed weakness.

Unquestionably, David is one of the most remarkable individuals in the entire Bible. He was described by Shaul's men in an almost unprecedented series of positive terms: "a talented musician and brave soldier, a man of war who is wise [understanding], [he is] a man of stature and God is with him"[4] – a description offered by these men, by the way, even before David had risen to prominence or accomplished anything of note. As the text reveals, he was not the perfect man, but he was the ideal king. He was a great warrior who was the "sweet singer of Israel."[5] He was a powerful monarch who was a master politician; he was a Godly king who brilliantly understood human nature. He succeeded both in his dealings with man and in his dealings with God.

David was able to firmly unite the nation under his leadership and to instill in Israel awareness and understanding of the Divine. He succeeded because he never lost touch with the simple shepherd boy he once was, nor with the God Who he knew elevated him to the throne of Israel. It was these very attributes that would characterize him throughout his life: a powerful ruler who nonetheless sought to keep his nation united and to rule only with their consent, and a successful king who recognized that, no matter how great his accomplishments, it was God to Whom he must credit his successes.

David versus Shaul: The Contrast

In the latter part of I Shmuel we read almost exclusively of the struggle between Shaul and David, between the present and the future king. It is not our purpose here to analyze that struggle but rather to underscore the sharp

---

3. I Shmuel 16:7.
4. Ibid. 16:18.
5. II Shmuel 23:1.

contrast between the two, a contrast that will help us understand why David's kingship succeeded while Shaul's did not.

Shaul failed twice in his military campaigns: he did not eradicate the Amalekites as he had been commanded[6] and he fell to the Philistines who, at his death, retained control over a significant part of the Land of Israel, reaching from their western coastal settlement almost to the Jordan River, Israel's eastern border.[7] These failures are revealed to us by the prophetic author of Shmuel in a most subtle manner.

As II Shmuel begins, we read how the report of Shaul's death was brought to David by a young Amalekite. The young man stated that he found Shaul on Mount Gilboa, pursued by the Philistines and mortally wounded. We already knew from the description in I Shmuel that the Philistine archers had wounded Shaul and that Shaul fell upon his own sword to avoid torture at the hands of the Philistines.[8] The report of this refugee from the war, however, differed from that which we read in Shmuel I. His claim was that Shaul was not yet dead when he found him, and upon the king's request, he stabbed him and killed him. We dare not miss the irony found in this story: Shaul was killed by both the Philistines and the Amalekite, the very nations that he failed to subdue. The prophet tells us that Shaul's failures came back to haunt him and eventually kill him!

As the story continues, we read of how David killed the Amalekite for daring to raise his hand against God's chosen king. The contrast is now complete: while Shaul was killed *by* the Amalekite, David *kills* the Amalekite; and while Shaul did not destroy Amalek, David successfully pursued and defeated the army of Amalek who had overrun his camp at Ziklag.[9]

The contrast is carried over to the struggle with the Philistines as well. In actuality, Shaul's failure to destroy Amalek was more a religious failure than a military one, as Amalek never really threatened the independence of Israel. Shaul's inability to defeat Philistia, however, was quite significant.

---

6. We read of the Amalekites still functioning after Shaul's war with them (see I Shmuel 27:8; 30:1–18; II Shmuel 8:12). These may have been individual nomadic clans who were not part of the war against Shaul, or it may be that Shaul simply destroyed all of the warriors but not all of the nation.

7. Although Reuven, Gad and Menasheh dwelled on the eastern side of the Jordan, the border given in the Torah was the Jordan River.

8. I Shmuel 31:3–4.

9. Ibid. 30:17; see also II Shmuel 8:12. We also read how David attacked the Amalekites regularly while serving Achish, the Philistine king of Gat (I Shmuel 27:8).

Rabbi Soloveitchik writes that it was one of the missions set out for Shaul as monarch. Rabbi Kalman Bar points to a commentary of the Vilna Gaon on the third chapter of the prophet Chavakuk. There, the Gaon states that Israel faced three classic enemies in the Bible: Moab, in the east; Edom, in the south; and Philistia, in the west. Moab was the archetypal enemy who sought to defile Israel and reduce her from her level of sanctity and spirituality, as Moab attempted to debase Israel by attracting her to immoral idolatry.[10] Edom was the model for all of Israel's enemies who sought to destroy her physically, as did Edom's descendant Amalek (and, by extension, his descendant Haman). The third enemy, the Gaon writes, was the most troubling.

Philistia, who tormented Israel, represents a unique enemy, for she seeks nothing positive for herself. She represents only the negative: those who sought only to prevent Israel from establishing a government or controlling the land. The Philistines, who despite the great need for water in the desert-like climate of the Middle East, chose to fill in Avraham's wells rather than use them, an attempt to deny Avraham any rights to the land or to the water,[11] are the same Philistines who, generations later, attacked Shaul as soon as he was anointed by popular acclaim[12] and besieged David as soon as he took control of Jerusalem and ruled over a united Israel.[13] Generation after generation, they were the nation who opposed Israel's possession of the land and her independence upon it. It was an essential function of any Israelite monarch to remove this threat, both for the sake of the nation and for the survival of his throne.

Clearly, this enemy had to be defeated before there could be a successful and lasting Israelite dynasty. The king's job was defined by the people themselves as "he shall lead us into war and fight our battles."[14] They made that request immediately after their war with the Philistines, realizing themselves the ongoing threat that the Philistines posed to the nation. But Shaul never succeeded in vanquishing the Philistines and removing them from the border of Israel. In fact, during his reign, Israel had become a vassal state to Philistia. We read the prophet's description of Israel's condition: "No blacksmith could be found in Israel, for the Philistines said: 'lest the Hebrews fashion a sword or spear'...so on the day of battle no sword or spear could be found in the

---

10. Bamidbar 25:1–2.
11. Bereishit 26:15.
12. I Shmuel 13:5.
13. II Shmuel 5:17.
14. I Shmuel 8:20.

possession of the army...."[15] Although Shaul was able to defeat the Philistines in a number of battles, he was never able to subdue them and remove them from the land. They remained a threat to Israel throughout his reign. And, of course, perhaps fittingly, it was the Philistine war that led to the demise of Shaul and the entire royal family.[16]

And then there was David. David rose to prominence as a young man because he defeated the Philistine hero Golyat (Goliath). His act of bravery brought victory to Israel and Shaul, who succeeded in chasing the Philistines back to their own cities.[17] Additionally, David, as general of Israel's forces years later, succeeded in defeating the Philistines again and again.[18] Upon close study, we see that the Philistines *never* defeated David in war, and by their own admission they feared him.[19] The contrast, therefore, is quite striking: the Philistines defeated Shaul in his final battle, while David's first victory was over the Philistine hero, Golyat; Shaul failed to vanquish the enemy, while David's subsequent victories succeed in subduing and humbling the Philistines. A successful Israelite reign was defined by its success in eliminating the Philistine threat. When Shaul died, the Philistines ruled over significant parts of Israel; when David died, Israel controlled Philistia and the intractable enemy no longer posed any threat to Israel at all.[20] Where Shaul failed, David succeeded.

David versus Shaul: The Conflict

The friction between David and Shaul began immediately with the rise of David's popularity. The text reveals how, after David's defeat of Golyat, the women composed a song of victory telling of how King Shaul had slain thousands of the enemy, while David, with his one act of bravery, slew tens

---

15. Ibid. 13:19–22.
16. One son of Shaul, Ish Boshet, does survive and eventually rules, although whether he fought in that final battle is a matter of conjecture.
17. I Shmuel 17:52.
18. Ibid. 18:30.
19. Ibid. 21:12.
20. By chapter 5 in II Shmuel, David had succeeded in chasing them from the land. The Philistines are never mentioned again in the books of the early prophets except to indicate a geographic location. The one exception is to be found in II Melachim 18:8 when we read of a final defeat of the Philistines by King Chizkiyahu. After hundreds of years of war and enslavement, the Philistines never again threaten Israel after David's reign.

of thousands.[21] Given the fact that God had already warned that He would transfer the royal power from Shaul to a more deserving person, Shaul was naturally suspect of anyone who would show leadership capabilities, especially one who now captured the imagination of the masses. Added to Shaul's understandable suspicions of David, the text reveals that God visited Shaul with an "evil spirit," and subsequent actions and reactions of Shaul reflect a disturbed personality, whose unbalanced behavior resembles that of a manic-depressive. The contrast between Shaul and David thus becomes even more obvious, for as the text comments, as God's spirit left Shaul it entered David. As a result, Shaul and David become polar opposites; one succeeding more and more as one failed more and more.

When we study the actions of Shaul we see a conscious strategy meant to deny David access to the throne and, eventually, the very right to live. On the day following the young women's victory chant, Shaul made two futile attempts to stab David, and, when David managed to avoid the spear, Shaul realized that "God was with him [David]." He then decided to make this heretofore inexperienced, untrained young man a commander in his army,[22] assuming that he would be killed by the Philistines and his "problem" would disappear. Of course, the opposite occurred, as David was highly successful in leading his men to victory over the Philistines and, as a result, became more and more popular within the nation. Shaul's "problem" grows.

We also read that Shaul had promised anyone who defeated Golyat the right to his daughter's hand in marriage. This was more than a simple reward guaranteeing the hero a prominent position in the nation. It is essential for us to remember that by marrying the king's daughter, a person became part of the royal family and, hence, a legitimate heir to the throne. This is something that, as we will see, was crucially important to David and something that David strove to hold on to even after Shaul's death.

Shaul had originally promised that David would marry his eldest daughter, Meirav. But rather than keep his promise, Shaul devised a number of strategies that he felt would keep David from the throne. When David humbly expressed his reluctance to accept such an honor (although David knew full well that he was destined to be the king), Shaul suggested that he "earn" the

---

21. I Shmuel 18:7.

22. Recall that David was so "untrained" in battle that he was uncomfortable wearing armor (I Shmuel 17:39).

right by bringing the corpses of one hundred Philistines to him.[23] Once again, Shaul hoped that such a task would lead to David's death, and once again Shaul was wrong. David brought back twice the number of Philistine corpses and his legend as the hero of Israel grew even more.

When the time came for the marriage, Meirav had already been taken as a wife. Commentators suggest different reasons why, including the possibility that she accepted the betrothal of another without her father's permission[24] or that she did not love David as her sister did.[25] But the reason might actually be quite simple: Shaul was reluctant to give David the hand of his eldest daughter, for that would place him even closer to the throne. He therefore arranged for David to marry his younger daughter, Michal, especially since she was deeply in love with David.[26] This too played into the hands of Shaul who believed that Michal would be a "distraction" to David and perhaps unwittingly lead him to his downfall. Of course, we see once again the fruition of God's promise that he would remove his spirit from Shaul and give it to another when, far from endangering David, Michal saved his life by protecting him from her father's soldiers, who were sent to kill him.

As mentioned previously, the rest of the book of I Shmuel deals with Shaul's pursuit of David, his attempts to kill David and his tearful admissions of David's righteousness. Yet even the deaths of Shaul and three of his sons did not guarantee David the throne. On the contrary, David's struggle for the throne of Israel had just begun.

The Struggle for Legitimacy

In stark contrast to Shaul, who actively attempted to thwart God's will and deny David access to the throne, David himself refused to do anything to usurp the power from Shaul, leaving it up to God, Who had promised him the rule of Israel. More than once David had the opportunity of killing the man who was trying to kill him, but he refused.[27] Although David had ample

---

23. I Shmuel 18:25. Actually, Shaul uses the derogatory term "one hundred foreskins," similar to the moniker David gives to Golyat "this uncircumcised one." In fact, throughout the Bible, the only specific nation referred to by this derogatory term was the Philistines.
24. See *Metzudat David*, I Shmuel 18:19.
25. Malbim, I Shmuel 18:19.
26. The only place in the entire Bible where it states that a woman loved a man!
27. See I Shmuel 24:6; 26:9.

justification to defend himself by killing Shaul, and although it would have meant that David would occupy the throne, he refused to do so. As a result, it took at least ten years from when David was first anointed until he finally took the throne.[28]

David's reluctance to harm the king was not born of fear. He was deeply reverent of the monarch and the monarchy, despite Shaul's attempts to kill him. He explains this reluctance to his men saying that he could never raise his hand against "the anointed of God," a king chosen by God Himself. This reverence for the kingship is what caused him to kill the Amalekite who stabbed Shaul, even though Shaul himself had requested him to do so.[29] It also explains why he killed the two brothers, Reichav and Ba'anah who assassinated Shaul's son, the king of the non-Judean tribes, Ish Boshet, despite the fact that David was at war with him.[30] Each time David seems incredulous at their acts of violence and asks the condemned assassin, "How is it that you did not fear raising your hand to murder God's anointed king?"[31] It was something that David, who had ample opportunity and ample reason to strike down the king, could never do. But David had another reason why he refused to kill Shaul, a reason that reflects David's absolute commitment to assure that he be regarded as a fitting successor to the Israelite monarchy.

It was David's ultimate goal to rule with the consent of the people and not against their will, as a foreign usurper of power. David refused to assassinate Shaul because he knew that such an act would be regarded as an attempt to overthrow the government and rule by force. Although David could have claimed the throne, as he was chosen by God and anointed by His prophet, he does not. With the Israelite monarchy in its infancy, David understood that it was essential to establish a stable government. Overthrowing the monarchy by force would be inviting civil war and would undermine the very purpose for which the people demanded a king: a secure government with peaceful succession to the throne. Imagine the precedent he would have set by murdering the

---

28. This number is derived from the fact that David took the throne of Yehudah when he was thirty years old, yet was anointed while he was a young man still shepherding the flocks. As he was subsequently sent with provisions for his older brothers in the army, he clearly was still too young to serve in the army, as the ensuing conversation implies (see I Shmuel 17: 28–29), meaning that he was not yet twenty years of age. One could even argue that he was anointed as young as fifteen or sixteen. But he certainly had to be younger than twenty.
29. II Shmuel 1:14.
30. Ibid. 4:11–12.
31. Ibid. 1:14.

first king of Israel, despite the many good reasons he may have had! Imagine what could have taken place (and almost did) upon the death of David himself. David goes through trials and tribulations trying to establish his throne in peace, as a result of the people's choice and not the people's fear.

There is no question but that David's desire to keep an easily fractured nation united as one was what drove David to act as he did. Understanding this concern of King David will help us understand some of his actions during his reign, for we see this trait of David throughout his reign, from his earliest years to his final ones. A few examples will illustrate how strongly this impulse affected David's decisions throughout his rule.

1. While negotiating a possible takeover of the non-Judean tribes with their commander in chief, Avner, David demanded that he first have his wife Michal returned to him. His ascension to the throne of a united Israel was made contingent upon the return of Michal because David wished to claim the throne as a legitimate heir to Shaul, his father-in-law through his marriage to Michal. He refused to take the throne were he to be regarded as a complete outsider, who overthrew the "legitimate" king. On the other hand, as son-in-law of the former king and as the popular choice of the leadership, he would be less likely to cause a rift in the nation.

2. Following the assassination of Avner, David openly curses his own general (and nephew), Yoav, for having committed the dastardly deed. He publicly mourns and eulogizes Avner, calling upon his own men to rend their garments and fast; he gives Avner a hero's funeral and arranges for his burial in David's own capital city of Hevron. All of these honors were granted to the man who had led his forces *against* David, yet they were given so that the tribal leadership and the common people would realize that David was not involved in the plot.[32] He wished to make it clear that he was not part of a cabal meant to violently overthrow northern Israel's government, for he did not wish to be seen as one trying to force his rule upon a reluctant population. By doing so, he hoped to keep the division between the tribes to a minimum and lay the groundwork for his eventual ascension to the throne.

---

32. The text indicates this clearly; see II Shmuel 3:37.

3. Even after the death of Avner and his king, Ish Boshet, David did not invade the remaining tribal territory, although the tribes were ripe for conquest as they were in political and military disarray. David avoids such an invasion even though the text itself indicates that there was growing support for David among the masses in the northern kingdom. Still, David waited years until the leaders of the tribes themselves requested that he rule over them. Only then did he agree to serve them, once again proving that he would not force his rule over the people and would govern only with the consent of the governed.

4. David's choice of Jerusalem as the capital of the newly united nation was also made with the overriding goal of keeping the nation unified. David rejected the possibility of remaining in his capital of Hevron, for it was closely connected to his tribe of Yehudah. He did not want to be considered the king of Yehudah who, due to a vacuum in the leadership of the other tribes, occupied their throne as well. It would cause resentment of the majority tribes and lead to a dissolution of the fragile union as soon as these tribes felt that they had "one of their own" to rule over them. David therefore immediately moved his capital from Hevron to Jerusalem. This move was significant. Besides the obvious historical and religious significance of the place, Jerusalem was more centrally located, closer to the northern tribes. Furthermore, Jerusalem had not yet been conquered by any one tribe[33] who could have claimed it as their own. In effect, it belonged to no one and so it belonged to everyone.

Even more fascinating, and perhaps more crucial, Jerusalem, according to the allotment of the land, was to be divided between two tribes, Yehudah and Binyamin. Could there have been a greater

---

33. The non-conquest of Jerusalem is a matter of discussion among the Rabbis due to the fact that it seems clear from the text (Yehoshua 10:10) that Yehoshua defeated Adoni Tzedek the King of Jerusalem and even killed him (ibid. 10:26). Furthermore, at the outset of the book of Shoftim (1:8), we learn that the tribe of Yehudah burned the city to the ground! Some believe that Jerusalem had been captured but was subsequently lost to the Jebusites. A fascinating approach of the Midrash Tadsheh (chapter 22) claims that there were two Jerusalems: the upper city that was part of Yehudah's portion and the lower city in Benjamin's portion. The Judeans destroyed the upper city and left it barren while the Benjaminites, as found in the book of Shoftim 1:21, chose not to conquer or even war against the lower city, leaving the Jebusites there. This lower city also had the name "Yevus," and this was the Jerusalem that was captured by David.

symbol of the unity of the nation, a greater reminder of the oneness of the people of Israel, than her capital, a city shared by the tribe of David and the tribe of Shaul? And that was precisely the message that David hoped to give to the people, for he too was the combination of both tribes: a son of Yehudah, a son-in-law of Binyamin! The conquest of Jerusalem was, perhaps, David's clearest act reflecting his fitness to be the Israelite monarch. Through this one act, David fulfilled the two major functions of the king: he accepted the designation of Jerusalem as a holy site, thereby representing God's will to the people, and he strengthened the bonds between the tribes, further uniting the nation.

5. When David's son, Avshalom (Absalom) rebelled, David was told "the hearts of the people are behind Avshalom."[34] David then flees from his capital, refusing to make a stand and battle his son. His reasons are clear. He would not want to have the local population suffer through a siege and perhaps death in a war, nor did he believe that he would find enough supporters to create an army that could oppose Avshalom, who had taken over David's armed forces. But an equally valid reason was David's reluctance to rule without popular support. Only after he escaped east of the Jordan did he find the support he needed, and only then did he succeed in raising an army to oppose his son's attempt to usurp his throne and kill him. Even after he was victorious, David did not return to his throne until he was invited to do so by the tribal elders. Even though David could have reclaimed the throne as the past regent, he again waited to be invited back to his capital by both the parts of his kingdom, the tribe of Yehudah and the northern tribes.

6. When escaping Avshalom, David and his men were confronted by Shim'i ben Gera, a member of Shaul's family, who cursed David as a usurper of the throne who was receiving his just deserts for having deposed the rightful king and royal family. Upon his return to Jerusalem, David, while crossing the Jordan, is accosted by Shim'i, who abjectly grovels before the king, begging for his forgiveness. Although Shim'i, a leader of the tribe of Binyamin, represents a real threat to the stability of David's throne, and although his act was deserving of a capital punishment, David refused to put him to

---

34. II Shmuel 15:13.

death, explaining "Should anyone in Israel be put to death today?"[35] David was not simply expressing the idea that it was a day of joy and celebration that he did not want to ruin by taking revenge. He was expressing another truth: any revenge exacted on this day would only further fracture the nation and strengthen his opponents. For the good of the nation he would swallow his pride and allow the deed to go unpunished.

This also explains why David failed to punish Shim'i even after he returned to the throne. However, once the kingdom was firmly established, he told his successor Shlomo to "deal wisely" with Shim'i. As he was a threat to him and his attempt to firmly grasp the reins of leadership, Shlomo was advised to "bring his old age to the grave violently."[36]

All of these examples make it abundantly clear that David was not only a "sweet singer," musician, poet and brave warrior, but he was also a brilliant politician who understood human nature quite well. And, when properly studying the text, we will uncover a humble personality who, as opposed to his predecessor, knew when to lower himself and when to assert himself. Nowhere is that clearer than in the story of Michal and David.

Like Father, Like Daughter

The story of David and Michal, the daughter of Shaul, reads like a true love story. It is a saga that begins with the love of a princess for the brave young hero whom she soon marries. It tells of the jealous father who tries to kill his son-in-law and the act of bravery performed by the princess to save her husband, although it meant endangering herself and her royal position. The story takes a tragic turn when the daughter is torn from her beloved husband, who fled the wrath of an unstable father-in-law king, and forcibly given to another. And the happy ending occurs when the dashing young man, now offered the throne of his father-in-law, refuses to occupy it unless his cherished wife is returned to him.

Unfortunately for all romantics, that is not the end of the story. The story of David and Michal ends in a puzzling and troubling fashion, related to us in chapter 6 of II Shmuel.

---

35. Ibid. 19:23.
36. I Melachim 2:10.

David had just completed what must have been the most spiritually uplifting day of his life. He had successfully moved the Holy Ark from the area of Kiryat Ye'arim to Jerusalem, thereby establishing the City of David as both the political and religious center of Israel. Throughout the pageantry, David celebrated with the people wearing a short linen jacket, the traditional garb of a servant of God and His Tabernacle,[37] and not the royal garments of a king. As he entered the city, Michal observed his behavior from her window and loses all respect for him.[38] Upon his return to the house Michal greeted him with the sarcastic comment of how royal and honorable he, as king, appeared before the commoners, and how surely they would lose all respect for him. David responded with the cutting remark that he had lowered himself, not before the commoners but before God – the same God who chose him as king in place of her father. He further argued that, rather than lose respect in the eyes of the people, they would now show him even more respect for having humbled himself before God. The story closes with the haunting fact that Michal had no children until the day she died.[39]

The story in and of itself is a fascinating one, for it helps give us insight into the personality of David. He is clearly "one of the people," dancing and celebrating with them, and even distributing gifts before bidding them farewell. Clearly too, he regarded this accomplishment as a gift from God and was sincerely moved by his ability to fulfill this dream of centralizing Israel's worship of God in his city of Jerusalem. We therefore perceive through this episode just how David lived up to the expectations of God and His prophet to be a servant of God and His people. Here he is revealed as the representative of God to the nation, reminding them of how his accomplishments were, in actuality, God's accomplishments, and he becomes a focal point for the people, being a popular leader who, through dint of his remarkable personality, unified the nation into one cohesive group.

But there is much more to learn from the story. And there is much about this episode that should trouble us. What happened to the love story? What

---

37. See I Shmuel 2:18.
38. The Hebrew expression ותבז לו בלבה implies a feeling of near disgust and revulsion toward David.
39. Our Rabbis disagree as to what this means. The Talmud takes the statement at face value, that Michal remained childless all of her life (Sanhedrin 21a), or that she had given birth earlier but had no more children from that time on, reflecting both God's and David's rejection of her (Rashi, ibid.); others suggest that she gave birth on the day she died, i.e., she died in childbirth.

happened to the relationship between Michal and David? Michal, who saved David when her father's men pursued him by lowering him out of the window (*b'ad hachalon*),[40] now verbally attacks David from what she spied from the window (*b'ad hachalon*).[41] The usage of identical phraseology is not coincidental. The prophet hopes to underscore the dramatic change in their relationship, reminding the reader to contrast the earlier episode with this one. Indeed, the contrast is so stark that it is even difficult for us to understand the tone of the dialogue between the two protagonists. After all, Michal was brought up in a palace and knew royal protocol well, so why does David respond so sharply to her words of criticism? And why would Michal be punished so severely, never being blessed with children? What is the underlying feud that destroys this loving relationship?

The division between David and Michal was actually a continuation of the split that separated David and Shaul, which reflected a completely different view of kingship and royalty in Israel.[42] As mentioned before, a key to success on the throne was the ability of the king to remove the Philistine threat.[43] Shaul loses the throne because he cannot defeat the enemy. A simple comparison of two battles against the Philistines will clarify Shaul's weakness and failure. Before Shaul is anointed king, the people battle the Philistines under the guidance and inspiration of Shmuel. There we read of how the prophet Shmuel gathered the people, prayed with them and inspired them to repent. They offered a sacrifice to God and then marched confidently to victory. In contrast, when Shaul must face the Philistines, we can sense the mood of panic that pervaded the camp of Israel. Whereas Shmuel was able to gather the people and form an army, Shaul watched as his gathered army dissipates and almost disappears. Shaul seems almost paralyzed, and without prayer or repentance he – instead of the prophet – offers the sacrifice, as he feared the complete desertion of his men and the resulting collapse of his army.

We find a similar pattern of behavior in Shaul's second battle against the Philistines, the battle we know as David versus Goliath (Golyat). Again we see Shaul as a frightened leader who is uncomfortably passive at a time when

---

40. I Shmuel 19:12.

41. II Shmuel 6:16.

42. The explanation I share here is based upon a lecture given by Rabbi Kalman Bar in Herzog College, July 2009.

43. The Philistines were really considered the "anti-Israel" nation. They are the only people in the entire Bible referred to as *arelim*, "uncircumcised ones," a clear contrast to the circumcised ones, Israel.

Israel needed faith and encouragement. Although Shaul had endured many weeks of Golyat's threats and insults, and despite the fact that he was in a near panic,[44] Shaul makes no attempt to pray, no attempt to call the prophet Shmuel; he does not even show any desire to sacrifice to God, although that had brought him victory in the last battle against Philistia.

Even when young David offers to fight Golyat, Shaul questions his abilities. When David tells Shaul of how he successfully protected his flocks and, with God's help, chased away the lion and the bear, Shaul remains silent, unconvinced, perhaps even confused. It is David who must continue and explain that God helped him then and would help him now as well.[45] In a clear role reversal that foreshadows the future events, it is David who plays the role of king, encouraging bravery when the nation was fearful, calling for trust in God when the people doubted their faith. It almost appears as if Shaul failed to see God's hand in his military victories or, worse still, denied that God was behind his military successes. As a result, when the women sang songs of praise and said that that Shaul killed thousands while David killed tens of thousands, Shaul's jealousy was not simply a result of having lower numbers. The women had revealed a truth that Shaul had refused to acknowledge: Israel was victorious but the victory was not his, it was David's; and because it was David's, it was God's.

Rabbi Yonatan Eibschutz offers a fascinating explanation as to the source of Shaul's resentment of the women's chant. Generally, we regard the terms *alafav* and *rivevotav*, "thousands" and "ten thousands," as synonymous and interchangeable. They indicate large numbers and often are not meant to be taken literally. But, he suggests, they actually are different and represent two different concepts. "Thousands," the lower number, represents those things that are common, normal and found in the natural world; "tens of thousands," the larger number, expresses that which is beyond the expected, the uncommon, the supernatural. Rabbi Eibschutz explains that Shaul saw the victories as being military in nature, simply part of the normal workings of the world. Shaul was praised with the term *alafav*, "thousands"; but David, who understood from the beginning that victory was God's, was praised with the term *rivevotav*, "tens of thousands," that which is beyond the expected

---

44. I Shmuel 17:11: "When Shaul and Israel heard these words of the Philistine, they trembled and feared greatly."

45. Ibid. 17:37. Notice how David must speak out again in verse 37 to explain to Shaul the point he was trying to make in verse 36 – that God will bring his victory.

and the natural. The chanting women recognized the difference and that disturbed Shaul. They realized that the two different terms reflect two different world outlooks that characterized each of these personalities.

As we apply this lesson to the story of David and Michal we realize that they were having the very same disagreement! Michal argued that, as king, David had to appear regal at all times. He had to build his dynasty as all kings on earth did: by commanding the nation's respect through creating an imposing and fearful royal presence. He had to be the glue that held the people together as one; he was to be their focus, their hope, their savior. It was he who led them into war and he who brought them victory in battle. He, therefore, had to retain a level of dignity at all times when appearing in public.

David responded that Michal reflected her father's way in leadership, a failed experiment. An Israelite dynasty, he argued, could never be built that way, for an Israelite dynasty could not be built upon the natural and the finite; it must be built upon that which was above nature, that which was the eternal. The people had to be taught that success for Israel would come as a blessing from above and not simply from the efforts exerted below. As the King of Israel, he was the instrument of God, Who brought salvation to His people. He, as king, was neither victor nor savior. He was God's instrument, God's servant and, through that, a servant of the people as well.

Michal may well have believed that she legitimized David's ascension to the throne; that David's marriage to her, the daughter of Shaul, is what made him king. Given that she was also David's first wife, she had every expectation that her son would be the heir to the throne, and her father's dynasty would be kept alive. But God thought differently. Michal would have no children because no heir to the Israelite throne should believe, as Shaul and Michal did, that victory belonged to the king. Michal would produce no heir, for it must be clear that David himself had earned the throne and that God, and God alone, legitimized David's dynasty by His choice of the young monarch. David, from his youth, understood that both dynastic rule and military victory belonged to the King of Kings. And this understanding, of course, was one of the essential ingredients that had to be part of the make-up of God's chosen king. David's dynasty would include none of Shaul's descendants who would repeat the mistakes of their ancestor.

David Sins...or Did He?

"He who says that David sinned is simply mistaken," states the Talmud.[46] The Rabbis were referring to the (in)famous episode of David and Bat-Sheva (Bathsheba), in which it appears at first glance that David was guilty of adultery with the wife of Uriah the Hittite. The Rabbis, however, explain that all of David's men issued divorces to their respective wives before going out to war. In this way, if they failed to return from war, their wives avoided the problem of the *agunah*, a woman whose husband may have died but had no witnesses to testify about his death. In that situation, the woman would remain in a state of limbo, married but with no husband, and unable to remarry as her legal status had not been established by any witness. Therefore, our Rabbis declare, David's act of intimacy with Bat-Sheva was not an act of adultery, for when her husband failed to return from war she was retroactively regarded as a divorcee at that time. With this clear declaration, our Rabbis set forth a challenge to all traditional biblical scholars and students: How can we understand the story of David and Bat-Sheva as found and implied in the text in light of the Talmud's declaration? Did David not sin at all despite ample references to his sin in the text? What were the rabbinic giants of the past conveying to the future generation?

In truth, we would be troubled by the story of David and Bat-Sheva even without this Talmudic comment. The story is well known. While his army is besieging the city of Rabbat Ammon, David spies, from his roof, a woman who is bathing. He inquires of her and finds out that she was the wife of a high officer in David's army, Uriah the Hittite,[47] who, at that time, was battling the Ammonites. David summons Bat-Sheva to his home and impregnates her. Upon hearing of the expected birth, David attempts to cover up his guilt by inviting Uriah back to Jerusalem in the hope that he would return and have relations with his wife, thereby letting everyone assume that the child was Uriah's. When this fails, David orders his general Yoav to place Uriah in the front line of battle where he is likely to be wounded and to tell the troops not to come to his aid. Indeed, this is what happens, and Uriah is killed in battle. Following the required period of mourning, David takes Bat-Sheva as his wife.

---

46. Tractate Shabbat 56a.
47. See II Shmuel 23:39 where Uriah is mentioned as one of the thirty-seven great warriors of David.

On the surface, we seem to be reading the machinations of a manipulative regent who refused to take responsibility for an act of (apparent) adultery with the wife of his own faithful officer – an officer who, at that same time, was risking his life for the king and the nation. And so, in order to hide his indiscretion, the king "arranges" for that loyal commander to die in battle. There are few, if any, redeeming features in David's behavior. This is certainly not the David who is so God-sensitive and moral, the David who is so close to his men and his nation, the David we have gotten to know in the course of twenty chapters. These, we feel, are rather the actions of a selfish king who believes that he is above the law – certainly not one who was to uphold God's law and serve as a model to the nation!

Increasing our puzzlement are the Talmudic rabbis who state that there was no sin at all, while the text makes it abundantly clear that David indeed did sin. In fact, the bulk of II Shmuel, from chapter 11 onward, focuses upon this sin and the ramifications of the sin. The rape of Tamar, the murder of Amnon, the rebellion of Avshalom and the resulting civil war are all a direct result of David's sin, and all are part of God's punishment of David, just as had been prophesied by Natan the prophet.[48] Even more problematic is the fact that the Bible itself has no hesitation in referring to the episode with Bat-Sheva as a sin committed by David. The prophet asks David: "Why did you reject God's law and do what is evil in His eyes?"[49] while David himself openly proclaims: "I have sinned to God."[50] Likewise, we find reference to the sin both in the book of Melachim[51] as well as in the book of Psalms.[52] In light of all this, we are challenged to try and understand what our Rabbis in the Talmud meant.

There are a number of approaches to understanding the rabbinic statement, ranging from those who relegate it to "midrashic" homily, not to be taken literally, to those who claim that the words must be understood as written, i.e., that David committed no sin and his behavior is simply beyond our ability to understand or judge. I prefer taking the middle road: David did

---

48. II Shmuel 12:11. Natan states: הנני מקים עליך רעה מביתך , "Behold, I shall bring you evil from within your very family," an apt description of what befalls David in the ensuing chapters.
49. Ibid. 12:9.
50. Ibid. 12:13.
51. I Melachim 15:5.
52. Psalms 51. The entire chapter deals with David's plea for forgiveness for his sin with Bat-Sheva.

not commit the actual sin of adultery, which would make him liable for the death penalty, but he was certainly guilty of a moral trespass for which God berates and punishes him. As we who read the story are shocked by this "non-Davidic" behavior, so is God. These may have been acceptable actions commonly practiced by other ancient rulers, but such actions would not be tolerated by the moral God from His chosen king. Nor should the rabbinic approach be regarded as a way of "whitewashing" David's actions.

In fact, we can see the textual support for the Talmud's puzzling statement and the probable source of this rabbinic opinion:

1. The prophet Natan while vigorously scolding David[53] never mentions an act of adultery. Rather, he criticizes David for arranging the death of Uriah, Bat-Sheva's husband, and then subsequently taking her as his wife. No mention is made, however, of any illicit relations between David and Bat-Sheva.

2. David, when confessing his sin, is careful to say "I have sinned to God," with the implication being that there was no sin committed against Bat-Sheva, Uriah or their marriage. This seemingly minor point is made more obvious upon reading psalm 51, David's plea for forgiveness after his sin. In it, David abjectly pleads for God's forgiveness and emphasizes that his sin was to God alone.[54]

3. The reference to David's misdeed made in the book of Melachim pointedly includes *only* that which he did to Uriah, calling his actions in this affair "the matter of Uriah the Hittite."[55] Again, no mention is made of his actions with Bat-Sheva.

It is essential, I believe, to understand the rabbinic approach and its explanation when attempting to make sense of this story. Doing so helps us come to the realization that being a king or a leader of Israel places greater responsibility upon one's shoulders, not simply greater privileges. David's true distinction is seen *after* his sin is exposed, for upon realizing what he had done and how he had angered God, he had but one reaction: "I have sinned to God!" David searched for no excuses, gave no rationalizations. David confessed. We cannot help but contrast this reaction to that of Shaul who, when confronted by the prophet with his sin, attempted to deny any

---

53. II Shmuel 12:9.
54. Psalms 51:6.
55. I Melachim 15:5.

responsibility and declared: "It is the *army* who spared the best of the sheep and cattle but only so that they could sacrifice to God."[56]

Remembering the book's theme of the struggles of creating the Israelite kingship and an ideal king, we cannot help but be impressed and inspired by the humility and simply humanness of David, who, as regent, could have had the prophet Natan killed for insolence in talking to the king[57] but reacts instead as a humble child who, admonished by his father, pleads tearfully for forgiveness. This also helps us understand why God quickly forgave David[58] but did not forgive Shaul. David retains the throne, while Shaul must forfeit his, for David admitted his sin and accepted its consequences. Additionally, David's sin was one of passion and human weakness while Shaul's sin was a reflection of a basic personality flaw. Shaul's sin of ignoring God's directive given straight to him – his decision to listen to the demands of his men over those of God – was regarded as an act of royal weakness that revealed his unsuitability to rule.

The Aftermath

It is far beyond the scope of this work to analyze every episode that followed the David–Bat-Sheva story, although each deserves analysis and attention. But it would be quite enlightening to look at the events that precede the rebellion of Avshalom and see what subtle messages the prophet leaves for future generations about David and Avshalom and the underlying themes that appear within the very wording of the text.

The story that catches our attention takes place soon after David's confession of guilt and the subsequent death of Bat-Sheva's infant. There, in chapter 13, we read of the infatuation of Amnon, David's oldest son and likely successor to the throne, with Tamar, his half-sister.[59] At the advice of his cousin and

---

56. I Shmuel 15:15.
57. See II Divrei Hayamim 24:20–22; King Yehoash kills the prophet Zechariah for this reason.
58. II Shmuel 12:13: "Indeed God has removed your sin...." We should be aware of the fact that God's forgiveness does *not* mean a removal of the punishment! The punishment is actually part of the process of forgiveness.
59. Commentators disagree as to whether Tamar was Amnon's half-sister, related through their father David, or whether she was merely a step-sister with no blood relationship to Amnon at all, being related only through the marriage of Amnon's father, David, to Tamar's mother. For our purposes, we will take the approach that Tamar was Amnon's half-sister, while she was a full sister to Avshalom, sharing both parents with him.

close friend Yonadav, Amnon feigns illness and requests from his father that he send his sister Tamar to his house to prepare some food so that he will have an appetite to eat something. David accedes to what seemed to be an innocent request, and upon removing all the attendants Amnon attempts to seduce Tamar. Rejecting his advances, Tamar pleads with him not to force himself on her; in desperation, she even suggests that he request her hand in marriage from the king. Refusing to listen, Amnon rapes Tamar and, perhaps in his guilt, feels immediate revulsion toward her, throwing her out of his house and locking the door so she could not return. Her full brother, Avshalom, finds her wailing and moaning outside Amnon's house and deduces what happened. He attempts to comfort his sister and eventually takes her into his home, where she remains together with Avshalom's family. David is greatly troubled upon hearing of these events, and Avshalom is greatly angered.

Two years later, upon celebrating the shearing of his sheep, Avshalom requests the presence of David at his party. Upon David's refusal, Avshalom convinces his somewhat reluctant (and suspicious?) father to send the crown prince, Amnon, to join all the other princes at the party. At Avshalom's command, his servants murder Amnon in revenge, and Avshalom himself flees to his maternal grandfather, Talmai, the king of Geshur.

That, in a nutshell, is the story. But it would be a mistake to believe that this is a story of passion and punishment alone. Beneath the surface loom powerful political forces that must be understood if we wish to fully understand these chapters. We have here a story of the use and misuse of power and the attempts to solidify a position as successor to the throne. Amnon, as the oldest son of David, was first in the line of succession. He was the crown prince – or so he saw himself. David had not yet indicated his choice for the throne,[60] and so there is a jockeying for that position between the two oldest sons, a struggle that would ultimately lead to open civil war and the very deposing (albeit temporarily) of King David from the throne.

From the very outset of the story, Amnon plays David against himself. His demand to satisfy his desire for Tamar, even though that was clearly improper, is an obvious replay of David's actions with Bat-Sheva. But the advice of the "wise"[61]

---

60. In I Divrei Hayamim 18:9 we read that God told David of the imminent birth of his successor and even what his name would be and why. This story is not included in II Shmuel, nor do we ever read that David expressed his choice for successor to anyone until he commanded that Shlomo be anointed king.

61. II Shmuel 13:3. There Yonadav is described as איש חכם מאד "a very wise man," better

Yonadav to have David himself send Tamar to Avshalom's house, places David in an untenable situation. In effect, it was he, David himself, who was to blame for placing Tamar in that situation in the first place! Who can David blame? What can he say? Amnon was simply repeating David's own misbehavior and doing so with David's help! And so, by having David send Tamar to his house, Amnon effectively silences David and any possible criticism he could give. Perhaps that is why Yonadav is introduced with the statement that he was "a very wise man."

This story also highlights an obvious change in the personality of David, perhaps part of God's punishment, perhaps a direct result of David's deep remorse over his sin. The warrior king who swept away his enemies and ruled his people effectively now becomes a passive pawn in much of what goes on around him. He who once manipulated others is now himself manipulated. He is fooled by Amnon into sending Tamar to his house, where she is raped; he is fooled by Avshalom into sending Amnon to his party, where he is killed. He is also misled by the "wise woman" of Tekoa into bringing Avshalom back from exile (chapter 14) from where he undermines David's rule, and he is then deceived again by Avshalom to grant him leave to go to Hevron, from where he begins his rebellion. David is even relegated to being no more than a passive onlooker during the battle for his very life and kingdom when his army battles Avshalom; and then he is ignored by his general Yoav, who kills Avshalom despite the king's clear and public command not to do so (chapter 18).

As we will suggest, it could very well have been this passivity and silence of David – and specifically his lack of reaction to what had happened to Tamar – that led to Avshalom's rebellion and assassination of his brother. If Avshalom could get no justice from the nation's highest judge, he would take matters into his own hands.

Amnon's rape of Tamar was more than an act of passion, however. The text is consistent in describing Tamar as the sister of Avshalom, and the reason is clear: the rape of Tamar was a statement by Amnon that he was the successor to the throne and could therefore take anyone he wished – especially his brother's sister. It was an act of wielding power over his brother, his rival to the throne,[62] much as David had misused his royal power to take Bat-Sheva from Uriah.

---

translated as "a very clever, crafty man."

62. The taking of women was an act of asserting one's dominance and legitimizing one's claim to the throne. David inherited Shaul's harem (II Shmuel 12:8); Avshalom takes David's concubines (ibid. 16:22); and Adoniyahu tries to marry Avishag (I Melachim 2:21).

In fact, even a cursory reading of this story would lead one to hear echoes of other biblical events. The author uses key phrases and words that appear elsewhere in an attempt to draw a parallel to what occurred in other places. Amnon's refusal to eat the food that Tamar prepared (וַיְמָאֵן),[63] his call to remove all people from his presence so that he could be alone with Tamar (הוֹצִיאוּ כָל אִישׁ מֵעָלַי)[64] and Tamar's rending of her multi-colored garment (כְּתֹנֶת פַּסִּים)[65] all echo back to the Yosef story, clearly meant to bring us back to another (near) fratricidal episode in early Israel. But the story we read in Shmuel has even stronger parallels to another story, also found in the book of Bereishit.

Amnon versus Shechem

Some have suggested[66] that the author of Shmuel had a clear agenda of contrasting our story to that of the rape of Dinah, the daughter of Yaakov, by Shechem, the son of Hamor. They point to the words of Tamar to Amnon in our story as keys to jogging our memory of these past events. Tamar pleads with her brother and says:

אַל אָחִי אַל תְּעַנֵּנִי כִּי **לֹא יֵעָשֶׂה כֵן בְּיִשְׂרָאֵל**, אַל תַּעֲשֵׂה אֶת **הַנְּבָלָה** הַזֹּאת! ...

"...No, my brother, do not rape me for *such a thing is not done in Israel*, don't do this *abomination*!"[67]

These words bring us back to the episode in chapter 34 of Bereishit, where we read of the reaction of the brothers to the news of the attack on their sister. There, we find the very same words being used:

---

63. II Shmuel 13:9; also used when Yosef refused the advances of Potiphar's wife (Bereishit 39:8).
64. II Shmuel 13:9; also used by Yosef before he revealed himself to his brothers (Bereishit 45:1).
65. II Shmuel 13:18; also worn by Yosef (Bereishit 37:3). Similarly, the very rending of the garment hearkens back to Yaakov's reaction upon hearing of Yosef's supposed death (ibid. 37:34).
66. Heard from Rabbi David Silber.
67. II Shmuel 13:12.

וַיִּתְעַצְּבוּ הָאֲנָשִׁים וַיִּחַר לָהֶם מְאֹד כִּי נְבָלָה עָשָׂה בְיִשְׂרָאֵל... וְכֵן לֹא יֵעָשֶׂה.

"...And the people [brothers] were saddened and very upset, for he had committed an *abomination in Israel*...as *such a thing was not done.*"[68]

The prophetic author makes conscious use of these terms in order to have us compare the stories. And indeed the parallels are striking. And so are the contrasts. Both stories center about the forcible rape of a sister, an unheard of act in Israel, and both are revenged by the brother(s). As readers, we are especially enlightened when we compare the events and the characters of each story. We can chart them as follows:

	II Shmuel	Genesis
Victim:	Tamar	Dinah
Perpetrator:	Amnon	Shechem
Avenger:	Avshalom	Simon and Levi
Father:	David	Yaakov

We can posit that the author's desire to remind us of the story in Bereishit is in order to highlight the sharp contrast between the behavior of the characters; this is something that will help us understand the ensuing story, one that focuses upon the relationship between Avshalom and his father.

In the Bereishit story, the guilty parties have certain redeeming features. Shechem, after the rape, is smitten with Dinah. He speaks to her hoping to woo her and even meets with her family in order to arrange for a marriage. Indeed, he is willing to do almost anything in order to marry her. He even agrees to be circumcised and has his entire town go through the surgery as well. In the Shmuel story, Amnon is smitten with Tamar only before he attacks her and speaks earnestly to her only to convince her to surrender to him. Whereas Shechem hopes to marry Dinah and to open the door of his home to this daughter of Yaakov, Amnon throws Tamar out of his house and pointedly locks the door of his home after her

---

68. Bereishit 34:7.

so she could never return.[69] We certainly cannot condone the behavior of Shechem, but his subsequent attempts to "make it right" leave the reader with a sense that he may have had certain positive qualities and that he felt real affection toward Dinah.

But the same cannot be said of Amnon. There is nothing positive in anything Amnon does throughout the story. His behavior is altogether abominable. From his scheme to bed Tamar and involve his unsuspecting father in that scheme, to the way he banishes his tearful victim and abandons her to a lonely life, Amnon is portrayed as a completely self-absorbed personality with absolutely no redeeming qualities. While we may judge Shechem in a somewhat positive light, we see only negative in Amnon.

David versus Yaakov

The contrast between the personalities in these similar stories does not end there. When Shimon and Levi take revenge for their sister by wiping out the entire city of Shechem, Yaakov, who until this point in the story was not heard from, admonishes them for their rash act. And although he argues against their deed based upon the practical realities of their situation[70] rather than the moral turpitude they exhibited, he is clear in his condemnation of the act. And if we needed any more clarification as to Yaakov's feelings about his sons' act of revenge, we need only turn to the final words he shares with his sons, where he condemns both Shimon and Levi for their violent and rash behavior.[71] Yaakov's children knew well how he felt about their actions.

In our story, however, David is painfully silent. The situation clearly cries out for a patriarchal response, but there is none. The author even leaves the reader with the expectation that David would say something. The text tells us: "King David heard of all these things and he was very upset...." We await the next verse that should tell us what David therefore said, what David did

---

69. There is much symbolism to the locking of the door. In Torah law, one who raped a virgin is, with her consent, bound to marry her and never to divorce her. This provided the woman, who would be regarded as "tainted" and likely not marriageable material, support and protection throughout her life (see Devarim 22:28–29). By sending Tamar out of his house, Amnon "closed the door" on her hope of ever having a normal life, which is why she is taken in by her brother, Avshalom.

70. Bereishit 34:30: "...I am few in number and they [the local tribes] will gather against me, so my family and I will be destroyed."

71. Ibid. 49:5–7.

in response. But we are left with a deafening silence. There is no response. David says nothing; David does nothing. We can, perhaps, understand David's predicament. He might very well have regarded this horrific event as part of the punishment God promised would befall him ("Behold I shall bring tragedy to you from within your own family"[72]) and therefore felt he must accept it silently.[73] He may also have felt that there was little he could say to his son, as he himself was guilty of a similar sin and, as we have seen, was responsible for endangering Tamar in the first place. Nonetheless, David was Tamar and Amnon's father, and we would expect to hear some words of admonition from him. Avshalom certainly expected as much.

This last point is most crucial. If we hope to understand Avshalom's behavior then we must understand his thinking. Avshalom hears and sees nothing from his father. He himself feels great responsibility toward his forlorn sister, taking her into his home and, interestingly, even naming his own daughter Tamar.[74] But he wonders about his father: Was David's reticence a sign of his acquiescence? Did David truly regard Amnon as his successor and therefore was reluctant to criticize him?[75] Avshalom doesn't know, and so he waits…for two years. It was only after two years of David's failure to react that Avshalom decides that he must.

Returning to the story in Bereishit, Avshalom sees himself as Shimon and Levi, avenging the honor of a sister. But he must also feel a strong resentment toward his father, who showed no desire to respond to the terrible act. This was considered an insult to Tamar, her mother and, by extension, Avshalom as well. If we keep the Dinah story as a model, we can understand why, upon hearing of the assassination of Amnon, David believes that all of the princes had been killed.[76] Not only did it make political sense – if Avshalom were jockeying for the position of crown prince he well may have killed all the "competition" – but it was also logical if he were copying the actions of Shimon and Levi – who, after all, wiped out the *entire* city!

---

72. II Shmuel 12:11.
73. See David's response to the curses of Shim'i ben Gera, II Shmuel 16:10–12.
74. This might connect to one aspect of the law of *yibum*, levirate marriage, where the brother-in-law who married his brother's widow names their first son after his late brother in order to perpetuate his name and memory (Devarim 25:6). Given that Tamar was not to be married, perhaps this was a way of perpetuating her name.
75. Interestingly, when David's son Adoniyahu later claims the throne, the prophet tells us that one of the reasons he believed that he was the rightful successor was because David had never admonished him. See I Melachim 1:6.
76. II Shmuel 13:30.

It is true that Avshalom committed murder,[77] a dastardly act. But, at this point in the story, most readers can identify with his wrath and perhaps even rationalize the murder of such a debased and unrepentant brother. Avshalom's defense of his sister and the manner in which he provided her with a home and sense of family also colors our feelings toward him. Even his escape to and forced exile in Geshur[78] plays upon the emotions of the reader. Like Yoav in the following chapter, we too would like to see Avshalom returned to his home and begin life anew. But Avshalom loses his heroic luster when subsequent events prove that his motives were not so pure. Indeed, we will see how much of Avshalom's actions were actually politically motivated and driven by his thirst for power.

David versus Avshalom

David's relationship with Avshalom was a troubled one, to say the least. After Avshalom's act of murder, he escaped to his grandfather in Geshur where he remained for three years. During that time, we are told that David recovered from the loss of his eldest and now pined for Avshalom, perhaps feeling the loss of two sons now. Nonetheless, David refused to allow Avshalom's return to Jerusalem and turned a deaf ear to the entreaties of his commander in chief, Yoav. Only after a talented woman (called a "wise woman") acted out a scenario devised by Yoav did David see the situation more objectively and allow his son to return.

In attempting to understand David's reluctance to bring Avshalom back, we must consider his conflicting emotions. David was torn between his feelings as a father and his duties as a regent. As father, he felt love and compassion for his son. As all fathers, he missed his son and longed to see him once more. Additionally, David might even have felt that he was to blame for the murder because he failed to reprimand Amnon for his actions. And haunting him as well must have been the realization that, as in the case of Tamar, it was he who sent Amnon to the celebration and ultimately to his death. A father's love, compassion and guilt played heavily on his emotions and would explain the somewhat puzzling fact that he missed Avshalom.

---

77. Actually, he merely arranged for the murder, having his servants commit the deed itself, something which echoes back to David's arranging for the death of Uriah through the sword of the enemy.

78. A city-state northeast of Israel where Talmai, Avshalom's maternal grandfather, ruled.

But David was also the king. The return of Avshalom would mean his return as the oldest surviving prince and, therefore, first in line for the throne. David, who rejected the use of violence as a way to secure the throne; David, who twice ignored the opportunity of killing Shaul and claiming the throne; David, who twice executed those who dared raise their hands against a king – this David could not imagine bringing back a son who used violence to enhance his position in the line of succession. Nor could he imagine that the people would accept one who was guilty of fratricide as their king. Furthermore, David did not wish to set a precedent for those desiring the throne in the future. As a king, David could not welcome back his son.

Yoav, on the other hand, as commander in chief had different concerns leading him to urge David to bring back his son. Yoav was concerned for the future and worried about insuring a peaceful succession to the throne. He rightfully viewed Avshalom as a threat to the throne – especially while he lived in Geshur. Away from the influence and control of his father, Avshalom could well gather an army of foreigners, and upon the death of his father claim the throne as his own. He would reinforce that claim by marching into Jerusalem with his army and, as oldest son, demand the kingship. Clearly, this could mean civil war and division amongst the people – exactly what the institution of kingship was meant to avoid! It was far preferable, therefore, to have Avshalom in Jerusalem where his actions could be monitored and somewhat controlled, he thought.[79] Indeed, Avshalom's rebellion breaks out only when he leaves Jerusalem and makes his way to Hevron. It is for this reason that Yoav urges David to bring the wayward son back to the capital.

David's actions upon his son's return also call for explanation. He allowed Avshalom to return, and yet for two years he refused to see him. One may well ask why David let him return if he did not forgive him for his act of murder, or why, if he did forgive him, he refused to see him. In light of our previous explanation, David's actions are quite understandable. In order to control and monitor Avshalom's actions and to satisfy his paternal longing, he invited his son back. But as king, David would refuse to give Avshalom the honor of an audience with him. I believe that David's words "he shall not see my face"[80] can be understood, as elsewhere in the Tanach, to mean "to curry

---

79. See I Melachim 2:36, where Shlomo demands that Shim'i ben Gera, who is a clear threat to his throne, remain in Jerusalem and suffer the punishment of death if he ever leaves. The reason there is the same as here: so that he could be controlled and his actions monitored.

80. II Shmuel 14:24: ‏ופני לא יראה‎.

favor,"[81] and not in their literal meaning, that he never saw his son. David, I suggest, may indeed have seen his son as a father but would not grant him a formal audience with the king, an honor that would imply a royal pardon for his act of murder and thereby place him in line for the throne.

This is why Avshalom turns to Yoav, the chief of staff, to arrange for the meeting and not to a close member of the family. It also explains Avshalom's insistence on seeing his father, an insistence so strong that he burned down Yoav's fields in order to force him to arrange that meeting. This was not the act of a loving and lonely son; it was the act of a conniving and power-hungry prince. Avshalom demanded a formal meeting with his father as king so that the people would see that he was back in the good graces of David and, by extension, the true heir to the throne.

These events reveal Avshalom's underlying agenda: to wrest the throne from his elderly father. We may, at first, identify with Avshalom's pain and anger; we may even seek to rationalize his behavior. But when we look back at his actions, knowing how he usurped the power from David, we come to realize that they were all part of a grand scheme designed and put into action by Avshalom well before his rebellion began. These were not the deeds of a hurt yet noble prince, but rather the carefully thought-out plans of a rebellious son to take over the kingship from his father.

Throughout the two years that Avshalom waited for his father's reaction to the rape of his sister, he planned his coup well. When he had his servants kill Amnon, he had convinced them not to fear retribution for their crime, explaining that "after all, it is I who has commanded you." This statement was not only meant as a commitment by Avshalom to shoulder the responsibility and blame for the crime, but also the prideful cry of one who saw himself as the next king. As the legitimate heir to the throne – the throne he believed was forfeited by Amnon through his immoral actions – Avshalom convinced his servants that he had the power and the right to condemn anyone, even his older brother, to death.

It is clear that this was always his plan. When he invited his father to his sheep-shearing festival, he expected David to refuse the invitation to something the elderly king would rightfully regard as unnecessary, below his dignity and possibly physically challenging. But he also knew that David would feel guilty refusing him, and he would use that guilt as a way of convincing David to "at

---

81. Bereishit 33:10: כי על כן ראיתי פניך כראות פני אלקים ותרצני.

least" send the eldest of the family to represent him and thereby extend some bit of honor to Avshalom.

This pattern of manipulative behavior continued after Avshalom's return to Jerusalem as well. He demanded an audience with the king and, when refused, he burnt down Yoav's fields (actually, once again, he had his servants do that), compelling the general to do his bidding. Once he returned to the king's good graces, he proceeded to undermine David's support with subtle and not-so-subtle criticism of the aging monarch,[82] slowly building support for a coup that would place him on the throne. Avshalom's tactics were certainly devious, done in an underhanded and dishonest fashion, and his attacks were especially pernicious, focusing as they did on those areas where David was particularly vulnerable. The text[83] relates how Avshalom first attempted to establish himself as the rightful heir in the eyes of the nation by arranging to have a special chariot and team of horses, as well as fifty men who preceded him acting as harbingers of his arrival. By doing so, Avshalom hoped to elevate his status above those of his brothers so that he would be considered the obvious choice to rule after David. It soon became clear to Avshalom, however, that he could not simply wait for his father to die in order to inherit the throne. He therefore took extraordinary steps to weaken David's grassroots support and to lay the groundwork for an eventual coup.

The text reveals that, while publicizing his elevated political position, Avshalom embarked on a campaign to present himself as "everyman," a simple common person with no pretensions of grandeur. When people would bow down to him, he would draw them near and embrace them. He would enter into personal conversations with them, and he thereby succeeded in endearing himself to the populace – at the expense of an elderly father who, it would appear, no longer wandered out amongst the masses. When we realize that one of David's great strengths was the close relationship he had with the commoners (recall the episode of dancing with them before the Holy Ark), we become more aware of the deviousness of Avshalom's plan.

However, most dangerous to David, and the kingdom as well, was Avshalom's attempts to portray David as an unfit king, one who judged unfairly and corrupted the judicial system. Preying on those who traveled to King David for judgment, Avshalom would accost them before they presented their case; listening to their arguments, he would agree that they were correct

---

82. II Shmuel 15:1–6.
83. Ibid.

but tell them that his father would never give them a fair hearing. By doing this, Avshalom ate away at the very unity of the nation, making the people believe that their king showed favoritism to one tribe over another or one family over another. Considering that one of the challenges that faced the early kings of Israel was to weave the tribes into one nation, and that truly David had succeeded in doing just this, Avshalom's actions were nothing short of treasonous and threatened the existence of the kingdom. But they were also successful.

The great question that often puzzles those who study this story is how could the people have abandoned David as they did, forcing him to flee and raise an army outside of his own city and his own tribe. Avshalom did not raise the banner of rebellion until he had support from most of the nation and from the army.[84] Understanding the effective and well-thought-out actions of Avshalom helps explain this strange phenomenon. What is important to remember is that most people must have considered Avshalom as the choice of the king so that they did not consider themselves involved in any coup. They were, after all, crowning David's son, the crown prince, as his successor.

Regardless of their reasons, the rebellion ultimately failed, although it succeeded in dividing the people deeply. It was only David's brilliant policy of appeasement and rapprochement that reassured the people that they would not be punished. His decisions to appoint Avshalom's general as his own chief of staff[85] and to forgive Shim'i ben Gera his trespass[86] indicated to the people that David was not interested in revenge and served as confidence-building acts that reunited the nation after this fractious episode.

In Conclusion

The final chapter of the book of Shmuel relates the story of the census taken by David, an act that angers God, Who visits a plague upon the people as punishment for the sin. As we pointed out earlier, this chapter, as well as the three previous ones, are not in chronological order, but make up a kind of addendum to the book, tying together random events and facts that help drive home the major theme of the book. We have previously discussed the common themes and bridges between these final chapters and the opening ones

---

84. Ibid. 15:13.
85. Ibid. 19:14.
86. Ibid. 19:24.

of the book of Melachim, as well as the common themes that tie together the opening chapters of this book to these closing ones.[87] However, before ending our discussion of the book of Shmuel, it would be beneficial and enlightening to analyze this final episode of the book.

As we have mentioned, David sins in this final chapter by holding a census to count the population of his kingdom. The purpose of the census is never revealed, although we are told that it was God who "tempted" David to sin.[88] It is logical to assume that its purpose was to let David know how many able-bodied men he had available in case he needed to conscript men for his army. The fact that David sends his chief of staff, Yoav, and his army to count the masses, rather than a governor or officer in charge of internal affairs, indicates that this was indeed David's purpose. The language used by Yoav when he reports back to David also implies a military purpose for the census, for he says: "There are eight hundred thousand *sword-wielding* men in Israel and five hundred thousand in Judea."[89]

The sin seems clear enough to those who are familiar with the Torah's dictates. In Shmot we read that no direct census may be taken: "When you count the Children of Israel, each shall give a ransom for his life to God when counted so that there will be no plague when they are counted. This is what they should give: one-half a shekel…"[90] As Rashi explains, this census of the people taken by David was indeed a direct one and therefore David trespassed the Torah's law.

And yet David's reaction upon realizing his sin seems to indicate a greater offense than the simple transgression of this one law. When David realized his mistake, he told God, "I have sinned *greatly* in what I have done…,"[91] a term he did not use even when confessing his sin with Bat-Sheva! What then made this action such a *great* sin? What is wrong with counting the people? What is the sin of census-taking? Radak comments that it is not census-taking itself that is inherently wrong but the fact that this census was simply unnecessary.[92] Although these approaches are logical, they don't explain the severity of the

---

87. See pages 59-69.
88. II Shmuel 24:1.
89. Ibid. 24:9.
90. Shemot 30:11–12.
91. II Shmuel 24:10.
92. Radak quotes a rabbinic statement also found in the commentary of Ramban on Bamidbar 1:2: "Whenever Israel was counted for a purpose, none were lost; but when they were counted for no purpose, there were losses, as in the time of David."

sin, which is clearly implied in David's reaction. Ralbag (Gersonides), on the other hand, takes a unique approach, which I believe properly defines David's precise sin and helps us understand its severity – especially in light of the king's responsibility.

Ralbag writes that by counting the military-aged men, David was placing his trust and reliance on the strength and size of his army instead of on God. When we recall the most basic lesson taught by Shmuel after his defeat of the Philistines – that victory belonged to God alone – and the great failure of Shaul in taking the spoils of the Amalekites – in effect asserting that the army was the victor and to them belonged the spoils – we realize that David's sin was more than a display of weakness at a time of temptation. It was a failure of royal proportions, for it undermined the very purpose of Israel's monarchy. One of the themes of this prophetic work was the importance of the Israelite king bringing the nation closer to God by attributing his military victories to God and letting the people recognize God's protection and salvation. Clearly then, this transgression of David's was more than a sin of personal passion; it was one of national import, for it contradicted the very purpose for which he was chosen.

The point made by Ralbag is that the very idea of counting the available soldiers implied two false things: (1) that they were "his" soldiers, that is, David's army, when in fact they comprised God's army, and (2) that they were the source of his strength, when, of course, God was. In effect, David's decision to count the men was an act that denied God as the source of Israel's strength and the force behind their victories.

To further illustrate the point, we refer to the recently quoted text from the book of Shemot. There, Moshe is told that whenever the population is counted, the census must be taken in an indirect fashion, i.e., through the collection and subsequent counting of the half-shekel coins. But if, as we posited, counting people indicates a sort of possession or control of those people, then even indirect counting should be prohibited; for, after all, the goal is ultimately to count the people and not the coins, so the same problem exists. This is precisely why the Torah goes on to direct Moshe to gather the coins and bring them to the Tabernacle, to God's place. By doing so, Moshe was proclaiming that these coins, representing each individual in Israel, belonged to God and not to any king or leader. This law was to remain applicable in the future as well: whenever a census would be taken it was done through coins that were then deposited in the Tabernacle or the Temple. Such a census is acceptable and, indeed, desired, but any other type of census leads to the false implication that those counted belonged to another and not to God.

The question that stood before David at that time is the question that the book of Shmuel was meant to answer for us: Is the king a servant of God through serving the people or is the king in control, serving no one, with the people serving him?[93] Shaul fails because, by ignoring the prophet's instruction and God's command, he sees himself in control. David succeeds because he places God's will before his own and the people's welfare ahead of his whims. He serves God and he serves the nation. When a king takes a census and does *not* bring the coins to the Temple – when he does *not* recognize God– then the act undermines the entire monarchy and everything it was to stand for.

Throughout the book of Shmuel, King David represented the best of the monarchy and repaired the damage to that institution caused by his predecessor. With this act, David appeared to have reverted to the mistakes of Shaul and undermined the entire experiment of kingship. His actions contradicted everything he had stood for up until this point and threatened to bring the monarchy back to square one. David looked back on his behavior and realized that this act flew against everything he believed and all the values that he exhibited throughout his life. This might explain why David, when he came to his senses (no pun intended), confessed the sin himself, with no warning and no homily or parable from the prophet. He knew that this foolish act of his went against his very nature, and when he was able to look objectively at his behavior, he rightly exclaims, "I have sinned *greatly*!"

In response to David's confession and entreaties, the prophet Gad offers David a choice of punishments: either three years of famine, three months of pursuit by an enemy or three days of a plague. It is a curious choice. After all, the Torah already ordained the punishment meted out for such an improper census: "...each shall give a ransom for his life to God when counted *so that there will be no plague* when they are counted."[94] The punishment is clear: a plague. Why, then, did God give David a choice? Also troubling is the simple understanding of David's response: "Let me fall into the hands of God, Whose mercies are great, and not fall into the hands of man."[95] What does that mean? What choice did David make? After all, both the plague and

---

93. As explained by Rabbi N. Helfgot.
94. Shemot 30:11.
95. II Shmuel 24:14.

the famine are divinely controlled. Why did God take these words to mean that David chose the plague?

In reality, David made no choice. David's response was an act of contrition and repair of his sin. What David was saying is that the choice was *not* his. He surrendered the decision to God, Who, after all, is He who controls all. After sinning by counting the people and regarding them as his, David now humbly bowed to God's decision, recognizing that He was the power that controlled all and therefore must be the One to pass judgment. Now that God meted out the punishment, David was able to successfully pray to save the people from suffering and eliminate the plague.

The book of Shmuel ends, as we have mentioned, with the purchase of the field of Aravna that would eventually become the site of the Holy Temple, a fitting bridge to the book of Melachim, in which we read of the construction of the Temple. But it is also a fitting ending because we see David in his finest hour. Not the great warrior, not the national hero, but the humble servant of God accepting His judgment and praying for mercy on behalf of his beloved nation. This was the true greatness of the man whose son will now attempt to carry on the dynasty in the same exemplary fashion as his father. The book of Melachim lets us know whether he successfully meets these challenges or not.

THE BOOK OF
I MELACHIM

ספר
מלכים א

From Dynasty
to
Destruction

OVERVIEW

The book of Kings, *sefer Melachim*, is a natural continuation of the previous book of Shmuel. Like its predecessor, its two sections are actually one complete entity, having been divided only later in history. The division itself is quite artificial, as the entire book is clearly written as one unit, with a common theme and purpose to both sections and a continuing, ongoing story of the kings of Israel and of Judea. Nonetheless, the early Church fathers divided the book[1] and chose to close the first part of the book with the death of the Israelite king Ach'av, although the prophet Eliyahu remains alive and continues his prophetic activities into the "second" book of Melachim.

Some have suggested that the author wished to draw a parallel between the opening of the book, which tells the story of the weak and sickly King David, and the beginning of the second part, which tells of the illness-injury of King Achazyahu, although the argument is far from convincing. It is more logical to opine that the primary purpose of dividing the book was to make it easier to

---

1. See overview section of I Shmuel. The reason why the Jews accepted these divisions made by Pastor Stephen Langton of Canterbury at the beginning of the thirteenth century, especially when so many of the chapter divisions run contrary to the traditional division of the chapters ("*ptucha*" and "*stuma*," "open" and "closed" sections) is explained by a medieval scholar: "I copied [the numbering of the chapters] from their books so that the Jews could quickly answer their questions [in their debates with Christian Biblical 'scholars'], as they challenge us every day and question our beliefs and our Holy Torah, and they bring their 'proofs' from the verses in the Bible and tell us 'Look, read such-and-such verse in such-and-such chapter in such-and-such book.'"

teach and learn as two short works rather than one long one. The division was therefore made as near to the midway point as possible, choosing the death of Ach'av and ascension of Achazyahu as the most logical coda, close to the middle of the forty-seven chapters yet not interrupting the Ach'av narrative.

Like the previous books in *nevi'im rishonim*, the internal structure of the book of Melachim is neatly "tied up" by parallel stories that serve as bookends to the prophetic work. Moreover, the stories also provide a dramatic contrast, underscoring the change that took place over the years from Shlomo to Tzidkiyahu (Zedekiah), the last of the Davidic regents. The book opens with the disagreement between David's sons over the succession to the throne, a struggle ultimately decided by King David himself. The closing chapters relate the power struggle between the sons of Yoshiyahu (Josiah) – Yehoachaz and Yehoyakim – but, in contrast to the opening chapter, this struggle was decided by foreign rulers: Pharaoh and Nebuchadnezzar. The opening chapters recount the construction and the magnificence of the newly built Temple and go into a detailed description of the appurtenances and vessels of the Mikdash. The final chapters, on the other hand, describe the destruction of the Temple and the list of holy vessels that were carried away by the enemy.

There is yet another reason that might explain the author's desire to draw the reader's attention to the difference between the promise of the early days of the Davidic dynasty and the disappointment and tragedy of its final days. The book of Melachim was written by the prophet Yirmeyahu[2] after the destruction of the First Temple and was addressed to the generation of the exile – who undoubtedly wondered how the house of the all-powerful God was destroyed by nations whose gods, they were told, did not exist. The book of Melachim and its lessons, therefore, were directed at those who saw the exile as a sign of God's "weakness" in the face of the Babylonian deities and the destruction of the Temple as a clear proof of the "defeat" of God by the gods of the enemy. In the book, therefore, the prophet reviews the history of the nation and shows how God had threatened the people with exile and warned the nation of the impending destruction. The prophet details the sins of Israel and her ongoing defiance of God and His laws.

---

2. Tractate Bava Batra 14b. We would be more accurate if we referred to Yirmeyahu as an author-editor, for much of the description of events from the earlier years was taken from the royal chronicles (mentioned throughout Melachim and Divrei Hayamim) as well as the writings of the earlier prophets who recorded the events of the time. This is clearly hinted to in II Divrei Hayamim 9:29, 20:34, 26:22, 32:32 and 33:19. These writings serve as primary sources for the book of Melachim and the book of Divrei Hayamim.

Yirmeyahu dramatically and convincingly shows how the exiles of both Israel and Judea as well as the destruction of the Holy Temple were punishments from God, payment for the infidelity of the nation. That generation and future ones had to understand that these were penalties brought about by the people's sins, and in no way should the nation believe that the defeat and exile of Israel was due to God's inability to overcome the enemy. On the contrary, the enemy was no more than a mere instrument in the hands of God, used to teach His nation a painful but necessary lesson. Through the lessons of this book, the prophet taught the people that it was Israel's faithlessness that brought upon them the destruction, not God's weakness.[3]

It is important that we keep the author's aim in mind so that we can fully understand why these specific stories, and not others, were included in the book of Melachim, especially when comparing them to the stories that were included in the book of Divrei Hayamim but not in Melachim.

As mentioned, the book of Melachim begins by continuing the saga of King David, now focusing upon his final days. Although the death of David might seem to be a more natural place at which to end the previous book – much as the first section of the book of Shmuel closes with the death of Shaul – it was the aim of the author to emphasize the almost seamless transition of power from David to Shlomo. Indeed, as the opening chapter tells us, Shlomo's reign began during David's lifetime, as the aging king witnessed the young monarch's first weeks of rule and, by doing so, guaranteed a peaceful succession to the throne. Perhaps the reader was also meant to see in this peaceful transition fruition of the divine plan to establish David's throne as the eternal ruling family of Israel, making this book a fitting closing to the book of Shmuel by reaffirming the theme of that book: the legitimacy of David's dynasty.

Together with this, the prophetic author of the book of Melachim, through his rejection of Bamah worship and his harsh criticism of Yerov'am's corruption of the accepted religion, clearly affirms the choice of Jerusalem and Shlomo's Temple as the unchallenged center of divine worship.

---

3. In truth, this is the same lesson that Moshe attempted to teach the nation before his demise. In the early chapters of the book of Devarim, Moshe points out how the people's sins had brought punishment upon them and how that would occur in the future as well if Israel were unfaithful to God. Moshe emphasizes that any defeat they may suffer at the hands of other nations would be a result of their infidelity, a punishment brought by God Who would use the nations as an instrument of His will.

Truthfully, one may logically question the prophet's decision to begin this book with the story of David's final days. As this is, after all, the book of Melachim, we should rightfully expect it to begin with the story of Shaul, Israel's first king or, at the very least, with the chronicle of David, Israel's first "successful" king. The author's decision to begin the book as he does, however, reflects a most essential truth, one important to understand when studying the early prophets. Appointing a monarch, and even establishing monarchy as a system of government, was not God's ultimate goal. Most important was establishing a dynasty, a line of succession, the rule of a son after his royal father. Until that would take place, there could be no real successful kings to speak of. In effect, the book of Melachim is the book of dynasties. Dynastic rule would guarantee relative stability in the government and provide the people with a sense of security.

Therefore, the opening chapter of Melachim should not be seen as the story of an aging monarch and the attempted rebellion of his son. Rather, we must see the chapter's focus as being centered on young Shlomo's ascension to the throne. This was what Israel had struggled for since the death of Yehoshua,[4] and only with the succession of Shlomo was a dynasty finally established; only now could there be a book of Melachim. The book proceeds to tell of the death of David and the reign of his son, a rule initially marked by unparalleled success and glory, but that ends with vocal opposition and near rebellion. In fact, the rest of the book deals with the division of David's kingdom, a split that occurred as a direct punishment for King Shlomo's infidelity to God and resulted in the eventual collapse of both monarchies.

Initially, however, the text goes into remarkable detail in describing the luxury and wealth of Shlomo's reign. One can almost understand the prophetic author, Yirmeyahu (Jeremiah), who, post-exile, waxes nostalgic about the "good old days" of Solomonic rule. We therefore read in detail the magnificence of both the Holy Temple and the royal palace, the abundance of food and delicacies upon Shlomo's table and even the exotic animals collected by the king. Clearly, the prophet hopes to record how the divine promise to Shlomo of unparalleled wealth, glory and wisdom was kept, but in doing so he also describes to the reader living in the future the high point of the Israelite monarchy: a time of peace, of military domination and political stability, of

---

4. The haunting question of the tribes in the beginning of the book of Shoftim (1:1), "Who shall lead us [into battle]?" can well be seen as a question that reverberates throughout the books of the early prophets.

financial growth and economic development. But all of this comes to a close as Shlomo's permissiveness[5] opens the door to idolatry and pagan worship not seen in the land since before the days of Shaul.

Throughout the book, the author deftly shifts focus from the Israelite monarchy to the Judean one in order to limit the discussion to the same basic time period. After describing the successful establishment of a "breakaway" northern kingdom, the book goes on to describe the efforts of her first king, Yerov'am (Jeroboam), to firmly establish an independent commonwealth, completely separate from its southern neighbor. To accomplish this, we read of his attempts to create a separate national religion, clearly differing from that of Judea and the ancient, Torah-based creed. Yerov'am sets up golden calves to be worshiped in Dan and Bet-El in lieu of the worship of God in His eternal capital. He eschews the tri-annual pilgrimages to the national religious center, fearing that such pilgrimages would eventually lead to a rapprochement with the Judean kingdom and its monarchy and the inevitable collapse of his sovereignty and independence.[6] He also appoints priests and attendants of his temples from the non-Levite tribes[7] and establishes a new holiday patterned after that which had been practiced by the people before the division of the kingdom.

The sins of Yerov'am serve as a valid precedent and set the pattern for future Israelite kings: though they differed in their level of Godlessness, they equally feared the return of their nation to Jerusalem and to the Davidic monarchy, and therefore they are consistent in keeping the worship of the false gods as the standard for the kingdom. The result was that each and every

---

5. Our Rabbis are insistent in pointing out that, despite the implications of the text, Shlomo was not directly involved in idolatry; such a thing would be unthinkable of the builder of the Holy Temple, one of whom it is said "and God loved him" (II Shmuel 12:24). Rather, he gave in to the demands of his many foreign wives and allowed the construction of temples and altars to their foreign gods in order to please them. This explains why the text never accuses Shlomo of actual idolatry, only of building places of worship for these foreign deities. See tractate Shabbat 56b.

6. I Melachim 12:26–27. According to the Talmud, Yerov'am actually prohibited his subjects from these pilgrimages, setting up sentries on the road to stop those who attempted to make their way to Jerusalem. See tractates Bava Batra 121b and Sanhedrin 102a.

7. One of the interesting results of these changes was the emigration of many Levites from the northern kingdom to the southern kingdom. They abandon their ancestral cities in the north since they were no longer receiving any of the priestly or levitic gifts. It is safe to assume, therefore, that a higher percentage of the tribe of Levi survived the exile of the ten tribes, as many of them had left the north years earlier. See II Divrei Hayamim 11:13–17.

king of Israel is described by the prophet as having done what was wrong in the eyes of God, even those kings who carried out God's command to destroy the family of their sinful predecessors. The tolerance of (and certainly the support of) idolatry by the king is the one factor used by the author to define the regent as wicked as opposed to righteous. This is true both of the Israelite rulers as well as the Judean monarchs.

The Israelite kings who sinned by tolerating idolatry are generally said to have "followed the wicked ways of Yerov'am." The first king had become the paradigm of a leader who causes his people to stray from God's laws. He is regarded in rabbinic literature as the archetype of the worst of villains, one who is a "*chotei umachti et harabim*," a sinner who leads many astray. The text completes the story of Yerov'am by describing the punishment that awaited him and the predicted fall of his dynasty with his son's loss of the throne. We then read of the events that impacted the early Judean kings, the ascension of the righteous Asa to the Judean throne and the succession of his son, Yehoshafat (Jehosaphat).

The final chapters of I Melachim are taken up by the fascinating stories of Ach'av (Ahab) and his antagonist, Eliyahu (Elijah), whose story continues into II Melachim. The struggle between the Ba'al worshiper and God's avenging prophet includes the dramatic confrontation between Eliyahu and the prophets of Ba'al at Mount Carmel, as well as the machinations of the wicked Queen Izevel (Jezebel) to acquire the field of Navot. We also read of Eliyahu's flight from the queen and the appointment of Elisha as the eventual successor to Eliyahu. The story of the clashes between the prophet Eliyahu and the king Ach'av ends, as does the first book of Melachim, with the death of Ach'av in a battle against the Arameans.

ANALYSIS

A Promising Beginning

King Solomon, whose Hebrew name, Shlomo, from the word "sha-lom," reflected the peaceful era in which he ruled,[1] was blessed from his very birth. This child, conceived as David comforted his new wife, Bat-Sheva, following the loss of their first child, was so dear to God that he sent His prophet to inform David of the special name God had for him: Yedidyah, "beloved by God."[2] We read nothing of his early life, although by tradition he was born in David's latter years and took the throne at the tender age of twelve, by which time he was already married and had fathered a son.[3] It was this awareness of his young age that moved him to request wisdom from God to properly lead the nation.[4] This request was not made simply to provide him with wisdom to judge those who came to him as the supreme

---

1. According to David in I Divrei Hayamim 22:9, it was God Who chose this name for David's son for this very reason, although this is not recorded in the book of Melachim.
2. II Shmuel 12:25. Interestingly, this "pet" name shares the same root form as the name of Shlomo's father, David (ד-ו-ד), as he too was beloved by God.
3. Although mentioned in a number of places we do read in Sifrei Bracha 36 the following quote: "Shlomo lived for fifty-two years." As he ruled for forty years (I Kings 11:42), he started his rule at the age of twelve.
4. I Melachim 3:7–9.

judge of Israel. As was true of the judges of an earlier era, "judging" included more than rendering legal decisions; it included providing leadership. Shlomo was well aware of the fact that his youth and inexperience would be viewed as a weakness that would encourage pretenders to the throne to challenge Shlomo and attempt to usurp his position.

The need for Shlomo to firmly take hold of the kingship was underscored by David on his deathbed. In his final recorded words to Shlomo, David urges his successor to deal severely with those who pose a threat to his rule and the very unity of the people, especially popular leaders who had already challenged David or opposed his choice of Shlomo as his successor.[5] David remained faithful to his goal of keeping the nation united until the very end of his life. He understood that the rise of a new king after his relatively stable rule of forty years could signal a struggle for the throne. This is why the book of Melachim begins with David's decision to have Shlomo publicly anointed and why David insisted on having his son begin his rule while he himself was still alive. In this way, he felt, no one could ever challenge Shlomo's rightful ascension to the throne. And this too was behind Shlomo's request for wisdom. He asked God for practical knowledge in the ins and outs of leadership so that he could silence any challenges to his rule and keep the nation united behind his kingship.

Following David's passing, Shlomo faced a brewing rebellion directed by his general, Yoav, and his eldest brother, Adoniyahu. Shlomo dealt firmly with this first threat to his throne as well as with a muted challenge from Shim'i ben Gera.[6] He also banished Evyatar, the high priest and long-time ally of

---

5. In I Melachim, chapter 2, we read of David's final directives to Shlomo, where he specifically tells him to deal harshly with Yoav, his general, and with Shim'i ben Gera of Binyamin. Shlomo was told in effect not to allow them to die peacefully.

6. At first glance, the story of Shim'i is difficult to understand, and Shlomo's reaction to Shim'i's misdeed seems somewhat harsh. But one must remember that Shim'i, who cursed King David when the latter was escaping from his rebellious son Avshalom (II Shmuel 16:7), was an influential leader of Shaul's tribe of Binyamin. He was able to gather one thousand men from his tribe to greet David upon his return to the throne, an act that undoubtedly affected David's decision not to punish Shim'i for his rebellious actions (ibid. 19:18–20). Nonetheless, David recognized that Shim'i, a member of Shaul's family, was a real threat to Shlomo's throne and warned Shlomo to suffer no breach from Shim'i. Shlomo realized that Shim'i's failure to follow his clear warning never to leave Jerusalem was more than a lapse of memory on his part. It was a defiant act meant to challenge Shlomo's power. Shim'i doubted that the new king would dare to punish him and risk a loss of support from his crucial tribe of Binyamin. Shlomo could not, and did not, allow this defiance to pass by in silence.

David, from Jerusalem, making it impossible for him to continue directing the ritual service and thereby effectively removing him from his post. This decision of Shlomo brings to fruition God's curse of the high priest, Eli, who was told that his descendant would lose the right to serve as the high priest and would forfeit his high office.[7]

Shlomo's success in removing these popular and powerful leaders strengthened his control of the kingdom by reducing the threats to his rule and enhancing his stature in the eyes of the nation, who now saw this young king as a confident and competent leader, one who would deal harshly with anyone who dared challenge his authority. Indeed, the text makes this quite clear when it introduces and closes these episodes with the words "and the kingdom was well established in Shlomo's hands."[8]

Divine Promises Realized

Interestingly, according to the text, all of these events occurred before God bequeaths Shlomo the gift of wisdom.[9] So too did Shlomo's marriage to the princess of Egypt, a clear proof of his growing importance and of the high esteem in which Israel was held, enough to have the ruler of the most powerful and dominant empire in the region choose to solidify an alliance with it. The gift of wisdom that Shlomo received from God, together with the promise of wealth, glory and fame, furthered his innate gifts; this serves as a theme for the story of David's son. Almost every chapter that follows can be understood in terms of these gifts, relating stories that show how God kept His promises to Shlomo.

The first indication of this is the well-known story of the two harlots and their argument over the newborn child, with both claiming to be the infant's true mother. Shlomo's verdict to divide the baby helped reveal the identity of the true mother and was seen by the people as evidence of Shlomo's divinely inspired wisdom and not as a result of simple knowledge

---

7. I Shmuel 2:30, 35.
8. I Melachim 2:12, 46.
9. It is not clear whether the events of I Melachim, chapter 2, occurred before Shlomo's dream and request for wisdom, or whether they occurred after but were included earlier since they connect closely to David's directives to Shlomo that open chapter 2. Certainly the story of Shim'i, which took place over a span of several years, seems to have occurred later in Shlomo's reign, as the text indicates that Shim'i remained in Jerusalem "for many years" before defying Shlomo and leaving the city (ibid. 2:39).

or legal training. This gift from God is what distinguished Shlomo and what inspired the nation to "be in awe"[10] of their king, despite his tender age.

The verdict in this case proved that God indeed granted Shlomo this gift of wisdom, while the description of his knowledge further demonstrates how God kept His word to Shlomo.[11] But the text is not satisfied with a description of Shlomo's brilliance alone, for the subsequent chapters record the extent of God's other gifts to His chosen king: unprecedented wealth and unequaled fame. And so we read of the lavish table spread in Shlomo's court, which reflects the number of noble visitors that graced his palace. The amount of food and types of delicacies that were consumed on a regular basis, as well as the number of attendants and overseers required to provide that food,[12] simply boggles the mind. The prophetic author goes out of his way to describe Shlomo's magnificent throne and palace, to record the exotic animals brought into his kingdom and even to detail the sources of Shlomo's wealth by recording the amount of gold and precious materials that were brought into the kingdom each year.

The Bible also reveals how God kept His promise of granting Shlomo fame and glory, showing how the king enjoyed widespread recognition in the ancient world. The text reports that Shlomo hosted many visitors and guests, including nobility from the many neighboring states. In addition, the local rulers hoped to solidify peaceful relations with Israel by marrying their daughters to Shlomo, which helps explain the large number of foreign wives that Shlomo had.

Included in the story of King Shlomo, of course, is the construction of the Holy Temple and the royal palace. The details related in these chapters describe construction that must have been quite remarkable in the ancient world; indeed it is even remarkable when we read about it today. These details include the dimensions of the Temple itself and a description of the amount of precious metals that were used. Especially moving is the prayer composed by the king for the dedication of the Temple in which he prays for the success of his Temple as a center of prayer and worship to God for Israel and, uniquely, for all of the nations of the world. The glorious and awe-inspiring Temple of Solomon was followed by the construction of his own palace; the residence of his wife, Pharaoh's daughter; and the fortification of Jerusalem, as well as other construction projects undertaken by Shlomo.

---

10. I Melachim 3:28.
11. Ibid. 5:9–15.
12. Ibid., ch. 4.

The final (positive) Shlomo story which describes the visit of the Queen of Sheba and her entourage is a fitting closing for these chapters, as it tells of all three divine gifts: Shlomo's wisdom, which he displays in answering all of her questions; his fame and glory, which had reached as far as the land of Sheba and inspired the queen's visit; and Shlomo's wealth and lavish lifestyle, which impressed the queen so that she "had no breath left in her."[13]

Upon reading these accounts, it becomes clear that the Solomonic era was the high point of Israelite history. It was a time of peace, as prophesied by God, a time of economic success and of national security. Shlomo had lived up to the great expectations God, his nation and his father had for him. Everything seemed perfect. But it wasn't. And what wasn't changed history forever.

From Temple to Tempest

The story of Shlomo as told in the book of Melachim bears no hint of criticism of or divine disappointment in Shlomo. For ten chapters we read only of his accomplishments and positive actions. We read of his wisdom, his wealth, his service to God and the growth of his fame. All of this changes when we reach the eleventh chapter. There we are introduced to "another" Shlomo,[14] one who married many foreign wives who eventually led him astray. The text reveals that during his later years, Shlomo constructed worship areas and temples for foreign gods to accommodate his foreign wives.[15] In fact, the entire tone of the book and its attitude toward King Shlomo change in this chapter. When the author portrays the growing importance of Shlomo by mentioning his marriage to the princess of Egypt, no word of criticism is uttered; on the contrary, it would seem that the marriage was presented as a source of pride to the relatively small Israelite kingdom. And yet when the marriage is mentioned again in chapter eleven, it is used as a proof of the king's misdeeds in marrying foreign wives.[16]

---

13. Ibid. 10:5.

14. Indeed, the change is so dramatic that, according to ancient legend, Shlomo was replaced by Ashmodai, the king of the demons, who was the one responsible for all the sins and failures of Shlomo. There really was "another" Shlomo!

15. Shlomo was *not* an idolater nor does the text ever say that he was. On the contrary, we are told only that "his heart was not fully with God as was the heart of his father, David," a description that would not be used were he an active idolater. It would seem that in his older age he simply gave in to the demands of his ever-growing harem of foreign wives.

16. The Talmud (Sanhedrin 101b) insists that the nation's growing dissatisfaction with Shlomo mentioned in this chapter was tied in to the honor and luxury he provided for the daughter of the Pharaoh.

It is fair to suggest that the earlier chapters that portray the idyllic state of the nation were taken from the writings of Natan, the prophet of David's later years and Shlomo's earlier ones. It is he who anointed Shlomo and, very possibly, passed from the scene before the corruption began. The description found in this eleventh chapter, however, could be the work of Achiyah (Ahijah) of Shilo, who warned Shlomo of his missteps and prophesied on the collapse of his kingdom. It was Achiyah who functioned during the later years of Shlomo and who appointed the first king of the northern tribes, Yerov'am.

And yet the beginning of Shlomo's downfall is foreshadowed in the final verses of the tenth chapter. There, after mentioning how Shlomo surpassed all contemporary kings in his wealth and his wisdom, the text reveals how much wealth was brought into his kingdom each year and how he had become a major purchaser of horses – so much so that he sent a contingent of his men down to Egypt in order to buy horses from merchants there. It is after these descriptions that the next chapter begins by criticizing Shlomo for his many (foreign) wives.

If one reads these chapters carefully, one cannot help but recall the laws that the Torah directed to a king. The book of Devarim presents specific laws that are incumbent upon an Israelite king. Of these, there are three laws meant to limit the king's power. The king is told: [17]

1. He may not have too many horses so that he not send people down to Egypt to increase the purchase of horses.

2. He may not have too many wives so as not to be led astray by them.

3. He may not have too much wealth.

The prophet's record of Shlomo's deeds follows the pattern of the Torah's prohibitions precisely: the purchase of horses for which he sent a contingent down to Egypt; the marriages to so many wives who, we are told, led him astray;[18] and the collection of so much wealth to support his luxurious lifestyle. We are presented therefore with Shlomo's trespasses of the three specific laws as well as the result of those trespasses, exactly as delineated in the Torah. The prophet's message is anything but subtle.

---

17. Chapter 17:16–17.
18. See Nechemiah 13:23–26.

But Whose Fault Is That?

And yet, one can argue that these were gifts granted by God Himself and not something for which Shlomo should have been criticized or punished. After all, the unsurpassed wealth was never requested by the king; it was God's gift to him. Likewise, God had granted him the gift of peace during his reign, something that may well have required Shlomo to marry these foreign women.[19] Why is Shlomo taken to task for the blessings that God gave him, blessings he never asked for?! Our Rabbis[20] find fault in Shlomo's hubris, in that he believed that he would not fall into the trap of "lower," less intelligent kings and be tempted to sin, as the Torah warned they would. He was confident that he could enjoy all of these excesses without trespassing God's dictates and therefore was not subject to these prohibitions.

But perhaps we can suggest another reason why Shlomo did bear the brunt of the sin and was held responsible for these actions. God's gifts to Shlomo were precisely that: God's gifts, bequeathed to His king as He saw fit. King Shlomo was not criticized for enjoying God's gifts but rather for not being satisfied with them. His actions indicate that he felt that God's beneficence was not sufficient for him, and he was therefore punished for his attempts to add to the gifts which God had granted him. Beyond the obvious fact that such activity reflected a certain lack of faith in God's ability to keep His promises and an unattractive trait of a hedonistic pursuit of material comforts, Shlomo's quest for greater wealth also blinded his own people to the fact that the true source of his wealth was God. Clearly these "wealth-amassing" expeditions would lead the nation to believe that Shlomo's economic success was due to the king's abilities and talents. When we recall that crucial to a king's mission was his ability to attribute his successes to God – for, as we've mentioned, he had to reflect God and not replace Him – we understand how Shlomo's actions failed this most essential test of a faithful Israelite monarch.

---

19. These foreign women all adopted the religious practices of the Israelites upon marrying the king. It was common practice throughout the ancient world, and indeed into the late Middle Ages and beyond, to adopt the religion of the nation whose king you have married. Rambam (*Mishneh Torah, Hilchot Issurei Bi'ah* 13:14–16) proclaims that it is impossible to believe that Shlomo, called "beloved of God," would have married these women without conversion. Rather, they converted, but their conversion was artificial, since they did so only to benefit from the wealth and standing of Shlomo, which is why the Bible refers to them as "foreign." Additionally, I would propose that these princesses came with a bevy of attendants and maidens who were not required to convert and brought in their idols and idolatry.
20. Tractate Sanhedrin 21b.

In order to clarify this point further we would do well to contrast Shlomo's actions with those of his illustrious father. When studying about King David's military successes we read of the great amount of booty and wealth he accumulated in his wars against the surrounding enemies. Tellingly, the Bible informs us: "These too David dedicated to God, together with the gold and silver that he set aside from all of the nations he conquered: from Aram and Moab and the Amonites, from the Philistines and Amalek and the spoils of Hadadezer...."[21] However, following the initial Temple construction needs, we never read that any of the wealth gathered by Shlomo was set aside for God or for His Temple.[22] What we *are* told is that the wealth brought into the kingdom by the king's fleets and the visitors to the kingdom was given directly to Shlomo.[23] We also read that Shlomo used the massive amounts of gold for ceremonial shields, for his royal throne and for his tableware. He used the gathered wealth for the purchase of horses, massive building projects and his lavish lifestyle.[24] But nowhere do we read that Shlomo set aside a portion of this wealth for God, as his father had.

This then is the focus of the criticism: Shlomo's active accumulation of wealth was used for his *own* aggrandizement and glory and not God's. This would explain Shlomo's investment in horses and chariots as well, for as the text reveals, he placed them not simply in specific cities around the land but also in Jerusalem "with the king,"[25] ostensibly for his own use. When we consider the additional fact that he taxed the people heavily in order to support this lifestyle, we better understand God's disappointment with his actions.

In similar fashion, Shlomo's marriages to his many foreign wives reflected a lack of faith in God's abilities to preserve the peace. There can be little doubt but that many of these marriages were entered into for political purposes, in order to insure peaceful relations with the surrounding nations. Nonetheless,

---

21. II Shmuel 8:11–12.
22. In truth, we are told (I Divrei Hayamim 29:2–3) that David had gathered much of the materials needed for the construction of the Temple. Except for the gold that Shlomo purchased from Hiram, we don't find any mention of Shlomo raising funds for the Temple, although he did gather the workers and artisans.
23. I Melachim 9:28.
24. Shlomo gathered ivory, which he used on his throne, and imported exotic animals into his kingdom such as monkeys and peacocks. He also gathered coral (עצי אלמוגים), which he used for musical instruments and to line his pathway from the palace to the Temple (Ibid. 10:12, 18, 21).
25. I Melachim 10:26.

the text is critical of Shlomo for his "love" of foreign wives and his desire to marry them, seemingly regardless of the political necessity. The author's telling verse "...it is to them that Shlomo clung in love"[26] implies a passionate attachment to these wives, not a marriage made simply for political convenience. How revealing is the prophet's choice of the word "clung" (דבק) whose first biblical use can be found in Bereishit (2:24) regarding a husband's attachment to his (one) wife! Shlomo's sin was not simply one of marrying more wives than permitted to a king but of marrying foreign wives, becoming enamored by them and surrendering to their demands. It is important not to minimize the impact of these marriages.

Subtly hidden beneath the Bible narrative is the success of both Shaul and David in removing the idolatrous influences that had plagued Israel since their arrival in the land. Shaul had so successfully removed the necromancers (אובות וידעונים) from the land[27] that, in his desperate attempt to contact God before his final battle, he could only find one hidden "ba'alat ov" in En Dor, whom he visited incognito. Likewise, nowhere throughout the reign of David do we read of any idols or idol worship, except those taken from the enemy as spoils of war.[28] This was no small accomplishment after the hundreds of years of widespread idolatry, well-documented in the book of Shoftim. And yet a mere generation after his father had passed on after completing the task of effectively erasing idolatry from the land, Shlomo, through his marriages to these foreign women, reintroduced the pagan cults to the land, allowing idolatrous altars and temples to be built, even situated on the mountain facing Jerusalem itself.[29] Need we still wonder why Shlomo is shouldered with the blame?

Rebellion against the Davidic Dynasty

Shlomo's excesses were tolerated at first by a population who still revered his father and saw in his lavish lifestyle a reflection of the newly acquired respect earned by Israel from her neighbors. But as the years went by and the luxuries increased, they became a drain upon the overly taxed populace. Shlomo's massive building projects must have been perceived as unnecessary,

26. Ibid. 11:2.
27. I Shmuel 28:3.
28. II Shmuel 5:20.
29. I Melachim 11:7.

especially during a prolonged period of relative peace when fortifying cities was not a priority for the people.[30] Furthermore, some of these projects did not benefit the people at all and, in fact, angered the people.[31]

Nonetheless, one could argue that the open rebellion would not have taken place had Shlomo kept the people united as one. The steps that King David took in order to have each tribe feel part of the nation[32] were ignored by his son. King Shlomo drew a clear line between his own tribe of Yehudah and the other tribes when he taxed the others at a higher rate than his own, an implication made in the text by the fact that the very first request made of the northern, non-Judean tribes of Shlomo's successor was to alleviate the heavy taxation of his father. A careful review of the twelve geographic areas that were required to supply Shlomo's palace needs monthly, areas delineated in chapter 4 of I Melachim, will show that the tribe of Yehudah did not share in that burden.

The very language used by the text also implies a forced servitude of these tribes. Yerov'am, the future king of northern Israel, was described as being in charge of "the burdens of the house of Yosef" (לכל סבל בית יוסף),[33] echoes of the description of Israel's servitude in Egypt.[34] So too we find phrases in describing Shlomo's work force that hark back to the slavery of Egypt: porters in charge of transporting the heavy stones and wood are called נושאי סבל, "the carriers of *burden*"; supervisors in charge of overseeing the labor, were called "רודים בעם,"[35] which reminds us of the biblical command לא תרדה בו בפרך,

---

30. II Divrei Hayamim 8:3–6.

31. Most notably was the palace built for the daughter of Pharaoh, a project Shlomo undertook once he completed the construction of the Holy Temple and of his own palace (I Melachim 3:1). Implied in the verse is that the princess of Egypt would dwell in the City of David only temporarily, i.e., until her palace was completed. It is not far-fetched to assume that an important and beloved wife such as the princess of Egypt (Sifrei Devarim, *Ekev*, ch. 52) would have expected, or even demanded, separate living quarters. Whatever the reason, it seemed to have been a source of friction and consternation among the people; see commentary of Mahari Karah, I Melachim 3:1. In II Divrei Hayamim 8:11, we read of Shlomo's own explanation for building the palace: "My wife will not stay in the house of David, King of Israel, for it is a holy [place], since the Ark of God had been brought to it." See also tractates Sanhedrin 21b and Shabbat 56b.

32. See I Melachim, ch. 4.

33. Ibid. 11:28.

34. Shemot 1:11: "in order to torment them in their burdens"; likewise Shemot 2:11: "and he saw their burdens."

35. I Melachim 5:30.

"you shall not work him ruthlessly";[36] and the people's complaint to Shlomo's son of their father's עול כבד, "heavy yoke," is a phrase used to described the yoke of Egyptian slavery.[37] These policies of Shlomo had the effect of tearing the people apart once more. The conscious attempts of the earlier kings to erase tribal differences that plagued the people throughout the period of the judges and their careful nurturing of a national identity were effectively destroyed by King Shlomo's actions. It is no wonder that the kingdom would disintegrate upon his death. It was he who began that process. The punishment fit the crime; indeed, the punishment *was* the crime!

Failing to Properly Succeed

The story of Yerov'am, the first regent of the northern kingdom, is more than a curious one. This Ephramite, after all, was described by the prophet as a "brave warrior,"[38] one whose obvious talents were recognized early on by Shlomo himself. Chosen by God to replace Shlomo, and leaving only a "shadow" kingdom to the Davidic line, it is clear that Yerov'am was meant to be the new David, that "ideal" king who would live up to all of the expectations God had for an Israelite monarchy. And yet he did not become that king. He did not build a dynasty. Nadav, the son who succeeded him, was assassinated in the second year of his reign. Yerov'am is gone and his dynasty is never established. He is remembered only for his wickedness and for the spiritual damage he wreaked upon the population, damage that eventually led to their exile. How could such a thing have happened to this outstanding personality, one who was chosen by God and invested by His prophet?

The answer to the question begins with understanding God's involvement in His world. God's blessings are not guarantees but opportunities. God may present an outstanding individual with a glimpse of what he *may* achieve in his life *if* he follows God's ways. As we saw in the case of King Shlomo, God's blessings do not guarantee success, for one is judged by what he does with those blessings. Yerov'am was blessed with great talents, and God granted him

---

36. Vayikra 25:43.

37. "I am the Lord your God, Who took you out of Egypt, from being slaves to them; I shattered the poles of your yoke and led you upright" (ibid. 26:13).

38. גבור חיל (I Melachim 11:28); in reality, this appellation implies far more than military prowess. It can be used to describe a person of means, a noble individual (Rut 2:1) or a person of accomplishment – as in איש חיל (I Melachim 1:42) or אשת חיל (Mishlei 31:10).

the opportunity of establishing the Israelite dynasty, a line of monarchs who would rule over the northern kingdom, *if* he followed in God's ways. This was clearly stated by the prophet Achiyah in his words to Yerov'am[39] when he explained to him that his success as monarch would be conditional on his observance of God's laws. Yerov'am had the potential to found an eternal dynasty but chose to ignore the prophet's warning to remain faithful to God and His laws.

But Why?

It is difficult to understand why any person would risk forfeiting God's guaranteed blessing by turning a back on the very power that provided the opportunities for success. Why anyone who heard God's word from His prophet would choose to ignore it is a difficult question to answer, despite the fact that the Bible is replete with stories of such individuals. In the case of Yerov'am, one can argue that, as history has proven, power is enticing – often leading people to believe that they need listen to no one. This could certainly have been the case with King Yerov'am, but I would suggest that in his case, the reason was far more basic.

Yerov'am lacked faith in God and, as a result, feared the loss of his kingdom. As he stated: "If the people bring their offerings to the Temple in Jerusalem their hearts will revert to their master, Rechav'am...and they will kill me...."[40] Yerov'am's decision to break away from God was not, therefore, a *religious* one; it was a *political* one. Yerov'am's fear that his nation, making three annual pilgrimages to the Temple in Jerusalem, would eventually overthrow his rule and return to the Judean kings led him to attempt and create a new identity for his nation, one distinct from their Judean brothers.

It was only natural that in the ancient world, where every nation had their national god, Yerov'am would seek to find worship that would make Israel distinct and different from Judea. If Ammon worshipped Molech and Moav worshipped K'mosh, if the Phoenecians turned to Ashtoret and the Philistines to Dagon, then the Israelites would worship the golden calf. Yerov'am therefore fashioned two golden calves, which he sets up in the northern city of Dan and the southern city of Bet-El, declaring that the people no longer need to make pilgrimages to a "foreign" country and city but could take pride in the

---

39. I Melachim 11:38.
40. Ibid. 12:27.

fact that they had their own God,[41] worshiped in their own unique fashion. The king was so committed to establishing an independent identity for his nation that he proceeded to build temples to these calves and appoint different priests to serve these idols, individuals that were not from the tribe of Levi (as the *kohanim* of the Torah were). He even established a different holiday on the fifteenth day of the eighth month, aping the celebration of Tabernacles (Sukkot) observed in Judea on the fifteenth day of the seventh month.[42]

It also seems clear that Yerov'am fancied himself as the founder of this "religion" and therefore as its high priest. It is remarkable to note the similarities between the actions of Yerov'am, the first high priest of "new" Israel, and those of Aharon, the first high priest of Israel. Yerov'am's choice of fashioning golden claves was not a random one: it was worship that the Israelites had already followed in the desert. And it was Aharon who fashioned the first golden calf. Likewise, Yerov'am, when proclaiming his new religion to the masses, exclaimed: "Behold your God, Israel, Who raised you out of the land of Egypt"[43] – language that echoed, almost word for word, the statement made to Aharon by the people when first seeing the golden calf he fashioned.[44] Nor can we ignore a subtle but almost shocking fact regarding King Yerov'am: he had two sons whom he named Nadav and Aviah, almost identical names to those of Aharon's oldest sons, Nadav and Avihu.

Might we suppose that Yerov'am "patterned" himself after the righteous high priest but used Aharon's few misguided deeds, though clearly condemned in the Torah (as were the deeds of his sons Nadav and Avihu), as precedent or rationale for his misdeeds? Whatever reason King Yerov'am had for rebelling against God, he successfully drags Israel down to his sinful level. And therein lies another puzzle.

And Why Follow?

Though we might understand the actions of Yerov'am, we still find difficulty in explaining the almost sheepish reaction of the nation who followed him, with no seeming resistance, into the practice of open idolatry. The nation

---

41. It seems clear that he did not wish to replace God Himself, changing the entire history of his nation, but rather His mode of worship, as will be explained.
42. I Melachim 12:31–32.
43. Ibid. 12:28.
44. Shemot 32:4.

had, after all, turned away from the worship of false gods many years earlier. Why did they allow themselves to be maneuvered and manipulated in such a fashion? How could Yerov'am have succeeded with such seeming ease? There are several responses to this question, none of which may be fully satisfying, but together may help us better understand the mindset of that day and the factors that led to the success of Yerov'am in leading the nation away from God.

First, not everyone followed the new king. Although the text in Melachim mentions no real opposition to Yerov'am, the book of Divrei Hayamim makes it clear that a significant portion of the people of the north joined their brethren in the south: "And the priests and the Levites from throughout Israel joined him [Rechav'am, the king of Yehudah] from their borders…. And besides them all those from the tribes of Israel whose heart desired to seek out Hashem, the God of Israel, came to Jerusalem to sacrifice to Hashem the God of their ancestors. These strengthened the kingdom of Yehudah and encouraged Rechav'am the son of Shlomo…."[45] With many of the strongest opponents to his changes already gone from his kingdom, Yerov'am had an easier time imposing these changes on his population with minimal resistance.

Second, we often fail to understand the depth of anger and resentment that the people of the north had toward the Davidic rulers. They had been made to feel as secondary citizens in the realm, shouldering a disproportionate share of the tax burden and treated unfairly by the Judean rulers. Recall that even at the very end of David's reign, there were strong elements of opposition to him from the north. He faced the degradation and curses of Shim'i ben Gera, an influential leader of the tribe of Binyamin,[46] who rejoiced at what he believed was David's abdication of the throne. Even after the coup of Avshalom was undone, David faced the attempted rebellion of Sheva ben Bichri,[47] who organized an opposition from the people of the northern tribes. The entire episode was sparked by a perceived slight to their honor when David allowed the Judeans to accompany him back to his throne although it was the Israelite tribes who first called upon him to return. As a result of this simple disagreement, some from the northern tribes sought to break away from David's rule.

---

45. II Divrei Hayamim 11:13, 16–17.
46. II Shmuel 16:5–8.
47. The episode is found in II Shmuel 20:1–22. This rebellion took place in the very final years of David's life.

To be sure, the uniting of disparate tribes after hundreds of years of relative independence would have taken more than one generation in any case. The actions of both Shlomo and Rechav'am, however, failed to further unite the people and, quite the opposite, actually gave impetus to those who opposed the Judean rule. If we understand this, we can better understand the view of Yerov'am that a new, independent nation required a new independent mode of worship. Those who followed their new king, I would submit, did so not as a rejection of their God but rather as a rebellion against their king. It was, as mentioned, a political decision – not a religious one.

Third, and perhaps the most compelling response to our question, Yerov'am convinced his nation (and perhaps was convinced himself) that it was *he* who remained faithful to the true worship, and David and Shlomo who had rebelled against God. He could have made the argument that Israel had always worshiped at modest religious structures, sometimes portable and temporary, and often at local altars. Since the destruction of the Tabernacle in Shilo during the time of Eli the high priest, the nation had offered their sacrifices at municipal sites, altars found in most of the cities (*bamot*), which were far more convenient for the local populace. Even the great prophet Shmuel, the very man who anointed David, worshiped at these places! Shmuel would travel from town to town and bless the town's sacrifices offered at these sites; he prepared both Shaul and David for their appointments as king at just such gatherings.[48] Did Shmuel not command Shaul to wait for him to make the pre-battle sacrifice to God – on a local altar?[49] Yerov'am may have made the convincing argument that if it was good enough for Shmuel why was it not good enough for Shlomo?[50] And he might have claimed that if was acceptable in the past, why would it not be acceptable in his day as well?

Yerov'am had yet another powerful claim against the legitimacy of Temple worship and may have even derided such worship. Speaking to the tribes in the north, Yerov'am could have argued that it was David himself who decided that his city, the City of David, was the chosen city. Calling on the collective memory of Israel, he could convince his nation that it was they

48. See I Shmuel 9:12–13 and 16:2–3.
49. Ibid. 10:8.
50. The prohibition of sacrificing outside of the Temple once it had been established as "God's chosen place" is found in Devarim 12:8–11, 13–18. The point being made is that Yerov'am may have questioned whether this was truly the place God had chosen or only the one David had chosen. He could have then argued that his temples, in Dan and Bet-El, were also legitimate places chosen by God for His worship, while still maintaining the legitimacy of worship on the local sites as well.

who were returning to the *original* religion as outlined to the people in the desert. It was Aharon, after all, the very first high priest, the brother of the lawgiver, who fashioned the first golden calf. He was merely bringing back the pure and simple worship of days past when there was no need for ornate edifices that required constant taxation for their upkeep. We can almost hear Yerov'am claiming that this was not God's Temple but Shlomo's Temple, and the tri-annual pilgrimages to the City of David were decreed by the dynasty of David, who were enriching themselves with the influx of visitors and maintaining their Temple with the taxes of the common people.

These arguments, hypothetical though they may be, are merely some of the possible arguments Yerov'am may have made to the people. It would be wrong to assume that the millions who lived in the north were ignorant or idolatrous. They were a majority of the nation who felt as outsiders, rejected or ignored by the government. Ultimately, then, the crucial prerequisite for monarchy – national unity – was forgotten by the monarchs, and the consequence was the creation of an irreparable split in the people. Without internal unity there could be no one king over Israel. The result was the creation of a political entity whose kings drew them further and further away from the legitimate worship of the One God as delineated in the Torah.

Due to Yerov'am's conscious decision to reject God's word in favor of amassing greater power for himself, he failed to build the dynasty God promised he could have. His line ended with the assassination of his son in the second year of his reign. Yet another short-lived dynasty ascended to the throne, and Ba'asha repeated the same sins of Yerov'am and lost his dynasty when his son was assassinated in the second year of his reign. Israel goes through a series of short-lived dynasties that create instability in the kingdom, whose subsequent history will continue to be marked by political intrigue, violence and assassination.

This period of instability is halted for a while with the ascension of Omri to the throne of Israel. Omri, about whose family we know very little, ruled Israel for twelve years,[51] during which he purchased the city of Samaria and established it as the new capital of the northern kingdom. Omri succeeded in founding a mini-dynasty that included himself, his son and two grandchil-

---

51. The precise duration of Omri's reign is unclear as his ascension to the throne was contested by Tivni ben Ginat for five years. Whether the twelve years of his reign included these five years or began only after the death of Tivni remains unclear; see I Melachim 16:21–23.

dren.[52] Although he is portrayed as a king whose wickedness surpassed that of all his predecessors, his deeds are all but forgotten as they pale in comparison to the corruption of his more infamous son.

Call Him Ach'av

Ach'av, the son of Omri, is generally recognized as the worst of all the Israelite kings. The text itself expresses that fact more than once. "And Ach'av, the son of Omri, did what was evil in God's eyes, worse than any [king] who preceded him."[53] The prophet continues to describe the wicked deeds of Ach'av and how they surpassed in their evil even the deeds of the corrupt Yerov'am. Ach'av built altars and temples for foreign gods and publicly worshiped them himself. Beyond the idolatry, the text accuses him of murdering innocents, including the prophets of God and Navot of Jezreel.[54]

To further accentuate the wickedness of this most vile of kings, the text repeats this characterization right before relating the final episode of Ach'av's life, his death in battle: "Indeed, never was there one like Ach'av who 'sold himself' to do what was evil in God's eyes…. He became depraved and followed the idols just as the Emorite, whom God had driven out from before the Israelites, had done…."[55] By simply reading through the text, we become revolted by the man and his misdeeds.

And yet, when we read the story again and focus on the nuances in the text, we will find that Ach'av's personality is far from one-dimensional and that perhaps he wasn't all that bad. The Talmudic scholars were indeed quite careful in their study of this figure, and they debate the stature of Ach'av. R. Yosef affirms the plain meaning of the text, that Ach'av was wicked and corrupt, while Rabbi Nachman states that "Ach'av was evenly balanced [between good and evil]."[56] Our Rabbis understood well that Ach'av was a complex

---

52. Omri's grandson Achazyahu died without leaving an heir, so the throne passed to the king's brother, Yehoram; see II Melachim 1:17.

53. I Melachim 16:30.

54. Although these murders were ordered by his wife, Izevel, he, as husband and king, is held responsible for them. See I Melachim 21:19 where Eliyahu accuses him of "murdering and inheriting."

55. I Melachim 21:25–26. Rabbi Hayyim Angel, from whom I heard many of these revelations about Ach'av, points to the prophet's comparison of Ach'av's actions to those of the Emorites as clearly implying that he would share the same fate and he too would be destroyed.

56. Tractate Sanhedrin 102b.

personality, an enigma whose true character can only be understood through a careful study of the Scripture. And so, although it seems obvious that Ach'av is guilty of two of Judaism's most heinous crimes,[57] the Bible subtly implies that things are not always as simple as they appear.

An indication of Ach'av's possible innocence (or relative innocence) can be found both in the initial condemnation of Ach'av's behavior and in the final one, where the text goes out of its way to blame that behavior on the influence of his wife, Izevel (Jezebel).[58] So Ach'av is portrayed as being wicked, but only passively so, a "too-willing" instrument of evil for his wife.

The Rabbis in the Jerusalem Talmud[59] express this idea through the fascinating story of Rabbi Levi, who after studying the text for six months, regarded Ach'av as being purely wicked – until the king himself appeared to Rabbi Levi in a dream and told him to study the end of the verse, the part that explained how he was manipulated by Izevel. The story continues that upon awakening, Rabbi Levi spent six months re-studying the text to find the positive in Ach'av's actions. Here too, just as in the tractate Sanhedrin of the Babylonian Talmud, the Rabbis seem to be showing a balanced approach in understanding the deeds of Ach'av, by stating that Rabbi Levi studied Ach'av in one way for six months, and after studying him for another six months, he saw the opposite.

The ancient Rabbis, ever sensitive to textual nuance, openly express the idea that Ach'av was "evenly balanced," and could not be judged as purely evil or totally righteous. It remains for us, therefore, to try and see the good in the behavior of Ach'av, attempting to put a positive spin to a character who, upon first glance, seems most wicked and negative.[60]

So What Was So Good?

We stated that, among his wicked deeds, Ach'av slaughtered all of God's prophets. And yet when the author relates the story to us, he states: "And

---

57. Murder (of the prophets and Navot) and idol worship.

58. I Melachim 16:31: "…and he took as a wife Izevel, the daughter of Etba'al the king of the Phoenecians *and he went and worshiped Ba'al…*"; ibid 21:25: "Truly, there was none like Ach'av, who 'sold himself' to do evil in God's eyes *as he was incited* [tempted, misled] *to do by his wife, Izevel.*"

59. Sanhedrin, ch. 10, halachah 2.

60. Indeed the majority of Rabbis in the Talmud (Sanhedrin 102b) strongly opposed the view of R. Nachman, insisting that Ach'av was the epitome of a wicked and idolatrous king.

when Izevel destroyed all of God's prophets...,"[61] blaming not Ach'av but his wife! At worst Ach'av was guilty of a sin of omission, perhaps being unaware of his wife's actions or, more likely, tacitly agreeing with them. And there is still the possibility, suggested by the commentaries,[62] that, far-fetched as it may seem, Ach'av had actively aided his God-fearing servant Ovadiah to hide the prophets and provide for their sustenance. This approach could certainly help us understand how, during a time of terrible drought and famine, Ovadiah was able to gather enough food and water to sustain one hundred individuals without the knowledge of his master, the king. What is clear is that it isn't clear! The very fact that the text does not implicate Ach'av in these murders gives us reason to propose other options and to consider the possibility that perhaps Ach'av was "balanced."

In the second "murder" story, Ach'av's involvement is also a subject of conjecture. In this story, Ach'av fails to act when Navot refuses to sell him his ancestral plot. It is Izevel who reassures her husband that she would acquire the vineyard for him[63] and, by doing so, "establish kingship [control] over Israel."[64] It is she, not Ach'av, who directs the city leadership to hire false witnesses and execute Navot based upon their false testimony. Ach'av was not directly involved in any of this. And yet, he clearly knew that his wife was planning and plotting something and clearly realized that he was now "inheriting" a field that was previously unavailable to him, all due to the sudden demise of its owner. Ach'av was guilty – but how guilty? Ach'av was evil – but how evil?

There are other actions of Ach'av indicating that he, like his nation, may have been torn between belief in the true God and acceptance of Ba'al as a deity to be worshiped as well. The man he retained as his main servant and faithful advisor was the righteous Ovadiah, whom the text proclaims "was very God-fearing."[65] Nonetheless, we do not read of any attempt made by the king to rid himself of Ovadiah's influence or to remove him from his influential post. When Eliyahu appears to Ach'av, the king argues with him but neither threatens to kill him nor attempts to imprison him. On the contrary! Ach'av is

---

61. I Melachim 18:4.
62. Malbim, I Melachim 18:4.
63. I Melachim 21:7. What she actually says is "I will give you the vineyard of Navot." (Or, "I will sell to you the vineyard of Navot," an obvious contrast to the statement of Navot in the previous verse, whose refusal to sell his vineyard was couched in the same terms.)
64. Ibid.
65. Ibid. 18:3.

open to the prophet's suggestion to gather all of the people for a "showdown" between Eliyahu, the prophet of the true God, and the 450 prophets of Ba'al. Furthermore, the king himself attends this debate. And when the fire consumed Eliyahu's offering, proving the sole and eternal rule of the true God, and the text relates that "*All* the nation saw, fell to their faces and exclaimed: 'Hashem, He is the [true] God; Hashem, He is the [true] God!'"[66] – would this not include the king as well? After all, he did subsequently allow Eliyahu to slaughter the idolatrous prophets with no word of rebuke toward him, and when Eliyahu then told him to quickly make his way to Jezreel to avoid getting caught in the coming downpour, he listened to the prophet, despite being in the midst of a long drought and there being no sign of rain. Ach'av believed; Ach'av listened. And when Eliyahu is forced to flee as a result of his actions, it is not Ach'av who was pursuing him but, once again, Izevel.[67]

The effect of these actions, or inactions, by Ach'av, one may suggest, is what led some Talmudic Rabbis to proclaim that he was not all bad, that he was "balanced." In fact, some later commentaries go as far as to claim that the king became a penitent, a *ba'al teshuvah,* and sincerely returned to God and the true worship of God alone.[68]

Wait…There Is More

If these arguments alone are not convincing enough to make us rethink the personality of Ach'av, then the text itself should certainly give us sufficient reason to. In the closing verses of both chapter 20 and chapter 21, Ach'av is portrayed as remorseful and sincerely moved by the prophet's words of admonition. Following the great victories over the powerful armies of the Aramean alliance, victories predicted by the unnamed prophet whose divine message Ach'av believed,[69] Ach'av frees the wicked king Ben Haddad after he agreed to Ach'av's conditions for peace. The prophet is angered by this action, seeing it as undermining God's miracles by releasing this enemy of Israel, who was responsible for the death of so many. The prophet confronts Ach'av and issues God's punishment: that he and his nation will suffer the fate that awaited the

---

66. Ibid. 18:39.
67. Ibid. 19:2.
68. Malbim, I Melachim 19:2.
69. In fact, Ach'av based his strategy in both battles upon the words of the prophet, another indication that he did not deny God or His powers; see I Melachim, ch. 20.

enemy. Ach'av's reaction is given in a simple phrase: "And the king of Israel returned home upset and angry."[70]

At first glance, these words seem unimportant. But when we consider that Ach'av had just completed routing Aram, the enemy that had tormented Israel for many years and posed an existential threat to the nation, this description of the victorious king who returns home and does not celebrate his victory or display any satisfaction over his accomplishment, indicates that Ach'av was deeply troubled by the words of the prophet and that he took God's admonition to heart. His is not the reaction of one who rejected God or His prophets.

Even more telling are the final verses of the chapter 21, which depict Ach'av's behavior following his confrontation with Eliyahu. Ach'av had just arrived in Jezreel to take over the vineyard of Navot in order to convert it into a royal garden abutting his palace (or, winter palace). Navot, as you may recall, had refused to sell or exchange the field, as it was his ancestral plot belonging to his family since the time of their entry into the land.[71] After Izevel arranged for the death of Navot and the confiscation of his property, Ach'av was able to possess the vineyard he so desired. Eliyahu confronts Ach'av with harsh words of admonition, including a description of the fate that awaits him and his descendants. Here, too, we read of how Ach'av took these words to heart, but this time we see his reaction in deeds. The king tore his garments and wore mourners' sackcloth in their place; he fasted and walked slowly, as was the wont of mourners and penitents.

God was duly impressed with the sincerity of these acts and pointed out to the prophet how the king had humbled himself before God. As a result of his contrition, Ach'av is spared living through the punishment: God pledges to begin his family's suffering only after his death. There is no question but that our Rabbis saw in these words that God Himself considered Ach'av's actions those of a sincere penitent. Ach'av, it seems, cannot be painted with but one brush stroke; he cannot be portrayed as being simply wicked.

Then again, just as we begin to reconsider this complex personality – just as we might be feeling remorseful over our condemnation of the king – we look at the text and realize that at the close of the previous chapter (chapter 20), Ach'av is also described as being remorseful as he returned home "upset

---

70. Ibid. 20:43.
71. According to the rabbinic understanding of the verse in Vayikra 25:25, one may sell such an estate only in the event of dire poverty.

and angry" after hearing the prophet's admonition. Such a reaction should have led, we would believe, to a marked change in Ach'av's behavior. And yet, immediately following this reaction, we read the story of the king's willing acquiescence to Izevel's machinations in acquiring Navot's vineyard. It is not coincidental that following the story of Ach'av's illegal confiscation of another's land he called on Israel to go to war against Aram for their illegal confiscation of Israel's land, and that it was in that very battle to lay claim to land that was rightfully his, that Ach'av lost his life. Had Ach'av truly changed? Was the lesson of Navot really absorbed? Did he mature spiritually? Despite the king's initial reactions following the prophet's admonitions, he remained basically unchanged: a complex personality who could be remorseful or wicked.

In the End

In the very final episode of his life, Ach'av remains that same enigma that he was throughout the saga that was his life, for after the text revealed his unchanged attitude of selfishness and insensitivity through the story of Navot, it begins the events that would lead up to his death: the battle against Aram. And in that story, we see positive signs of Ach'av's sincere return to God and a selfless concern and sensitivity for his nation.

Ach'av decided to war against Aram for her possession of Israelite land. He turned to the righteous king of Judea, Yehoshafat (Jehosaphat), for aid in the war and, indeed, formed an alliance with the southern kingdom to face the Aramean enemy.[72] He agreed to Yehoshafat's request to "ask of God" before the battle, and gathered four hundred prophets of God. These prophets proved to be false ones and in fact misled Ach'av by convincing him to go to battle. But they *were* prophets of God and *not* the prophets of Ba'al![73] And although

---

72. Yehoshafat is condemned by the prophet Yehu for agreeing to this alliance, especially after the prophet of God told Ach'av that Israel would be defeated and that he would lose his life if he went to war; see II Divrei Hayamim 19:2–3.

73. Actually, both Radak and Ralbag argue that these were indeed prophets of Ba'al, as Ach'av himself was a worshiper of Ba'al and the prophets were clearly false. They further claim that the only reason why they prophesy in the name of God is because King Yehoshafat, a worshiper of God, was present and had to be convinced to go to war. Rashi, on the other hand, points to tractate Sanhedrin 89b as support for his view that these were indeed prophets of God who simply did not receive true prophecy but claimed that they did; due to their fear of the king and his queen Izevel, they simply said what Ach'av wanted to hear. The difficulty with this view is how it interprets Yehoshafat's remark "Is there no prophet of God here whom we can ask?" (I Melachim 22:7). Possibly, the Judean king was requesting a prophet of God whose prophecies

the king chose to ignore their advice, he did believe them! This would explain why Ach'av chose to disguise himself before entering the battlefield – yet he reassured Yehoshafat, the king of Judea, that he need not do so. Ach'av feared that he would die just as the God's prophet Michayahu had predicted.

And indeed he does. A fitting end to this sinner, we might think. But is this the last impression we are left with? Not at all!

The text continues by describing how Ach'av was mortally wounded in the battle and how he ordered his chariot driver to take him out of harm's way, away from the battlefield. But rather than abandoning his army in search of medical aid, Ach'av, we read, remained in his chariot. Unable to stand on his own, he is "propped up" in his chariot, overseeing the battle and urging his men to victory. Much as Moshe did during Israel's first military encounter, their battle against Amalek,[74] Ach'av too stood over the battlefield hoping to inspire and strengthen his troops. Ultimately, God's will was done; the battle was lost and the prophecy was realized. But the haunting vision of the wicked king giving his final breaths in the service of his people leaves the reader emotionally torn between the two conflicting views of this most enigmatic personality.

And an Addendum[75]

When eulogizing Theodore Herzl in 1903, Rav Avraham Hakohen Kook, the legendary first chief rabbi of Palestine, pointed out that only two rulers in the book of Melachim were killed in battle: King Yoshiyahu and King Ach'av. Ach'av, the king of Samaria, was considered the most morally corrupt and actively idolatrous of all the monarchs. He was a man who engaged in and readily encouraged the spread of pagan cults. He defiled the land with his idols. Yoshiyahu, the Judean king, is described as a most righteous ruler who opposed any idol worship, who removed all of the appurtenances of foreign gods that made their way into the Holy Temple and destroyed any remnant of

---

had already been proven correct – an experienced prophet, rather than these whose veracity had yet to be tested. Given Ach'av's presence at Mount Carmel and the fact that he personally witnessed the defeat of Ba'al, it is not unreasonable to believe that he summoned prophets of God – or at least those who claimed to be – rather than those of Ba'al.

74. Shemot 17:9–11.
75. I heard this story from Rabbi Yoel Bin Nun.

pagan cults from the entire kingdom.[76] Yoshiyahu was the "anti-Ach'av."

Despite the clear contrast between these two rulers, there is a Talmudic view that both will have a portion in the world to come. Rav Kook explained that regardless of Ach'av's earlier sins, the fact that he, like the righteous Yoshiyahu, died defending the Israelite nation was sufficient reason to guarantee him a future reward. There are, by rabbinic tradition, two Messiahs: the descendant of Yosef (*Mashiach ben Yosef*) and the descendant of David (*Mashiach ben David*). Each of these, argued Rav Kook, represents a different type of Jew. The better-known Messiah of Judea is the "Yoshiyahu" Jew, one who remained committed to God and His Torah, who kept the holiness of Israel alive even in the Diaspora and thereby guaranteed the survival of Israel as God's chosen nation. The lesser known Messiah is the "Ach'av" Jew, who lost his commitment to God's Torah but remained identified with his people through his attachment to the nation and his love of the land. Both, claimed Rav Kook, would be necessary to build a future for the Jewish nation in Israel.

Regardless of one's reaction to Rav Kook's approach, what seems clear to a student of Tanach is how *un*clear Ach'av's legacy is. He remains, indeed, an enigmatic figure who, even thousands of years after his death, does not cease to fascinate us.

Yet, equally fascinating is the personality of Ach'av's antagonist, one who brought God's word to the king, the character whose life story bridges the two sections of the book of Melachim – the legendary prophet, Eliyahu.

---

76. See II Melachim 23:4–5 for a detailed account of Yoshiyahu's campaign against idolatry.

THE BOOK OF
II MELACHIM

ספר
מלכים ב

Ignored Prophecy,
Corrupted Royalty,
Destroyed Kingdom

OVERVIEW

The second book of Kings chronicles the collapse of both the Israelite and the Judean kingdoms, a result of their moral perversions and abandonment of God and His laws. The text takes us through stories of internal strife as well as episodes describing the external threats facing both kingdoms. One can see the book as a record of the struggle of king versus prophet, of temporal ruler versus spiritual guide, and even of the Heavenly King versus a mortal one.

This perspective, although true, can lead to an oversimplification of the book, which is in actuality the record of a difficult and involved period of history. The struggle of an Israelite regent to assert his control; the legitimacy of his reign over a nation who regularly experienced military coups and political assassinations; the challenge facing the Judean ruler to establish his throne and his authority, while accepting the role of a constitutional monarch whose power was limited by Torah law at a time when surrounding kings ruled with unlimited power – these concerns make the royal actions described in the book of Melachim more than simple choices between right and wrong, as twenty-twenty hindsight might see them. There was far more facing the king than what meets the eye of a casual reader. Understanding those factors that might have impacted the decisions of the various rulers is crucial to our understanding of the events that unfold in the book of Melachim.

In II Melachim we read of the activities of the prophet Elisha, student of and successor to Eliyahu. The close parallel between the actions of these two prophets seems to indicate that perhaps Elisha was sent to complete the mission of Eliyahu.[1] Elisha's demise is followed by a description of the growing military power of the northern kingdom – power that granted Israel victory over its brothers in Judea and even over its implacable enemies in Aram. In fact, Israel succeeds in extending its influence further than it had since the time of King Shlomo. Yet their military domination was short-lived, and during the following years a series of weak kings and short reigns, marked by assassination and corruption, bring Israel to the brink of destruction. As the Assyrian Empire begins to dominate the entire Middle East, the northern kingdom is invaded, defeated and exiled from the land, never to be heard from again.

The fate of the southern kingdom was to be similar, although it would take another 150 years until the Judeans are defeated and exiled. In the final chapters of the book of Melachim, we read about some of the most remarkable personalities in the Tanach: the stories of King Chizkiyahu (Hezekiah) and his relationship with the prophet Yishayahu (Isaiah). Chizkiyahu's sincere prayers that led to the flight of the Arameans and resulting failure of their invasion, and the miraculous extension of his life, contrast dramatically from what appears to be the growing corruption and idolatry of the Judeans. As well, the wickedness of King Menasheh (Menasseh) that seals the fate of the southern kingdom[2] stands in bold contrast to the righteousness of his successor and grandson, King Yoshiyahu (Josiah).

These final chapters relate the collapse of the kingdom: the corruption of the last kings, the Babylonian invasion of Judea and the failed rebellions against Babylonian rule. The book ends by relating the destruction of the Holy Temple, as well as describing the exile of the Judeans and the fate that awaited the political leaders of Jerusalem. With the assassination of Gedaliah, the Babylonian-appointed (Jewish) governor of Jerusalem, by his co-religionists, Judea loses its final hope even for some limited type of independence. The prophet, however, does not close the saga before relating the hopeful development of King Yehoyachin's release from prison, his elevation above the other captive kings and his being given the honor of eating at the king's table throughout his life.

---

1. As we will discuss, when Eliyahu stands at Mount Sinai and complains to God that he was unable to complete his mission, God responds by, among other things, charging him to anoint Elisha as a prophet *tachtecha*, "in your stead." It is for this reason that I chose to discuss the activities of Eliyahu in the II Melachim chapter even though most of his story is included in the first book of Melachim – in order to compare the lives of these two prophetic giants in the same section.
2. II Melachim 24:3.

ANALYSIS

AND IN THIS CORNER...

God's agent chosen to oppose the wayward King Ach'av and bring Israel back to the worship of the true God was one of the great figures of Jewish history: the prophet Elijah – Eliyahu Hanavi. As the king's antagonist, Eliyahu risked his life numerous times to confront Ach'av and bravely proclaim God's message to him. And yet this figure is no less difficult to understand than is Ach'av. Eliyahu was truly a man of mystery, and from the very beginning of the Eliyahu story the reader often finds himself with more questions than answers.

The prophet's story begins with no introduction to the character or any explanation of his mission. Consider the opening words: "Eliyahu the Tishbi, a resident of Gilead, said to Ach'av: 'I swear by the God of Israel Whom I serve that there will be no rain or dew except by my word.'"[1] Who is this man? What occurred that precipitated these words? Was he even commanded by God to declare a drought? Had he been involved in an ongoing feud with the king? None of these questions are answered in the text! On the contrary, the text seems purposely obtuse and vague, leaving much to the consideration of the reader. Eliyahu is unique among the major prophets in that the text never

---

1. I Melachim 17:1.

reveals his father's name[2] nor do we even learn what tribe he is from. This shadowy figure who occupies such an important place in Jewish tradition remains throughout his saga a mysterious and mystifying personality.

The Lonely Man of Prophecy

Interestingly, it is not the text alone that leaves so much about Eliyahu to the imagination; rabbinic sources too are sparse and provide little information regarding Eliyahu's early life. While the patriarch Avraham's beginnings are also largely ignored in the text, midrashic literature and rabbinic tradition is rich in describing his early years. Yet regarding Eliyahu there is very little in rabbinic writings that helps us understand this important prophet or that offers us a reason why he was chosen to carry out God's will. I would suggest that this is no coincidence. And the mystery of the prophet known as Eliyahu is not one limited to those who would live thousands of years after him. He was a puzzle to his contemporaries as well, who saw him as being an incomprehensible and almost mystical figure. And, as we shall see, they had good reason to see him as such.

Eliyahu was a "loner." He was one who was much more comfortable with God than with people. He had little to do with the politics of the nation; he commented only on the internal, spiritual life of the people. As opposed to his contemporary, Michayhu, and his successor, Elisha, Eliyahu was not known to foreign kings nor did he ever advise the Israelite monarch regarding war or peace. And while his student, Elisha the prophet, could be found in the capital city of Samaria or the Israelite town of Dotan, we find Eliyahu secluded from the people, living in caves and fed by birds, hiding in a foreign country and running into the wilderness. Even when he was met by the righteous Ovadiah, whom rabbinic tradition identifies as the prophet of that same name,[3] he appeared totally unaware of who this individual was or the remarkable acts of bravery he had performed.[4] Eliyahu was so detached from the

---

2. Although the ancestries of the prophets Gad, Natan and Ido, as well as six of the "minor" prophets (Amos, Michah, Nachum, Chavakuk, Chaggai and Malachi) are similarly unknown, it is rather troubling that the parentage of such an important prophetic personality – one who is the focal point of the text and of many of the events for so many chapters – should remain hidden from the reader.
3. Tractate Sanhedrin 39b.
4. I find it especially significant that Ovadiah seemed almost incredulous when he asked: "Was it not told to you that which your servant had done when Izevel was killing off the prophets of God?" (I Melachim 18:13).

nation that he had no idea of what had transpired during his years of absence. He then all but ignored the saintly Ovadiah, who referred to him as "my master, Eliyahu," when telling him: "Go and tell your master [Ach'av]."[5]

The text underscores the contrast between these two righteous individuals when it describes Ovadiah as a man who lived with the people, in the capital, in the palace where he served the wicked regents, and nonetheless retained his saintliness, while Eliyahu fled from his land and detached himself from his people in order to remain righteous. Ovadiah saved the lives of one hundred true prophets, hiding them in a cave, feeding them and providing them with water, while at the same time Eliyahu hid away, saved no one and was provided sustenance by others.[6] It is important to take note of this, for unless we understand the detachment and distance of Eliyahu from the people, we will fail to understand why he was seen by his contemporaries as such a mystical figure and how God attempted to teach and direct Eliyahu throughout his prophetic activities.

The Mysterious Man of God

From the very outset of the Eliyahu chronicle, the prophet was a "wanted man." Having declared a drought that would end only "upon my word,"[7] Eliyahu was a marked man, for the Israelite king Ach'av and undoubtedly many of his subjects were convinced that Eliyahu could end the drought whenever he wished.[8] As a result, he was sought after and pursued throughout the region, even in the surrounding lands, in Ach'av's attempt to bring him back and force him to end the drought. For three years, Eliyahu hid near the Jordan River and, subsequently, in the village of Tzorefat in Phoenecia, while the king searched futilely for him. Eliyahu had, it seemed, disappeared.

---

5. I Melachim 18:7–8. Similarly, when explaining his presence at Mount Chorev to God, Eliyahu states: "And I alone remain [from among God's prophets]" (ibid. 19:10), totally ignoring the activities and accomplishments of Ovadiah, not to mention the one hundred prophets who almost lost their lives.

6. The contrast is even starker when comparing the language used to describe Eliyahu's behavior (I Melachim 17:3–6) with that of Ovadiah (ibid. 18:4).

7. I Melachim 17:1.

8. Ironically, this is similar to the opinion quoted in the Talmud that God granted Eliyahu three powers usually reserved for God alone: the power to revive the dead, to open the womb and to control the rainfall; see tractate Sanhedrin 113a.

When, after three years, at God's command, Eliyahu suddenly appeared before Ovadiah, even this righteous officer of Ach'av feared that Eliyahu would disappear as mysteriously and suddenly as he had appeared, and cause the king to vent his wrath against Ovadiah for having allowed Eliyahu to escape.[9] "And the wind of the Lord will carry you to – I don't know where...,"[10] said Ovadiah, expressing precisely how the masses viewed Eliyahu's rare and unexpected appearances.

This air of mystery continued to surround Eliyahu when, following his contest with the prophets of Ba'al, he urged the king to hurry to Jezreel in order to avoid the impending downpour that would herald the end of the long drought. The king hitched up his chariot and left Eliyahu at Mount Carmel – yet when he arrived at Jezreel he was greeted by the prophet himself, who, though traveling on foot, miraculously (and in the king's eyes, mysteriously), outraced the king's chariot.[11] It is therefore no wonder that after Eliyahu was taken heavenward, the student prophets (בני הנביאים) refused to accept the fact that he was gone forever and insisted on searching for him for three days. Tellingly, when explaining to Eliyahu's successor, Elisha, their desire to search for their master, they use the same phrase as Ovadiah did: "...perhaps *God's wind has carried him away* and brought him to some mountain or valley...."[12] The people saw Eliyahu as one carried away by the wind of God and "deposited" in any place where God desired him to be, whether at the Jordan, in Phoenecia or mysteriously appearing in Jezreel before the king. It is in keeping with the mystifying personality of Eliyahu that the author of the book of Melachim, as well as rabbinic interpretations, may have purposely obscured Eliyahu's origins as well.

The Two Eliyahus

In attempting to understand the fascinating story of this great prophet and the lessons it bears, the reader may uncover two different approaches. The most obvious approach is one that sees the story of Eliyahu as a tale of good versus evil: Eliyahu, God's prophet, versus Ach'av, God's betrayer. At its very essence this certainly is the story. But the *Tanach* is far too serious

9. I Melachim 18:12.
10. Ibid.
11. Ibid. 18:46.
12. II Melachim 2:16.

a work to be taken at face value alone. With a more nuanced approach and a closer analysis of the text, we can perceive that there is more to both personalities than simply representing pure good and unadulterated evil. We have already seen how Ach'av was viewed by the Rabbis as being a complex and multifaceted personality. I believe that by applying the same analytical approach to Eliyahu, we will find that there is a more nuanced way of viewing his character as well.

The story of Eliyahu seems straightforward enough. When we are first introduced to Eliyahu, we find him warning the people of the impending drought, a punishment from God for their faithlessness to Him. The punishment should have come as no surprise to the people, as it is consistent with the explicit warning found in the Torah: "Be careful lest you become foolish and stray [from God] and worship other gods and bow down to them. God will become angry with you then *and hold back the heavens so there will be no rain....*"[1]

The Torah's punishment for idolatry is drought and subsequent famine, and the prophet's pronouncement reminded the wayward nation of just that.[2] After delivering his prophecy, Eliyahu, at God's command, went into hiding for three years, ostensibly to escape the wrath of a vengeful king and the angry masses. After a three-year exile, during which he was fed by the ravens at the stream of Kerit and by the poor widow in Tzorefat, Eliyahu received the command to return and appear to Ach'av so that God could break the drought and once again send down rain for the people. Eliyahu arranged a contest against the prophets of Ba'al at Mount Carmel in front of Israelites from around the nation. Eliyahu was successful in his contest with the idolatrous priests, and the people, beholding the truth of God's power, prostrated themselves before God and proclaimed: "Hashem, He is the [true] God."[3] Eliyahu commanded the new believers to capture the priests who had misled them, and he subsequently slaughtered them in the Valley of Kishon.

---

1. Devarim 11:16–17.
2. The Rabbis in the Talmud (Sanhedrin 113a) express this very idea. They describe a conversation between Ach'av and Eliyahu in the home of the mourner Chiel of Bet-El, who had lost his sons after rebuilding the destroyed city of Jericho. Eliyahu explained to the king that the tragedy was the result of Yehoshua's curse of anyone who would rebuild Jericho (see Yehoshua 6:26). Ach'av responded that this could not be. After all, if God's own curse of drought (as punishment for idolatry) was never realized, how could Yehoshua's curse come to fruition?! As a result, God sent the drought.
3. I Melachim 18:39.

The drought was broken, the people became believers and Eliyahu's victory was complete. Or so it seemed.

Unfortunately the victory was but short-lived. Immediately following the great contest at Mount Carmel, Eliyahu was forced to flee from Izevel, who had threatened to kill him, to the kingdom of Yehudah. There, an angel commanded him to eat and drink in preparation for a forty-day journey, which eventually brought him to Mount Chorev, better known as Mount Sinai. At the holy mountain, God questioned Eliyahu's presence at the mountain. He repeated his questions twice and received the exact same responses from Eliyahu both times: that he was forced to flee because he was God's avenger and the people had abandoned their covenant with God, destroying His altars and killing His prophets. Finally, God instructed Eliyahu to return and replace the king of Aram, anoint a new king of Israel and appoint Elisha as prophet in his stead.

The story of Eliyahu continues, but the events at Mount Chorev and the conversation between God and His prophet cry out for explanation – one that will provide a key to understanding this classic story and to uncovering fascinating textual undertones that will impact our perception of Eliyahu and his mission.[4] And so, we first turn to this troubling dialogue between God and Eliyahu at Mount Sinai in an attempt to understand it more fully.

Eliyahu and Moshe

When God questioned Eliyahu as to why he was at Mount Sinai we are rightfully astonished. After all, it was the angel of God who sent him on his journey to the holy mountain! What was the purpose of God's question? Clearly, God does not need to be informed of what or why. He poses questions to individuals in order to evoke specific responses and, hopefully, to force the responder to objectively reflect upon his own actions.[5] So what response did he expect from Eliyahu? What reaction did he hope to draw out of the prophet?

A serious study of the entire story seems to suggest that God was sending a pointed message to Eliyahu. Most students of the *Tanach* immediately sense the close parallel between the story of Eliyahu and that of Moshe. As Moshe separated

---

4. Much of this analysis is based upon the approach of the Malbim; see I Melachim, ch. 19.
5. So it was with God's questions to Adam (Bereishit 3:9), to Kayin (ibid. 4:9) and to Bil'am (Bamidbar 22:9).

from the people following their sin, so did Eliyahu. As Moshe did not eat or drink for forty days and nights while on Mount Sinai, so Eliyahu does not eat or drink for forty days and nights on his way to Mount Sinai. As Moshe hid his face upon hearing God speaking to him, so Eliyahu covered his face when hearing God's voice. As Moshe is placed "in the cleft of the rock" as God's glory passed before him, so Eliyahu stood at the opening of the cave as God's glory passed before him.[1] Eliyahu was asked to go through these series of actions in order to learn what was expected of him as a prophet, a spiritual heir of Moshe.

So when God asks Eliyahu "Why are you here, Eliyahu?" He hoped to receive a "Mosaic" response. He wanted to hear a defense of His people by the prophet as he had once heard from Moshe.[2] Perhaps Eliyahu would describe the victory at Mount Carmel and how it was only the wicked monarchs who had led the people astray, or perhaps he would cry out to God on behalf of the suffering nation. He therefore placed Eliyahu in the exact place where Moshe pleaded with God[3] to forgive the sinful nation their sin of idolatry, in the hope that Eliyahu would do the same. God asked him the question "Why are you here, Eliyahu?" to teach him that he belonged *with* the people. He tried to teach Eliyahu that the people needed him to teach them and to inspire them as Moshe had. True faith cannot be brought about through legislation or even through miracles; true belief in God requires education and inspiration, patience and perseverance. That is what Moshe had done and what Eliyahu should have been doing. Hence God's question was a form of rebuke: "Why are you here, Eliyahu," demanded God, implying "and not with the people when they need you most?"

When Eliyahu responded with accusations *against* the people, God needed to impress Eliyahu with the true nature of his mission: to be a defender of the people, to be their teacher and inspiration, but certainly not to be their accuser and prosecutor.[4] And so he told Eliyahu to stand by the mouth of the

---

1. The Malbim opines that this was the very same place where Moshe was placed, which is why the definitive "*the* cave" is used here. See his commentary also for the numerous parallels between Moshe and Eliyahu.

2. As explained in *Seder Eliyahu Zuta*, ch. 8.

3. Moshe was placed in the "cleft of the rock" (Shemot 33:22), which commentators identify as the opening to the cave on Mount Sinai.

4. This idea is beautifully expressed in Shir Hashirim Rabbah, ch. 1, where the cake Eliyahu ate before journeying to Mount Sinai was called עוגת רצפים, for it should "destroy the mouths" (רצוץ פיות) of anyone who would speak ill of Israel. This is similar to the "cleansing" of Yeshayahu's "impure" mouth that had referred to Israel as an "impure nation" by having his lips touched by hot coal, ובידו רצפה, by an angel of God; see Yeshayahu 6:6.

cave and wait for God's spirit to pass before him. However, God explained, the spirit would not be found in the powerful wind or fire or noise but rather in the silent whisper. God hoped that Eliyahu would accept His message that, in the same fashion, Eliyahu could help God's spirit enter the hearts of the people only through the "silent whisper" – that is, through patient explanation and sincere love of God's nation, not through threats, droughts or heavenly fire.

And so, after finding God's spirit in the silent whisper, Eliyahu was again asked by God why he was there, hoping to evoke a response that would indicate that Eliyahu had indeed understood God's message. Instead, Eliyahu repeated the same accusations and criticisms of Israel.[5] He had not absorbed the lesson God had hoped to impart to him. Eliyahu remained the "zealot," one who fought God's battles by himself and in his own way.[6]

Doing It His Way

The truth is that Eliyahu was ever the loner. That fact is made clear in this "post-victory" story when he chose to run away from the people precisely when they needed him most. He even goes so far as to abandon his own attendant back in Beersheba and wander into the desert by himself. But this facet of his personality is not revealed here for the first time. This was a trait that actually had been apparent from the very beginning of Eliyahu's prophetic activity. Perhaps he chose this kind of life to separate himself from the wickedness of Ach'av and the idolatry of the people that surrounded him. Perhaps, as suggested, he was interested in self-improvement and spiritual elevation and, when his miracles failed to move the people sufficiently, he saw it as his own failure and lack of spiritual strength.[7] Perhaps, facing an antagonist as extreme as Ach'av, who regarded the pagan god Ba'al as Israel's God, he too went to extremes. Or, perhaps, it was simply part of his nature. In any case, it would seem that this was not the most fitting characteristic for a prophet who had

---

5. That point is well made by the fact that verse 14 of chapter 19, Eliyahu's second response, is a word-for-word repetition of verse 10, Eliyahu's first response.

6. Our Rabbis equate the personality of Eliyahu with that of Pinchas, grandson of Aharon the high priest, who was described as בקנאו את קנאתי בתוכם, one who had vented God's wrath against the people (Bamidbar 25:11), a phrase close to the words Eliyahu uses to describe his own activities on God's behalf, 'קנא קנאתי לד, "I have taken vengeance for God" (I Melachim 19:10, 14).

7. Malbim, I Melachim 19:3.

to mix with the people and understand them in order to change their ways. And when we read the Eliyahu story with this personality trait in mind, we see a very different picture of the events and better understand the message God wished him to share.

When Eliyahu first appeared on the scene, he proclaimed to all that there would be no more rain except at his word. Missing from this declaration, however, was the name of God. "Except by my word," he proclaimed, and not "by God's word." Although at first glance it seems logical to assume that Eliyahu was talking in the name of God, something the people would have understood as well, a deeper analysis of the events and of Eliyahu's personality might lead us to a different conclusion. Many see Eliyahu's act as an independent decision, made by the prophet to force the people back to the worship of God. According to this view, God had given Eliyahu the freedom to "rein in" the people by granting him the power to deny the people rain.[8] It was, therefore, Eliyahu's decision alone to bring the drought, something that was not ordained by, or, as we will see, even acceptable to God.

Understanding God's Way…

God had wanted Eliyahu to identify with the nation and their suffering so that Eliyahu would better understand the impact of his actions and that he best pray for the Israelites, not punish them. And so He told the prophet to flee to the stream of Kerit, where he was forced to rely upon ravens[9] to provide him with food. After one year the stream dried up due to the drought, and Eliyahu was directed to Tzorefat, where he was dependent upon the generosity of a poor widow and her son. Traditional commentators see these events as a message to Eliyahu from God. The ravens, ordinarily known for their cruelty and lack of pity, had mercy upon Eliyahu and daily brought him the food he needed. Shouldn't Eliyahu then have exhibited comparable compassion for his people?[10] In a similar fashion, God dried up the stream of Kerit, Eliyahu's only source of water, for the purpose of letting Eliyahu feel the suffering of those who, because of his decree, now lacked water, in

---

8. See footnote 14 of this chapter.
9. I Melachim 17:6. The Hebrew *orevim* (עורבים) is generally translated as "ravens," although Radak also quotes the possible translation of "merchants."
10. Radak, I Melachim 17:4.

the hope of encouraging him to call for an end to the drought.[11] According to these views, therefore, God was trying to influence Eliyahu and impress upon him what he, as a prophet, should have been doing, even before their confrontation at Mount Chorev. Eliyahu, however, failed to respond to God's subtle messages.

But God did not give up. Instead, He placed Eliyahu's fate into the hands of a poor widow. Consider what Eliyahu faced: he was to be supported by a non-Israelite, an idolater[12] – a woman who was poor and, without a husband, had no visible means of support. The woman also had to feed her son, and when Eliyahu met her she was down to her last bit of flour. Was this how the prophet should have lived? Was this the level to which he had fallen? Or was this yet another test and message from God? And was it not also an attempt to teach Eliyahu a lesson of what the Israelites now faced – relying on others for food and sustenance and even more likely to turn to idolatry, a result of the brutal drought he decreed upon them?

Once again, however, Eliyahu seemed unmoved by the lesson.[13] He seemed untroubled by the suffering. And so God waited until Eliyahu grew closer to his hosts, and He then took the life of the widow's son. Eliyahu attempted to bring the child back to life by placing him on his own bed. God, however, did not respond immediately and remained unresponsive even after Eliyahu prayed to Him. Instead, God waited until Eliyahu did more than simply pray to Him for help; He wanted the prophet to become directly involved with the fate of the child. Only after Eliyahu placed himself on top of the child, with all of his body parts corresponding to the child's as an act of identification with the youth, does God respond to Eliyahu's pleas. Only when Eliyahu connected to the suffering of the people and became one with them did God answer his pleas.

And see how revealing the reaction of the grateful mother is! The widow, who had blamed Eliyahu for the death of her son, now exclaimed that she finally realized that Eliyahu was truly a man of God. For although Eliyahu's promise that she would survive the famine had been fulfilled, she was, perhaps

---

11. Rashi, I Melachim 17:7 (paraphrasing the Talmud, tractate Sanhedrin 113b).
12. Though we do not see her actively worshiping idols, she was of an idolatrous nation, Phoenecia, and we have no reason to assume that she did not worship her national god.
13. One might well understand Eliyahu's anger at the nation after seeing how a non-Israelite, a Ba'al worshiper, had enough faith in the word of God given through Eliyahu to share her very last morsels of food with him, while God's own people lacked the faith that he would provide them with the rain they required, which led them to rely on the false god, Ba'al.

unwittingly, expressing God's subtle message that an *ish Elokim*, a "man of God," is one who alleviates suffering and removes pain, one who would pray to God on behalf of another, one who truly empathized with those in distress. A man of God must be one who brings life, not death.

…But Not Learning God's Way

It is no wonder, therefore, that after these events – after Eliyahu had brought life back to the lifeless child – God turned to him and told him that it was time for him to bring life back to the suffering land and nation. He commanded Eliyahu to confront his nemesis, Ach'av, so that God could then bring the rain and break the drought.

But Eliyahu's actions are again puzzling. Again, Eliyahu does it his own way. Rather than confronting Ach'av, he met with the king's righteous servant, Ovadiah, and, even after speaking to the king, he did not decree an end to the drought but instead called for a contest with the idolatrous prophets on Mount Carmel. Eliyahu, the zealot, knew that he must eventually cry out for rain, but he refused to do so before proving God's dominion and punishing those who had denied it. He began by exhorting the people to follow the true God alone, he teased the false prophets who failed to get a response from their god and, when the time was right, he rebuilt the altar and cried out to God, Who answered him by sending down fire from the heavens.

And it worked! Eliyahu left Mount Carmel victorious. The false prophets were killed, the people pledged their allegiance to the true God and even the stubborn king bowed to the dictates of the prophet. Eliyahu had been vindicated! But not all went as it should. God responded, but only after a rather lengthy plea from Eliyahu. The people went back home, but no rain had fallen yet. Eliyahu proceeded to climb to the top of the mountain and pray for rain, but God again did not respond – neither the first time nor the second. In fact, Eliyahu had to turn to God seven separate times, sending his attendant back each time to see if any clouds were gathering, and only after the seventh prayer did a cloud appear.[14]

Can we sense in God's reluctance a certain irony? Just as the false god could not respond to his prophets, so God now would not respond to Eliyahu. Do

---

14. Interesting to note as well is the usage of the term ויגהר, "and he crouched" – the only time in all of *Tanach* that this term is used for prayer. It seems to depict an Eliyahu who was once again isolating himself from the outside world and turning in to himself.

we see here a mild rebuke of Eliyahu, who was told by God to bring the rain, but did not? Indeed, Eliyahu's euphoria lasted for but a day, and the actions of the fiery prophet on Mount Carmel had only a limited effect, for the seer who called for fire from the heavens to consume his offering and to destroy those who would harm him[15] – the very same prophet who would go up to heaven in a fiery chariot[16] – learned at Mount Chorev that 'לא באש ה, God cannot be found in fire.

It was there as well that the prophet learned that his mission to draw the people back to God would be given to another. God's declaration that "those who escape the sword of Haza'el will be killed by Yehu and those who escape the sword of Yehu will be killed by Elisha"[17] is His message to Eliyahu that the power of punishment was not given to him; punishment would be meted out instead by God's chosen agents. Eliyahu would continue to function, but only in relationship to the king. He would no longer deal with the people. He had failed to make any lasting impact on the nation despite the miracles and punishment he had brought. Now Eliyahu was left with the task of passing down his mantle of prophecy to the man who would be his successor, Elisha.

The Contrast: Eliyahu and Elisha

We are not told of any prior relationship Eliyahu may have had with Elisha. From the text, it seems that before he was commanded to appoint this successor, he had no connection with him at all. As we read of Elisha and his personality, it becomes clear that he is quite different from his master and predecessor. We read of the two prophets only at the very beginning of their relationship and at the very end, at the moment when Elisha was chosen and on the day that Eliyahu was taken.

From the very beginning, it seems that the relationship of teacher to student was not as close as one would expect. Eliyahu arrived at Elisha's home and said nothing to him. He did not inform Elisha that God had chosen him to succeed Eliyahu as prophet. Instead, strangely, he tossed his mantle at him. The handing of a garment to another as sign of his succession to the post is something that had been done earlier in the Bible: Aharon's son, Elazar,

---

15. See II Melachim 1:10, 12.
16. Ibid. 2:11.
17. I Melachim 19:17.

donned the priestly garments upon the death of his father,[18] and, unwittingly, Shaul handed his uniform and weapons to David.[19] But in this story, Eliyahu seems to have been testing Elisha, something he continued to do throughout their relationship. It appears that Eliyahu was not very impressed with God's choice. Rather than find a scholarly, mystical introvert, deep in prayer or study in his house – much as Eliyahu might have been – he met Elisha while Elisha was plowing the field with his workers. He refused to hand over his mantle to Elisha and instead he tossed the mantle at him, testing if he truly understood the significance of the act.

Elisha does pick up the mantle, he does understand its significance, but he also seems to have angered Eliyahu with his behavior. Why? Elisha disappointed Eliyahu because he asked permission to bid farewell to his parents before following Eliyahu. Eliyahu sarcastically remarked, "Go back! What have I done to you?"[20] Eliyahu was actually implying that he expected Elisha to follow immediately, as the call to prophecy demands no delay. Through this simple episode we start to sense the clear contrast between the great prophets, a contrast that characterized their prophetic activities as well.

Eliyahu was the man with anonymous parents. We do not know their names, even though biblical personalities are generally identified by their father's name. We never read of Eliyahu making reference to them or having any conversation with them. Elisha, on the other hand, is identified by his father's name and does not leave his home without bidding them farewell. Eliyahu fled from the people, remaining isolated, distant and always the "loner." Elisha, on the other hand, was in the fields with his workers when we meet him, where eventually he would share a celebratory meal with them. Eliyahu was sustained by a poor, righteous widow; Elisha sustained a poor, righteous widow. Eliyahu ignored the people's thirst for water; Elisha responded to the people of Jericho in need of water. Eliyahu, isolated from his fellow prophets, failed to help them at the time of their need, leaving it up to Ovadiah to feed them; Elisha himself fed the prophets during a time of famine. Eliyahu took food away from the people; Elisha shared his gift of food with the people.

The contrast is obvious and dramatic. It is therefore not surprising that there seems to be little in common between the personalities of the two

---

18. Bamidbar 20:28.
19. I Shmuel 17:38.
20. I Melachim 19:20.

prophets who were, by nature, so different. And yet, despite their divergent personalities, the two complemented each other as Elisha carried on the work of his master.

Eliyahu's Final Chapter

The final day of Eliyahu's life lacks any real drama for the reader – or, in fact, for his contemporaries who lived through the event. The text begins the story with the words "On the day that God took Eliyahu to heaven in a storm"[21] and proceeds to tell of how Elisha, and all the prophetic "students"[22] as well, knew that Eliyahu was to be taken from them on that day. Nonetheless, Eliyahu revealed none of this to Elisha, who by that time had been Eliyahu's attendant for a while.[23] He remained, as always, mysterious and distant. We are therefore not surprised when Eliyahu tried to separate from Elisha, hoping to die alone, by himself, just as he had lived.

So he traveled from Gilgal to Bet-El and from Bet-El to Jericho, eventually reaching the Jordan River. We would be remiss if we fail to see a message in Eliyahu's journey through the specific cities, Bet-El and Jericho. Before beginning the entire saga of Eliyahu, the author tells of the rebuilding of Jericho during the days of Ach'av: "In his days, Chi'eil of *Bet-El* [re]built the city of *Jericho*; with [the loss of] his eldest son, Aviram, he laid its foundation and with [the loss of] his youngest son, Seguv, he set up its doors, thereby fulfilling God's [prophetic] word to Yehoshua bin Nun."[24] Eliyahu understandably saw these two cities as living testimony to the wickedness and corruption of the people: Jericho, which, by God's word, was to remain in a permanent state of destruction as an eternal reminder of God's power and victory over the false deities of Canaan, was defiantly rebuilt by a resident of Bet-El, where the corrupt Yerov'am set up his false deity, copying the cults

---

21. II Melachim 2:1.
22. The term *benei nevi'im*, literally the "sons of the prophets," speaks not of the biological heirs of these seers but of their spiritual heirs (see Rashi, Devarim 6:7). It refers to schools of prophecy in which exceptional young men would study how to reach a level at which God would choose to rest His spirit upon them. From numerous references in the Bible, it seems that these individuals would, at times, possess a prophetic spirit and sense future events.
23. Elisha, certainly at the outset of his prophetic career, was known as "he who poured water upon the hands of Eliyahu" (II Melachim 3:11), that is, one who faithfully served and attended to the needs of the great prophet.
24. I Melachim 16:34.

of the Canaanites. And yet even here, in these "cities of sin," the man who told God that no prophets remained but he, was shown that there indeed remained prophets to the true God!

Throughout this day of travel Eliyahu attempted to discourage his charge from accompanying him; it appears that he was testing whether God regarded Elisha "worthy" enough to see his final departure. And in each of the cities, in Bet-El and in Jericho, the students of the prophets questioned Elisha as to whether he knew of the impending departure of his master; apparently, they too were not very impressed with Elisha or his prophetic abilities.[25] And almost as if to confirm these very doubts, Eliyahu, before making his way to the Jordan, told Elisha to remain in Jericho with the other prophets, thereby implying that he was no better than they. Yet, throughout that day, Elisha refused to abandon his master.

On a certain level, it is difficult to understand Eliyahu's attempts to discourage Elisha other than see them as a test to prove his worthiness. And if we carefully scrutinize the language of our text, we will see that the very phrases utilized by the *navi* hint to that exact fact.[26] Three times Eliyahu tells Elisha שב נא פה, "please stay here," and three times the narrator tells the reader וילכו שניהם, "and they both walked on." In these simple phrases we hear the clear echo of the greatest test imposed upon Avraham: the binding of Yitzchak, his son. There, the Torah quotes Avraham as telling his attendants שבו לכם פה, "please stay here," [27] and twice it describes the father and son ascending the mountain to fulfill God's will as וילכו שניהם יחדיו, "and they both walked on, together."[28] We see the author's comparison of the successful separation of Avraham from his attendants, who were not worthy of witnessing this act of faith, with Eliyahu's unsuccessful attempts to separate from Elisha, who was, after all, worthy of seeing Eliyahu's departure. Elisha passed the test, but did he prove to Eliyahu that he was a fitting successor to the great prophet?

Eliyahu's testing of Elisha continued until the very end of his life. Eliyahu granted Elisha a final request before he would be taken away, but when Elisha

---

25. In fact, they seem rather surprised when Elisha returns after the ascent of Eliyahu with the master's prophetic abilities and exclaim: "The spirit of Eliyahu has descended upon Elisha!" (II Melachim 2:15).

26. I am indebted to R. Amnon Bazak for these and other revelations in the Eliyahu-Elisha saga.

27. Bereishit 2:4.

28. Ibid. 22:6, 8.

responded: "Grant me a double portion of your spirit,"[29] Eliyahu would not agree. Eliyahu, even now, was reluctant to grant such a request, explaining that his request was a difficult one and the gift, therefore, would be conditional. Elisha would be given his request but only if God would grant him the privilege of witnessing Eliyahu's ascent heavenward. Elisha wanted his teacher to bequeath a double portion to him much as the eldest son receives an added portion of his father's inheritance above that given to his siblings.[30] The granting of such a gift would be seen as an admission by Eliyahu that Elisha was his rightful spiritual heir, as the oldest son was first to succeed a father. But even this was denied him, for the master challenged his student once more with his final test.

There is yet another sign of Eliyahu's reluctance to bequeath the mantle of prophecy on to Elisha, even at the very end of his life, and that symbolism is quite clear. Upon meeting Elisha for the first time, Eliyahu, rather than place his garment on the chosen successor, tossed his cloak at him and left it for Elisha to pick up. In the final moments of his life on this earth, as the chariot of fire[31] separated the two who were crossing the Jordan, Eliyahu once again did not place his mantle on Elisha but instead left it for the student to pick up – indicating that Elisha was charged to "pick up" from where Eliyahu left off and implying that whatever his student would accomplish would be the result of his own labors and his own efforts and not due to the master's blessing. It would seem that Eliyahu never regarded his mission as having been fulfilled or passed to another, and he was therefore reluctant to pass on his mantle to another. And, to a certain degree, God saw it that way as well. This might explain why Eliyahu is the only figure that the Bible clearly describes as never having died but rather as having been taken into heaven. It is also perhaps why the last verses of prophecy in the entire Bible – the final words delivered by the latest of the prophets, Malachi – speaks of God sending Eliyahu once more to prepare the people for "the great and awe-filled day of God."[32] Eliyahu would yet return to complete his mission.

---

29. II Melachim 2:9. The rabbis discuss whether a double portion meant twice of what Eliyahu was granted, or, as I have chosen to accept, double what the other prophets were to be granted.

30. Devarim 21:15–18.

31. It is interesting to compare the departure of Eliyahu and his lifelong antagonist, Ach'av. Both find their end while in a chariot, but whereas the chariot of Eliyahu was filled with a holy fire and bound for heaven, Ach'av's chariot was drenched with his blood and bound for Samaria where he would be buried in the ground.

32. Malachi 3:23.

Elisha: Building a Reputation

Elisha began his career by picking up the cloak of his master. More essentially, he could not cross back onto the western side of the Jordan until he touched the waters with Eliyahu's mantle and called out for help from "the God of Eliyahu." Only then did God respond to his prayers. Elisha's career would be based upon that of Eliyahu and would build upon the accomplishments and teachings of his master. But this would be the last time Elisha would need to call upon the merits of his teacher. Once he returned to Israel proper, he was *the* prophet, who would make his name known through his own deeds and accomplishments and, in the process, build a reputation among his contemporaries that equaled and perhaps even surpassed that of the fiery Eliyahu.

As we have seen, Eliyahu and his career could best be symbolized by fire. His refusal to soften his courageous stand against the king or his zealous defense of the Eternal God highlighted his belief that there could be no compromise with idolatry and that evildoers must be punished. Like fire, he could warm the people so that they could sense the presence of God; and, like fire, he could destroy those who challenged his belief in God. He brought fire down from heaven and he went up to heaven in a chariot of fire. Elisha, on the other hand, could best be symbolized by water. He slowly nourished and educated the people about God's expectations from them and watched as they gradually grew in their belief and faith. And while Eliyahu's first prophetic act was to withhold water from the people, Elisha's first prophetic act was to bring potable water to the people.

From the very outset, it is clear that Elisha did not command the respect of all and would have to establish himself as God's agent to the nation. Upon his return from crossing the Jordan and separating from Eliyahu, Elisha was greeted by the student prophets, who remarked that Eliyahu's spirit had settled upon Elisha. Nonetheless, they refused to listen to him when he told them not to search for the departed master, as Eliyahu was indeed gone; instead, they insisted on forming a search party to seek him out. After a futile search proved Elisha right, Elisha left Jericho and made the steep climb into the Samarian hills, where he is teased by young men from Bet-El, who cry out, "Get out, you bald one!"[33] We are certainly troubled by Elisha's seeming overreaction to their hurtful taunts: he cursed them, and as a result bears came out of the forest and tore apart forty-two of them.

---

33. II Melachim 2:23.

We are also puzzled by the mocking words of the young men when they called him "bald one" – what were they saying exactly? Perhaps the characterization of Elisha as a "bald one" was a derogatory way of saying that Elisha was not as holy as Eliyahu, who was a *ba'al sei'ar*, "one with much hair."[34] Like a nazirite, who refrained from cutting his hair, Eliyahu had long hair; and, like a Nazirite, he too had isolated himself from the people,[35] something that was not true of Elisha. Possibly echoing the comments made by their parents, these youngsters derided Elisha as not being on the same level as his teacher. He was not as "holy" because he was "bald;" unlike his master, he was not hermit-like but seemed "too accessible" and approachable, no different from other student prophets. The lesson of God's choice of Elisha and of the prophet's lofty level of sanctity was taught at the expense of the lives of these taunting youngsters. His reputation grew.

Elisha proceeded back to Israel proper, traveling from the Jordan to Jericho and from Jericho to Bet-El, and eventually to Gilgal, in effect retracing the steps he had previously taken with Eliyahu. He who had once been thought of as being no greater than the local student prophets, the man who was considered by many to be no more than a mere attendant of Eliyahu, now returned to these cities to firmly establish that he was the chosen successor of their teacher. It was he, and he alone, who saw their master taken from them, as the prophets of Jericho looked from a distance and failed to see the wondrous departure of Eliyahu. He took that precise route, for he was determined to repair his reputation and establish his presence and accessibility to the people. He even returned to Mount Carmel, the site of Eliyahu's greatest triumph; but unlike Eliyahu he did not run away from the people and flee into the desert to be alone. He made his way to the people, to Samaria, the capital of the northern kingdom, to be close to the nation and accessible to the king. And indeed he was.

Of the People, For the People

Elisha had such an impact on the people and its history that the prophetic author of the book of Melachim focuses, almost exclusively, on his life and deeds. For five chapters, the book of Melachim becomes the book of the

---

34. Ibid. 1:8.

35. This was commonly done by Nazirites in order to avoid possible contact with one who was impure, something that was prohibited to them.

prophet, telling the story of Elisha, with King Yehoram being almost tangential to the story. The book relates to us Elisha's exploits in Jericho and Bet-El as well as in Samaria. We read of his counsel to the kings of Israel and Judea regarding their war against Moab, as well as his advice to the poor widow on how to pay off her debts. The episodes included in these chapters clearly depict Elisha as a prophet who was close to the people, one who fed the *benei nevi'im* (student prophets) during a famine and miraculously was able to feed one hundred people with a small gift of food he received.

Most notably the story of Elisha and the woman from Shunam, so similar to the story of Eliyahu and the widow from Tzorefat,[36] serves as a powerful depiction of the differences between the two prophets and further underscores the special relationship the citizens of Israel had with their prophet. At the very outset of the story, we read of Elisha traveling among the people, passing through the cities and villages often enough to gain the attention of the wealthy woman. She regularly hosted Elisha during his visits and, together with her husband, decided to build an extra room in their house where the prophet could stay whenever he passed through. The woman's words to her husband, "Behold, the man of God passes through regularly,"[37] reflects Elisha's practice of going to the people, as opposed to Eliyahu's practice of avoiding the people and appearing before them only infrequently and haphazardly. Furthermore, we learn from this story that it was his practice to stay with the local population and not reside outside the city. Most interesting, however, is the portrayal of the relationship Elisha had with the citizenry, one of whom insisted on building a room where he would be comfortable rather than have him stay outside, the common practice of wayfarers. Once again we have an indication of how reachable Elisha was in contrast to Eliyahu, who, as we have seen, was remote and inaccessible.

As the Elisha narrative continues, we learn that the prophet was a well-known figure even outside of Israel, with the respected general of Israel's enemy, Aram, seeking him out to cure his *tzara'at*.[38] The prophet's acquiescence to the request of Na'aman, the enemy general, to cure him of his affliction – indeed, Elisha's insistence that King Yehoram send the general to him, as well

---

36. Both are taken in by women, both reward their hosts, both are entreated to save the sons of their hosts and both revive the dead sons of their hosts in the same exact manner.
37. II Melachim 2:9.
38. A disease, generally translated as leprosy, although most commentators agree that it is not similar to the leprosy of today.

as his refusal to accept any remuneration for effecting the cure – provides us with insight into how Elisha functioned as a prophet. He was interested in spreading the knowledge of the true God through acts of kindness rather than through punishment and suffering.

Elisha's "educational" activities as well were not limited to the spiritual struggle of Israel. Having advised King Yehoram regarding military matters, Elisha was also sought after by the enemy. The final result saw their bewildered Aramean army blindly follow the prophet, who brought them to the capital of Samaria into the hands of King Yehoram and the Israelite army. But even here, Elisha would not allow the king to capture the glory, warning him not to kill the enemy but to send them back to Aram. He explained his reasoning to the king, telling him: "Would you be killing those whom you had captured by yourself?"[39] In other words, is it right for you to be killing these people, thereby taking the glory for their destruction, if you were not the one to capture them? Since the enemy was humbled by a miracle of God without any involvement of the Israelite army, the prophet felt it wrong to have the king destroy the enemy army and be credited with the victory. Here too we are granted a glimpse of Elisha the inspiring figure, who preferred sending even non-believers back to their capital, there to retell the wonders of God to their countrymen, and not allowing any human to claim credit for that which was God's victory.

Such behavior made Elisha a widely respected figure in the enemy's land as well as in Israel itself. The Israelite king asked to be told stories of Elisha's miraculous acts while the king of Aram inquired of Elisha whether or nor he would recover from his illness. And here too the author presents another contrast between Elisha and Eliyahu. The second book of Melachim begins with the story of the king of Israel who inquired of the false god of Ekron, Ba'al Zebub, whether or not he would recover from his injuries, an act that both God and Eliyahu decried; this led Eliyahu to tell the king that, as a punishment, he would indeed die from his wounds. It is the sad story of the king of Israel who would not inquire of his God through the prophet of Israel. And yet, here we find the king of Aram similarly concerned about his recovery but not inquiring of his own gods but of Israel's God, through Israel's prophet, Elisha!

---

39. II Melachim 6:22.

The Final Years

As Elisha's life drew to a close, the condition of Israel worsened. The growing power of their northern neighbor, Aram, threatened their very independence as King Chaza'el, anointed by Elisha as per God's directive to Eliyahu,[40] all but destroyed the Israelite army,[41] a consequence of their sinfulness. Elisha remained close to the Israelite kings, advising and teaching them so that, even as he lay on his deathbed, Elisha was visited by the king, Yo'ash. He told the king to shoot arrows out of the window and prophesied that these would be the "arrows of victory for God, arrows of salvation from Aram."[42] Rather than isolate himself from his beloved nation at the end of his life, Elisha offered prophecies of hope and salvation for the nation.

It is important to note that, upon realizing that Elisha was dying, the king cried aloud, repeating the very words first said by Elisha when his master was taken from him: "My father, my father, the chariot and horsemen of Israel!"[43] But whereas Elisha made his declaration standing alone, as the student of a great teacher, he himself is addressed by the king of Israel, who was echoing the sentiments of an entire nation. This episode sums up the differences between the two prophets in the simplest terms: one prophet who was never understood and often reviled by his nation and one who was deeply loved and respected by his nation and the surrounding peoples. Eliyahu left his people in a supernatural event, while Elisha died and was buried as all men are. Eliyahu, after his death, would return to herald better days.[44] Elisha, after his death, succeeded in bringing the dead back to life.[45]

But neither succeeded in preventing the exile of Israel.

The Beginning of the End

After the death of Elisha, the spiritual life of the nation deteriorated dramatically. At first, God, in His mercy, saved Israel from oppression and possible destruction, freeing it from the iron fist of Aram with the death of its

---

40. I Melachim 19:15.
41. II Melachim 13:7.
42. Ibid. 13: 17.
43. Ibid. 2:12.
44. Malachi 3:23.
45. II Melachim 13:21.

king, Chaza'el.[46] Similarly, He sent salvation to the nation through the military campaigns of Yerov'am son of Yo'ash (often called Yerov'am II), who, though no more righteous than his predecessors, was granted victory over Israel's enemies and restored Israel's borders to their original extent. The text explains God's intent in using an idolater to bring salvation to His people with the statement: "For God saw the intense suffering of Israel…and that there was no one who would help Israel. And God never thought to obliterate Israel's name from under the heavens, and so He saved them through Yerov'am, son of Yo'ash."[47]

The merciful God provided Israel with the opportunity to witness His hand in their salvation and, hopefully, turn back to Him as a result. However, Israel remained blind to the divine hand that helped them, much as they had during the period of the judges, and due to that stubborn blindness, the wayward nation sealed their fate.

The final years of the northern kingdom were marked by military weakness and political instability. In the last forty-one years of its existence, Israel saw six different kings and coups that included four assassinations of the sitting regent. The exile that had been prophesied since the rule of Yerov'am, the first Israelite king, came to be. However, even when punishing His nation, God encouraged Israel to repair their evil ways: by bringing the exile in stages, God thereby provided the nation with time to look at their deeds and return to God.

During the reign of Pekach, the Assyrians exiled the residents of the northeastern regions of the kingdom, an event that precipitated the assassination of the king. The new king, Menachem, threw his fate in with his northern neighbor, Aram, and together with this traditional enemy invaded his brothers in Judea. The invasion caused Assyria to intervene on behalf of Judea and kill the king of Aram. Although Menachem was not punished with more than paying tribute to the Assyrians, eventually Shalmaneser, the Assyrian monarch, suspected him of joining Egypt in a plot against Assyria. Menachem's failure to pay the tributes brought the Assyrian hordes to Israel,

---

46. Chaza'el threatened the southern kingdom of Judea as well when he invaded the Judean kingdom and captured Gath. His plan to capture Jerusalem was thwarted only when the Judean king Yeho'ash sent all of the wealth gathered by his predecessors and all of the riches found in the temple treasury and the royal treasury to the Aramean king.

47. II Melachim 14:26–27. A similar declaration is made when explaining God's help in Israel's victory over Aram and King Chaza'el; see ibid. 13:23.

where they imprisoned the king and, after three years of siege, captured the capital city of Samaria and exiled the nation.

The Middle of the End

Throughout the record of Israel's moral decay the prophetic author is careful to remind the reader that the southern kingdom of Judea was also drifting away from God.[48] And although the political situation was far more stable in the southern kingdom, with the Davidic line still intact, the final twenty-two years saw the reign of four different kings, two of them ruling for three months only. Furthermore, the religious practices of the kings were increasingly displeasing to God as many of these kings turned to pagan worship. The righteous rule of Chizkiyahu brought an end to the idolatry that ran rampant throughout Judea, as he destroyed any object that was worshiped by the people, including the bronze serpent fashioned by Moshe that the people had begun to venerate.

Especially fascinating is the story of God's defeat of the Assyrian army, by responding to Chizkiyahu's prayer and breaking their siege of Jerusalem. When the king died, it appeared that Judea had turned away from their sinful ways, but the reign of the righteous Chizkiyahu provided but a temporary change in the immoral behavior the people had adopted. Unfortunately, Chizkiyahu was succeeded on the throne by his twelve-year-old son who would undo all the good his father had done and in the process become the most notorious king of Judea.

The fifty-five-year reign of Menashe (Menasseh) was the longest reign of any Israelite or Judean king and was filled with corruption and moral depravity. Menashe was an idolater who actively spread the pagan cult throughout his land, even defiling the Holy Temple with pagan altars and the idol of Ashera. He was a murderous regent who "filled Jerusalem [with blood] from end to end,"[49] leading God to tell His prophets that Jerusalem would share the same fate as Samaria. The effect of this long period of corruption on the people of Judea was devastating. Over the years they lost their knowledge of the Torah as the wicked king had, apparently, destroyed many of the existing copies of

---

48. "And Judea, likewise, did not follow God's commands and [instead] followed the practices of Israel" (II Melachim 17:19).
49. II Melachim 21:16.

the law.[50] There appeared to be little hope for the nation who had been led astray by their renegade regents.

Until Yoshiyahu (Josiah) appeared.

The End of the End

King Yoshiyahu was the most remarkable king of Judea, for he was brought up in a pagan world and yet dramatically changed his ways and those of his nation. The religious revolution took place during the eighteenth year of his reign when, in the process of repairing and strengthening the Temple's structure, the high priest discovered a Torah scroll.[51] The scroll was brought to the king and its contents read by the scribe Shafan. Upon hearing the words of the Torah – words that undoubtedly included the tragedies that would befall the people if they failed to uphold the laws – the king tore his clothes and demanded that the high priest "seek out God." The Temple leadership approached the prophetess Chulda, who informed them of the inevitable destruction of the city and its inhabitants, a punishment decreed by God and precipitated by the people's wicked ways. Nonetheless, the prophetess continued, in view of Yoshiyahu's sincere feelings of regret and repentance, he will not see the punishment, for God will postpone the destruction until after his death.

Upon hearing the words of the prophetess, the king gathered representatives from the entire land, and in the Temple itself, he read the words of the Torah to them. He then entered them into a covenant with God in which they agreed to uphold the words of the Torah and follow all of the laws of God. He proceeded to destroy all remnants of idolatry and paganism from Judea, including the temples of these false gods and their functionaries.[52] When the king had completed his campaign, he called upon all of the people to observe the paschal sacrifice as commanded in the Torah – with the result that there was a widespread observance of this ritual, the likes of which hadn't occurred for hundreds of years, since the period of the judges. To further underscore

---

50. As we will see, twenty years after Menashe's death, a scroll of law was discovered hidden in the Temple and it caused a religious upheaval, as the words of the Torah, that had clearly been unknown, were read to the king.

51. According to II Divrei Hayamim 34:3, this religious reform began a full ten years before the discovery of the Torah scroll in the Temple.

52. The full extent of Yoshiyahu's extermination of idol practice is described in II Melachim, ch. 23.

the accomplishments of this outstanding personality, the text goes out of its way to declare: "Never before in Israel was there a king [like Yoshiyahu] who returned to God with all of his heart and soul, nor would there be another after him."[53]

As students of the *Tanach*, we expect to read of the positive impact that Yoshiyahu's actions had upon God's decision to punish Judea. But instead this uplifting story ends with five verses that seem to ignore all of the remarkable deeds that the righteous king had performed. The text relates that despite all Yoshiyahu had done, God remained angry with the people and still planned to exile them. And then, almost as an afterthought, the author tells us that Yoshiyahu led an army to confront the Egyptian Pharaoh and his army, who were marching to a campaign against the Assyrians. And, during this battle, in the town of Megiddo, King Yoshiyahu was killed.

But Why?

The death of the saintly king during battle presented the nation with a crisis of faith.[54] Simply put, the question that must have haunted them, and the question that those who study the episode today must answer, is: How could tragedy like this befall such a righteous king? The people of Judea had every right to believe, as we ourselves do, that a leader whom the Bible attests was unequaled in his sincere return to God should not have suffered the ignoble end that he did. And unless we can understand why such a tragedy occurred – that is, what sin was committed that so displeased God – we can never believe in any leader, no matter how righteous he may be – because even if he may be worthy of God's favor, we may not be.

In fact, one may argue that this event may have been the reason why the population was not heedful of the warnings issued to them by the prophets of that time. After all, if their great king – one they may have even believed would bring them the ultimate redemption from their oppressors – if he could be killed despite his righteousness, then what chance did they have? We will therefore attempt to understand the underlying mistake of King Yoshiyahu, and by doing so, I believe we will also uncover the underlying message of the prophets contemporary with the last kings of Judea.

---

53. II Melachim 23:25.
54. Indeed, Rav Yoel Bin Nun, from whom I heard these thoughts, opined that it remains a crisis of faith for all Jews even today.

The first question we should address is: What was the king doing in Megiddo? It was a city in the northern part of the land and not even part of his kingdom! Why would he care about the Egyptian army passing so far from his land? The answer lies in the text itself, where we can uncover the underlying assumption of Yoshiyahu and, quite possibly, the other Judean kings. Rav Yoel Bin Nun posits that the kings of Judea regarded themselves as the kings of *all* Israel, even the northern provinces. Following the exile of the northern tribes, a small population of Israelites still remained, a fact seen clearly when the book of Divrei Hayamim tells us that King Chizkiyahu "sent letters to all of Israel and Judea – even to [the tribes of] Efraim and Menashe,"[55] clearly regions of the former kingdom of Israel. Chizkiyahu further called out to them to join their brethren in Jerusalem for the paschal service and urged them: "Return unto the God of Avraham, Yitzchak and Yisrael; let all those who have survived the hand of Assyria return."[56]

Yoshiyahu, like his great-grandfather, saw himself as the regent of the remnants of the northern kingdom. When eradicating foreign worship from the land, we read how Yoshiyahu purified not only the cities of Judea and the city of Jerusalem but also "the cities of Efraim and Menashe and Shimon, even up to Naftali."[57] Of course, we also know from the first section of the book of Melachim that Yoshiyahu was destined to burn the remains of the false priests on the altar of Bet-El, something that he indeed did, even though Bet-El had been the capital of the north. But, as the text informs us, the Judean king does the same to "all the temples throughout the cities of Samaria,"[58] carrying out God's directive to the prophet Yirmeyahu given during his reign: "Go to the north and speak these words and tell them: 'Return faithless Israel....'"[59]

Clearly, Yoshiyahu saw himself as regent of Samaria and her inhabitants as well as the king of Judea, a probable result of the diminished Assyrian

---

55. II Divrei Hayamim 30:1. There is, furthermore, archeological evidence of Israelite settlements in the area of modern-day Tel Aviv as well as the region of Kibbutz Yavneh, from the period of Yoshiyahu's reign.

56. Ibid. 30:6. The chapter goes on to describe how the runners brought the message of the king to the tribes of Menashe and Efraim, and even as far north as Zevulun, urging those remnants from the exile to return to the worship of the true God. Unfortunately, most mocked the king's call with only some (from the tribes of Asher, Menashe and Zevulun) responding to the king's declaration.

57. Ibid. 34:6.

58. II Melachim 23:19.

59. Yirmeyahu 3:11.

presence in the land, a fact that the king took advantage of. It is for this reason, therefore, that Yoshiyahu went up to Megiddo to confront the Egyptian force; he was, after all, the defender of all Israel. But given this truth, our second question is even more troubling: What sin had Yoshiyahu committed that led him to die in that battle?

We can find the answer within the words of the prophets of the time, for within their admonition we can infer what shortcomings the people had and what expectations God had for the people and their kings. The earliest prophecies of Yirmeyahu were offered during the reign of Yoshiyahu,[60] and there we read of the failure of the king's reforms. God, we are told, bemoaned the fact that, despite what had happened to the northern kingdom years earlier, despite the exile and destruction that befell the Israelite nation, their Judean brethren refused to learn their lesson and continued in their sinful ways. This chapter, as our Rabbis comment, proves that the repentance of Judea was not sincere. The king may have legislated the practice of the Torah's laws but never, effectively, educated the Torah's values to the nation. And so, the people's observance was a result of outer pressure, not inner commitment. As a result, upon the death of Yoshiyahu, the people returned to their idolatrous ways. It was due to this insincere repentance that God refused to change His decree or even postpone the exile.

Although this helps us understand the limited effectiveness of Yoshiyahu's efforts, it still fails to explain his death in battle. It is extremely important for us not to underestimate the historical impact of his death. In a very real sense, the loss of the king marked the beginning of the destruction of Judea, Jerusalem and the Holy Temple. He was, after all, the last real independent Judean king, as those who succeeded him were controlled by Babylonia; indeed they were little more than puppet rulers who were appointed to and removed from their thrones at the whim of the Babylonian monarch.[61] In fact, the twenty-two years that followed Yoshiyahu's death were marked by tragedy after tragedy, internal upheaval and calamitous events that led up to the inevitable exile.

---

60. See Yirmeyahu 3:6.

61. Rav Bin Nun proposes that Yirmeyahu's famous prophecy of Israel's return to her land after "serving the king of Babylonia for seventy years" (Yirmeyahu 25:11), a prophecy whose calculation has always stymied commentators, might well be understood if we begin counting the seventy years from the death of Yoshiyahu (609 BCE), for it would then conclude the year of the proclamation of Cyrus the Great (539 BCE).

In light of all of this, our remaining question is even weightier: Why did this righteous scion of the Davidic line; a king who labored to fill his land with *tzedek* and *mishpat*, righteousness and kindness, as God had demanded of His kings; the individual who expanded Israel's borders and cared for *all* of the nation – why did he find his end in Megiddo? Why did he fall in battle, bleeding to death in his chariot, precisely as the wicked King Ach'av had?[62]

The answer is actually provided for us in the words of the prophets. A recurrent theme throughout the prophecies of the pre-exile period is God's rejection of all types of political and military alliances. The common idea that flows from the words of the various seers is Israel's need to rely upon God and God alone. "Efraim is like a foolish dove that lacks wisdom; they call to Egypt, they go to Assyria,"[63] cried the prophet Hoshea, while Yirmeyahu berated King Yoshiyahu with the question: "Why do you follow the road to Egypt...and why take the path to Assyria...?"[64] This same condemnation had been delivered by Yeshayahu to King Chizkiyahu, who chose to rebel against Assyria; in his words, "Woe to those who turn to Egypt for help, who rely on horses and depend upon chariots because they are many...but do not call out to God and do not seek Him out."[65] Both Israel and Judea were warned numerous times not to rely on other nations, not to seek out alliances and not involve themselves in political intrigue.

God desired Israel to rely fully on Him and find their security in their faith in God, for just as He had conquered the land for them so He would protect them. It was a message that, unfortunately, was seldom heeded. But beyond God's demand that Israel place their trust in Him alone was also His desire that Israel be a model for the nations, above the petty politics and military alliances that characterized the power struggles of that time. He favored neither the southern empire of Egypt nor the northern power of Assyria; He opposed Chizkiyahu's rebellion against Assyria as well as Yoshiyahu's revolt against Egypt. God favored an independent Israel secure in her reliance upon Him and spreading His word to the world.

This, then, was the sin of Yoshiyahu, the righteous king who chose to ignore the message of the prophets and the message of God. His interference

---

62. See I Melachim 22:35.
63. Hoshea 7:11; see also ibid. 12:2; 14:4.
64. Yirmeyahu 2:18.
65. Yeshayahu 31:1.

in a battle that was not his, his decision to confront Egyptian forces who were not threatening his land, was not only a failure of military intelligence, it was a failure of religious commitment and faith in God.

The End, Like the Beginning

Ultimately, the failure of the kings of Judea and the kings of Israel was the failure God and the prophet Shmuel feared when acceding to the people's request for a monarchy. As mentioned, the basic theme of all of the books of the early prophets is the theme of kingship: the establishment of a dynasty that could produce rulers, unite the people, bring them closer to God and help them build that perfect society demanded by God, a society dedicated to sanctity, justice and kindness. To accomplish that, the king had to eschew all personal glory and understand that the hand of God was behind all of his accomplishments. If he truly understood that, he would not bother with alliances or political machinations. He would be a model of faith to his nation and teach them by example to rise above petty local politics and place their faith in God. Those kings who did so were successful; those who did not, made the exile inevitable.

As the book of Kings ends, we become more aware of its underlying purpose. The generation who witnessed the destruction of their Temple and the exile of the bulk of their population looked back with shock at what had happened to its once glorious past. They struggled with religious questions: What happened to the future they had been promised? What happened to the eternal Temple they had worshipped in? What happened to the all-powerful God they believed in? It was to this tragic generation that Yirmeyahu addressed the writings of these prophets. These contemporaries were made to understand that it was not God who had been "defeated" nor was it the enemy who had destroyed His Temple. By reminding them of their past, Yirmeyahu taught them that it was their own sins and misguided actions that had brought the inevitable exile, punishment for their wayward behavior, and that it was God Who had destroyed His Temple, after His nation had ignored the warnings of His prophets.

Fittingly, *sefer Melachim* closes with the release of King Yehoyachin from Babylonian imprisonment and his elevation above all other defeated kings, becoming an honored guest at the table of the Babylonian regent for the rest of his life. By adding this "addendum" to his book, the prophet reassures the nation that there is still hope for them. Indeed, as their sins had forced them into exile, their repentance would bring them back.

An important message to that lost generation.

An important message to all generations.

ABOUT THE AUTHOR

Rabbi Neil N. Winkler received his BA in history and his MS in biblical studies from Yeshiva University, and his rabbinic ordination from the Rabbi Isaac Elchanan Theological Seminary. A dynamic educator for over forty years, Rabbi Winkler serves as the Coordinator of Tanach studies of Yeshivat Moriah, the Moriah School in Englewood, New Jersey, where he has taught since 1978. Throughout these same years he has also served as spiritual leader of the Young Israel of Fort Lee, New Jersey, and as officer and board member of numerous rabbinic organizations. As teacher and guide for students competing in the International Bible Contest, Rabbi Winkler has seen over thirty of his students win the national championships and compete internationally in Jerusalem, with a number achieving the title of *Chattan/ Kallat Hatefutzot*, the Diaspora champion. Rabbi Winkler and his wife Andrea are the proud parents of five children and nine grandchildren.